THE QUEST FOR VOICE

The Quest For Voice

On Music, Politics, and the Limits of Philosophy

THE 1997 ERNEST BLOCH LECTURES

LYDIA GOEHR

OXFORD
UNIVERSITY PRESS

OXFORD
UNIVERSITY PRESS

Great Clarendon Street, Oxford OX2 6DP

Oxford University Press is a department of the University of Oxford.
It furthers the University's objective of excellence in research, scholarship,
and education by publishing worldwide in

Oxford New York

Auckland Bangkok Buenos Aires Cape Town Chennai
Dar es Salaam Delhi Hong Kong Istanbul Karachi Kolkata
Kuala Lumpur Madrid Melbourne Mexico City Mumbai Nairobi
São Paulo Shanghai Taipei Tokyo Toronto

Oxford is a registered trade mark of Oxford University Press
in the UK and in certain other countries

First published by Oxford University Press 1998
First published in paperback
by Oxford University Press 2002

British Library Cataloguing in Publication Data
Data available

Library of Congress Cataloging in Publication Data
Goehr, Lydia.
The quest for voice: on music, politics, and the limits of
philosophy: the 1997 Ernest Bloch lectures/Lydia Goehr.
p. cm.
Based in part on lectures given by the author at the University of
California, Berkeley; some of the material in chapters 1, 4, and 5
previously published in altered form.
Includes bibliographical references and index.
1. Music—Philosophy and aesthetics. 2. Wagner, Richard,
1813–1883—Aesthetics. 3. Romanticism in music. 4. Music—19th
century—Philosophy and aesthetics. 5. Music—Peformance.
6. Music and state—Germany. I. Title.
ML3845.G64   2002   781'.1—dc   98–14763
ISBN 0–19–816696–6

3 5 7 9 10 8 6 4 2

Typeset by Best-set Typesetter Ltd., Hong Kong
Printed in Great Britain
on acid-free paper by
Antony Rowe Ltd.
Chippenham, Wiltshire

For my
Father

What is outer is what is inner, raised to the condition of a secret. . . . Everywhere there is a grammatical mysticism. . . . Grammar. It is not only the human being that speaks—the universe also speaks—everything speaks—unending languages.

(Novalis)

[Y]our whole life must become an endless melody.

(Wackenroder and Tieck)

The greatness of poets should be measured by what they leave unsaid, letting us breathe the thing unspeakable to ourselves in silence. It is musicians who bring this unspoken mystery to clarion tongue, and the impeccable form of their sounding silence is endless melody.

(Wagner)

One can say, as a general comment on Wagner as a musician, that he has given a language to everything in nature that until now has made no attempt to speak; he does not believe that some things must inevitably be dumb. He plunges even into dawn and sunrise, into forests, fogs, ravines, mountain peaks, the dead of night and moonlight and discovers a secret longing in all of them: they want a voice.

(Nietzsche)

Acknowledgements

There are so many who have helped me in this project. I cannot name them all, but I do thank them all. First, I thank the members of the Music and Philosophy Departments at the University of California at Berkeley for inviting me to give the 1997 Ernest Bloch Lectures, out of which this book originated; the experience could not have been more rewarding. I am deeply indebted to my dear friends, former colleagues, and students from Wesleyan University, most especially Brian Fay and Victor Gourevitch. I am grateful to my new colleagues and graduate students at Columbia University for all manner of good suggestions. I also thank many friends who have helped me in my thinking either recently or in moments long past but not forgotten:

From philosophy: Phillip Alperson, Noel Carroll, Joseph Chytry, Arthur Danto, Kate Elgin, Steve Gerrard, Hannah Ginsborg, Stefan Gosepath, Danny Herwitz, Patricia Herzog, Gregg Horowitz, Tom Huhn, Robert Kaufman, Martin Jay, Richard Kuhns, Elijah Milgram, Amelie Rorty, Robert Sharpe, Hans Sluga, and Barry Smith.

From music: Daniel Albright, Katherine Bergeron, Karol Berger, Juliane Brand, Reinhold Brinkmann, Bojan Bujić, John Butt, David Caddis, Walter Frisch, Susan Gillespie, Tom Grey, Stephen Hinton, Joseph Kerman, Kim Kowalke, David Levin, Alfred Mann, Estele Olevsky, Mel Strauss, Richard Taruskin, Leo Treitler, and the members of the Stanford Opera Group.

I offer a special thanks to my editor, Bruce Phillips, his assistant, Helen Foster, and the copy-editor, Laurien Berkeley, at Oxford University Press for their excellent advice and for making my experience with OUP a thoroughly agreeable one. Many thanks also to Lynne Withey at the University of California Press at Berkeley for producing the American edition with such generosity and encouragement.

I am extremely grateful to Bernard Williams and to John Deathridge, as also to my four anonymous readers, for reading the manuscript in its entirety and for their insightful criticisms and recommendations for correction.

I thank Amy Ayres, Curtis Church, Jonathan Neufeld and Michel Singher for their editorial help. I am grateful to Lawrence Schoenberg for making material accessible from the Schoenberg Archive at the University of Southern California. I thank David and Bette Caddis for lending me a room with a spectacular view.

Last but by no means least, I thank Rickey Calleo, whose Boccaccian love of fishing into the depths of the singing voice has been my daily source of inspiration.

Some of the material in this book has appeared elsewhere. In Chapter 1, I use material from my: 'Music has no Meaning to Speak Of: On the Politics of Musical Interpretation' (in M. Krausz (ed.), *The Interpretation of Music: Philosophical Essays* (Oxford, 1993), 177–90); 'Political Music and the Politics of Music' (in P. Alperson (ed.), *The Philosophy of Music*, Special Issue, *Journal of Aesthetics and Art Criticism*, 52/1 (1994), 99–112); 'Schopenhauer and the Musicians: An Inquiry into the Sounds of Silence and the Limits of Philosophizing about Music' (in D. Jacquette (ed.), *Schopenhauer, Philosophy, and the Arts* (Cambridge, 1996), 200–28); and 'Writing Music History' (*History and Theory*, 31/2 (1992), 182–99). A much earlier version of Chapter 4 appears in S. Frith (ed.), *Performance Matters*, an issue of *New Formations: A Journal of Culture/Theory/Politics*, 27 (Winter 1995–6), 1–22. A modified version of Chapter 5 appears in R. Brinkmann and C. Wolff (eds.), *'Driven into Paradise': The Musical Migration from Nazi Germany to the United States* (Berkeley, Calif., forthcoming). I am grateful to the editors and Presses for permission to reuse this material.

L.G.

New York City, 1998

Contents

Introduction

What is musical meaning? Where does it reside and how can it be known? Does it make a difference to its meaning if the music is composed with or without words, as a symphony or as a song? Why is it thought that music can express human feelings with an immediacy not possible in other languages or arts? What is contained in the claim that music is autonomous, or that it is prophetic and can articulate a 'politics for the future'? These are some of the questions the German Romantics asked about music. In this book I try to answer these questions by focusing on the view that music means something, not just because it is a well-formed symbolic language, but because when human beings engage with this language they express something about themselves as human beings. That something, in Romantic terms, approaches a subjective freedom expressed within and against objective constraints.

In this expression endures an ancient activity that once signified a philosophical quest for the cultivation of the soul and a political quest for freedom. This activity was originally captured by the Socratic concept of *mousikē*. Reconnecting music to the original aspirations of *mousikē* has an advantage for us today insofar as it allows us to recognize music's broad philosophical and political significance and its autonomy. For, as paradoxical as it sounds, connecting music to *mousikē* demonstrates that music is philosophical and political already by virtue of music's being *autonomously musical*.

Schopenhauer and Nietzsche contributed much to establishing this connection. Yet I focus far less on these or, indeed, on any other philosophers of German Romanticism. Hegel and Feuerbach would have been obvious choices. Rather, I focus on Richard Wagner: with an impact unparalleled he demonstrated in theory and in practice the wide-reaching significance of thinking about philosophy and politics in terms of music, and music in terms of philosophy and politics. He showed the dangers of losing the musical in our music, the meaningful in our philosophy, and freedom in our politics. He showed these dangers in two ways: sometimes by resisting them, sometimes by succumbing.

This book describes Wagner's attempted restoration of the concept of *mousikē* into modern musical practice. He introduced the concept to serve as an antidote to a prevalent mode of musical thinking he believed was overly constrained by formalism. To achieve this end, he employed two concepts of the musical. He spoke of restoring an older, metaphorical concept of the musical to accompany a more modern, literal one. The older concept captured music's broadly human and metaphysical significance; the newer concept attended devotedly to music's tonally moving forms. The older captured the 'extramusical' domain of 'the inexpressible'; the newer the 'purely musical' domain of 'the expressible'. Under formalism's influence, Wagner argued, musical practice was increasingly favouring the literal concept at the expense of the metaphorical, the empirical at the expense of the metaphysical, the modern at the expense of the premodern, the expressible at the expense of the inexpressible, the purely musical at the expense of the extramusical, the freedom of music's content at the expense of its freedom of 'speech', and, finally, the musical work at the expense of its performance. Wagner tried to revolutionize the practice by indulging in the antagonistic play of these oppositions.

Yet this book investigates the connection Wagner helped forge between music, philosophy, and politics not merely for the sake of understanding the nineteenth century, but also to resituate our contemporary thinking specifically about formalist claims to music's autonomy. Recently, these claims have been subject to all manner of academic and cultural attack and rejection. Given the current understanding of these claims, the attacks have usually been warranted. And yet to rid ourselves of our commitment to the principles with which these claims are associated creates more problems than it solves. A common tendency at present is to use the terms 'the musical' and 'the extramusical' with apologetic quotation marks. Certainly, quotation marks show our concern, but they hardly provide an adequate solution. My hope is that a rereading of the early history of the formalist claims might give their terms a renewed and acceptable contemporary use.

To this end, I argue for a position of enhanced or critical formalism. However, this position is best grasped if readers approach this book not so much as about Wagner as about philosophical method;

for, though I treat many aspects of his thought, I focus somewhat idiosyncratically and with stringent selectivity on his musical, political, and philosophical arguments on the limits of formalism. I extrapolate these arguments from his large *opus*, not always or just because they are right or coherent—sometimes they are neither— but always in such a way as to show simultaneously their progressive and their regressive potential. Wagner rejected the false security promised by the emerging formalism of the nineteenth century, a security that depended on severing the musical from the political. But in rejecting this security, he revealed (as I said earlier, both by resisting and by succumbing to) the risk that an argument about musical meaning that has the most progressive political potential can be appropriated so easily to work for the most regressive ends. He showed from both sides the very dangerous tightrope we walk when we allow the political to work in the domain of the musical. This is why I have written about Wagner: he so perfectly demonstrated the risk. It was an obvious choice, but not always a happy one.

Chapter 1 offers a general introduction to the theme of expressing the inexpressible. It treats the elusive Romantic motifs of secrecy and silence as they resonate within the philosophical and musical domains. It introduces these motifs with a discussion pertaining to our contemporary interest in the topics of formalism, autonomy, and censorship. It introduces the problematic distinction between the purely musical and the extramusical. This discussion quickly leads to concerns with philosophical method and the strangely paradoxical role the concept of the purely musical has played in articulating them. The concept of the purely musical, I argue, functioned as a metaphor in the nineteenth century to capture philosophy's silence or that which was philosophically unsayable. Against the background specifically of Schopenhauerian and Nietzschean concerns with philosophical method, Wagner is introduced.

Chapter 2 investigates the paradoxical relations between rules and creativity, conditions and exemplars, and tradition and innovation, specifically in connection with the revealed and concealed relations that emerge between aesthetics and politics in Wagner's *Die Meistersinger*. This chapter offers a close reading of the opera's libretto from beginning to end. The libretto corroborates many of the aesthetic principles articulated in Kant's *Critique of Judgement*.

Chapter 3 investigates the formalist–transcendentalist debate over the content of instrumental music and opera as a disguised cultural debate over autonomous expression and the emancipatory power of voice. It addresses the contentious debate between Wagner and Hanslick against the background of Rousseau's *Essay on the Origin of Languages*. It contains the central argument of my book for a revised reading of music's claim to autonomy. This argument resituates the concept of the musical by shifting our emphasis from a work's form and content to music's function of expressing or voicing the inexpressible through performance.

Chapter 4 attends to competing ideals of visibility and invisibility in modern performance practice. It seeks the rationale behind the demands either that we should see or that we should not see our performers. It compares two conceptions of performance, one which gives a formalist priority to the *work* performed, the other an anti-formalist priority to the *performed* work. This comparison forces us to revise our usual understanding of the relation between work and performance. To justify this revision, I compare Wagner's ideals for Bayreuth and its concealed orchestra with the more contemporary ideals of invisibility associated with recordings. The latter are represented through the arguments of Glenn Gould. I argue that the different sets of ideals point to a shared interest in aesthetic transfiguration and the ends and End of art. I conclude by returning to my methodological concern, specifically to the question of how a philosophical theory should accommodate the kinds of conflict of ideals or competing conceptions that sustain the open character of our practices.

Chapter 5 presents the final argument and conclusions of my methodological enquiry, but in terms much closer to home. It explores the relation between creativity, expression, and national identity with regard to the expulsion of mostly Jewish composers from Nazi Germany. This exploration focuses on a Romantic–Modernist legacy that demands that musical expression transcend national identity at the same time that it be rooted in such. Wagner played a significant part in shaping this double legacy. Yet the stress is given in this last chapter to showing the painful realities with which composers were faced when they found themselves having to test it.

Each chapter assumes a distinctive style. To each I have tried to give the character of an essay. As essays they can be read (almost) as self-sufficient. Indeed, readers less inclined towards philosophy might find it useful to begin with the last one first. However, there is a single philosophical argument uniting the chapters. This argument claims the advantages of using a metaphorical concept of the musical as an anti-systematic restraint on systematic philosophical theory. I describe the advantages in different ways, but tying them together is the claim that 'doubleness', as I call it, serves as a successful technique by which to produce a philosophical theory that respects its own systematic limits or, in other words, sees through its tendency towards systematization. This respect enables a theory to accommodate the primacy of the practice it seeks to describe and prescribe. Doubleness supports a theory of open and critical practice. It closely recalls traditional dialectics, yet it does not depend upon establishing too strong a teleological development in which oppositions are brought to their (pre)determined syntheses. Instead, it serves more moderately to preserve both in theory and in practice the two or more sides of conflicts, sides that often serve one another by being at hand to be denied. Each chapter attends to several of these historical and metaphysical conflicts. Each, in its own way, is intended to persuade readers of the musical and political benefits of employing the philosophical technique of doubleness.

1

Secrecy and Silence:
An Introduction to Music and
its Metaphor

But music speaks a loftier tone
To tyrant and to spy unknown,
And free as angels walks with men
Can pass unscathed the gaoler's ken.

(Grillparzer[1])

1. On the Musical and Extramusical

Consider three paradoxical proclamations: first, Orwell's: 'the opinion that art should have nothing to do with politics is itself a political attitude'; secondly, Goethe's: 'You cannot escape from the world more certainly than through art; and you cannot bind yourself to it more certainly than through art'; and thirdly, Adorno's: 'music represents society the more deeply the less it blinks in its direction'. Though they were uttered in very different times and places, these proclamations share the rationale of protecting music, literature, and the arts from the threat of the moralizing censor, where the censor symbolizes a social or moral unfreedom. I borrow part of my opening thought from Nietzsche's *Twilight of the Idols*, specifically from his comment on 'l'art pour l'art' (section 24): 'The struggle against *purpose* in art is always a struggle against the *moralizing* tendency in art, against the subordination of art to morality. *L'art pour l'art* means: the devil take morality! But this very hostility betrays that moral prejudice is still dominant.'

---

[1] Written for the composer Ignaz Moscheles; quoted in R. J. Goldstein, *Political Censorship of the Arts and the Press in Nineteenth-Century Europe* (New York, 1989), 155.

This chapter begins by considering the paradoxical position into which the traditional claims of musical formalism have been placed, especially the claim that music exists for music's sake. My consideration is mostly conceptual; in so far as it is historical, it sweeps broadly through the nineteenth and twentieth centuries. It initiates one of the major projects of this book, to offer a broad philosophical and political reading of the claims of both musical formalism and autonomy. This reading is intended to counter the tendency, demonstrated increasingly in this century, to read these claims in a devotedly positivistic way. This devotion, I shall argue, originated in the nineteenth century in a deep concern with philosophical method that generated not merely a theoretical disagreement, but a full-blown cultural war, over what it means for music to be musical. This book is about that war and the part Wagner played in it.

I take as my evidence the elevated Romantic discourse of the European musical world. I have long wanted to understand how one of its most common claims, that purely instrumental music has no cognitive or referential meaning, but just 'specifically musical' meaning, could function conceptually in an argument against music's censorship and for its claimed freedom.[2] Positing a meaning for music that is unknowable in cognitive terms, and understood only by a musically educated elite, has seemingly provided composers an effective defence against censors who are said to have judged music according to false criteria deriving either from society's determinations or from their own 'pathological' tendencies. These censors have identified in music all sorts of purportedly dangerous elements, but composers have been able to defend themselves by denying that these identifications correspond to the real meaning of their works.

Given the formalist tendency to regard music's meaning as

---

[2] In this section I shall be introducing themes I have discussed in some detail in my 'Writing Music History', *History and Theory*, 31/2 (1992), 182–99; 'Music has no Meaning to Speak Of: On the Politics of Musical Interpretation', in M. Krausz (ed.), *The Interpretation of Music* (Oxford, 1993), 177–90; and 'Political Music and the Politics of Music', in P. Alperson (ed.), *The Philosophy of Music*, Special Issue, *Journal of Aesthetics and Art Criticism*, 52/1 (1994), 99–112. Note, also, that throughout this book I will generally be using terms such as 'Romantic', 'formalist', and 'modern', sometimes as coincident with one another, sometimes as oppositional, sometimes as picking out specific movements and sometimes broader world-views. As context demands, I shall also be using the terms 'political', 'moral', and 'social' sometimes as synonymous and sometimes with their various, more specific meanings.

residing solely in its 'tonally moving forms', composers have been able to assume an advantage over artists working with representational and referential mediums. They have not had to employ an Aesopian or underground language, as other artists have historically had to do. They have just had to stick firm to their claim that any extramusical references to feelings or emotions, to programmatic content, to visual or verbal association, or to social, political, or moral values are false, because they do not emanate directly from their referentially or conceptually meaningless notes. The musically meaningful and the musically beautiful, Eduard Hanslick wrote in his famed treatise on musical aesthetics, 'is self-contained and in no need of content from outside itself. . . . [I]t consists simply and solely of tones and their artistic combination.'[3] Of course, given their own moves towards abstraction, other artists have increasingly been able to advance a similar defence. In their defences, artists have often and quite explicitly aspired to music's purely formal, 'content-free' condition.

But there has always been a serious confusion in the defence that music is only about its notes. For if this defence is taken literally, then composers have not really needed it at all, because the charge that their music is significant in ways that might bother the censors has been unwarranted from the start. If their music is meaningless in all terms other than those specifically musical, then their increasingly common defence that 'I am merely a musician' or 'I only compose notes' has been truthful. Yet the problem with this sort of defence is that it has been disempowering. Music, it has implied, should matter musically, but not in any other way. 'Especially in recent times,' Hegel once observed,

music has torn itself free from a content already clear on its own account [i.e. from poetic speech] and retreated . . . into its own medium; but for this reason it has lost its power over the whole inner life, all the more so as the pleasure it can give relates to only one side of the art, namely bare interest in the purely musical element (*das rein Musikalische*) in the composition and its skilfulness, a side which is for connoisseurs only and scarcely appeals to the general human interest in art.[4]

But if, for Hegel, the interest in the purely musical rendered music less powerful as a fine art, for others, the same interest proved it

---

[3] *On the Musically Beautiful*, tr. G. Payzant (Indianapolis, 1986), 28.
[4] *Aesthetics: Lectures on Fine Art*, tr. T. M. Knox (Oxford, 1975), ii. 899.

most powerful. In part, I want to suggest, the interest here was strategic.

Consider this century's McCarthy trial of the composer Hanns Eisler. Eisler chose to, and found that he could, defend himself against the accusation that his music was 'communist', by claiming that it had no extramusical meaning. Having devoted his public musical life to broader social or political ends, ends which were explicitly communist, he still maintained that, even if these ends might be evident in Brecht's words (words he had used in his songs), they were not evident in his accompanying notes. He was not being entirely disingenuous, but he was also not being entirely truthful. He did believe that his musical notes could be political or revolutionary, but if they were, they were so only in an 'abstract', 'formal', or 'philosophical sense'.[5] It was a sense that apparently allowed his notes to appear as non-political and as merely musical.

Long before Eisler, other composers had also spoken of directing their musical work towards the betterment of humankind or to society's transformation, Here, again, the commitment usually proved more abstract than concrete. Indeed, it seems an abstract argument was required if one was properly to account for how, say, Beethoven's revolution in symphonic form had contributed, as so many claimed it had, to the betterment of humankind. The most common argument of abstraction rested on the claim that political or social concerns with humanity were, in the act of composition, transfigured or realized into purely musical terms. In being so realized, their expression was rendered purely musical. But precisely this realization threw the formalist claim into paradox. For formalism's commitment to the purely musical suggested now that though the music appeared as purely musical, its significance might none the less still be extramusical.

What is 'the extramusical' and how is it related to 'the purely musical'? Theorists typically use the term 'das rein Musikalische' to capture music's 'unique technical characteristics', or music's constitutive properties of sounds in their rhythmic and dynamic combinations. 'Das Aussermusikalische' is intended to capture everything else, i.e. everything that is not 'formally' or 'specifically' musical. Yet, I want to suggest, in its historical connection to 'das

---

[5] I have discussed this case in detail in my 'Political Music and the Politics of Music'.

Musikalische', the term 'ausser' has proved ambiguous, and sometimes strategically so, because it has carried (without termino-
logical differentiation in German) the connotations of 'non',
'extraneous', or 'outside' and of 'beyond', 'extra', or 'something
more', and these two sets of connotation have not always been the
same. I also want to suggest that it has been just the ambiguous use
of 'ausser' that has enabled the formalist claim to function in a
paradoxical state.

If we distinguish the concept of the extramusical from that of the
non-musical, then we can claim initially that whereas the non-
musical might play no role in our understanding of the musical,
the extramusical none the less does. Historically, the extramusical
seems to have accommodated precisely those properties of the
musical world that are not specifically musical, yet have given to
pure music its broader human and expressive significance. Traditional philosophical distinctions help capture the relation in which
extramusical properties have stood to merely or specifically musical ones. We might see them related as contingent to essential, as
extrinsic to intrinsic, as relational to monadic, as shared to unique.
But though comparison with these distinctions helps capture the
uneven or lopsided relation in which the extramusical has stood to
the musical, it does not explain it. For such comparison fails to
capture the paradoxical sense in which extramusical significance
has been tagged onto the specifically musical core as somehow *both*
relevant and irrelevant to the latter.

Indeed, the strange character of the extramusical reveals something that logical clarification could never capture by itself, namely,
what has really been at stake in musicians wanting to delimit the
borders of their purely musical domain so precisely, and why, as a
consequence, they have relegated all the other somehow relevant
factors to this uncomfortable 'extra' place. To identify what is at
stake, one might turn to a historical approach of the sort I pursued
in my book *The Imaginary Museum of Musical Works*. There, I
focused on the emergence of the concept of a work. After publication, I realized I had also traced the emergence of music's modern
claim to autonomy, but I did not see then how problematic that
claim was. The book described the development around 1800 of a
specifically musical practice of composition, performance, and reception severed from both its traditional, occasional service to
Church and court, and its age-old dependencies on poetry and text.

Yet it gave insufficient attention to the need for this new musical practice to reconnect itself to all these now extramusical elements under the modern condition of its emancipation. Music's emancipation, Carl Dahlhaus has written most appropriately, '"sequestered" music into a realm of its own', leaving musicians of 'delicate conscience . . . torn hither and thither between cries of art for art's sake and pronouncements on the social mission of art'.[6]

The emancipation had depended on distinguishing the musical from the *non*-musical to help separate out the aesthetic domain from that of the historical, social, moral, or political. And though it looked thereafter as if music's emancipation justified a purist concern only with musical or aesthetic matters, it really meant that musicians should be concerned with *extra*musical matters, but in purely musical or aesthetic terms. Against this background, the formalist claim to autonomy became a claim about the freedom of music's means of expression: music could address issues that were outside, or *ausser*, its scope, but not because it was functioning as a 'handmaiden' in service, say, to 'religion or politics'. This sort of service, modern theorists claimed, had too long controlled music's production in its pre-emancipated state. Music should now engage with and within the world purely musically, as an independently regulated language. Under this reading, music could claim to be both purely musical and extramusical: it is just that music would carry its extramusical significance, as Baudelaire once put it, 'by means peculiar to itself', or in Hegel's, Heine's, and sometimes even in Hanslick's terms, according to 'its own aim'. In other words, by thinking about music more as an independent language than as a separated domain, we begin to see that if music wanted to express something extramusical, then it could do so through its free and purely musical address. 'The extramusical' was capturing here the mediation, we might say, of the non-musical by and in the independently and purely musical.

Of course, by admitting a connection to, or an interest in, the world, musicians had constantly to prevent their emancipated music from returning to its purported former servility to non-musical demands. Music's emancipation marked a deeply defensive period, a strategic period of 'great refusal' in which the best way to protect music from the unwanted interference of society or

---

[6] *Nineteenth-Century Music*, tr. J. Bradford Robinson (Berkeley, Calif., 1989), 194–5.

its censorial representatives was rhetorically to claim that social assessments of music were non-musical, though allowing when pressed that they might really be extramusical. To believe they were non-musical was purifying but potentially disempowering to musicians; to believe they were extramusical was a way to preserve music's independence, while allowing also that it might be acting as a powerful social language.

Composers demonstrated their refusal by taking advantage (though not always consciously so) of the confusion between the non- and the extramusical. But they also gradually found a stronger argument of protection. They increasingly asserted their independence not only from a former servility to social institutions, but even from the threat of socialization by institutions that purportedly acknowledged their freedom. The argument lying behind their retreat into the ivory tower had been given them by Goethe, but it increasingly became Marxist and dialectical: though modern bourgeois institutions acknowledge the independent interests and ends of its music and musicians, they none the less constrain that freedom solely by virtue of their being social institutions. As such, they tend towards the type of conformism that disempowers musicians, either by taking their formalist claim to its purist extreme or by turning their music into 'mere entertainment'. Under such bourgeois conformism, the censors always win because music ceases under these conditions to be threatening in social or political terms.

An even more complex paradox had now appeared in music's formalist claim to autonomy. To claim that music is free was to acknowledge, first, that through the independent employment of its musical forms, music could articulate social ends by 'prophesying' ('in a philosophical sense') an art or politics for the future; but, secondly, that those ends would conflict with the ends that define the status quo. Music expressed the conflict itself, because while it asserted itself as a free or alternative means of expression, it would always also reflect (through its materials) the society that had given rise to it. The argument privileged music: it rested on the assumption that whereas conventional social dynamics tended historically towards the maintenance of the status quo, a would-be autonomous music aspired towards a liberation from it. This aspiration alone constituted music's great refusal, or, in Adorno's later phrase, its 'perennial protest'.

Music's refusal has been cast in other ways. One way I favour draws on an equation derived from strains of Critical and liberal political theory. One may say that music's *freedom from* external constraint gives music a *freedom to* express itself in, with, and on its own terms, which in turn gives it a *freedom to* express or reflect upon society at a critical distance. By combining music's *freedom from* with its *freedom to*, music achieves its desired position in society—its *freedom within*. The key to this notion of *freedom within* is the idea that music is immanent and social, but it is not merely or instrumentally social. Rather, it aspires to be resistantly social through its purely musical form. Again, this description captures music's demand (of course, only when it has this demand) to be entirely formally significant and thoroughly socially empowered.

In my *The Imaginary Museum*, I marked the emergence of the work concept at the beginning of the Romantic era and characterized that era as containing two steps or moves in aesthetic theory. I named these steps the *transcendental* and the *formal*. These steps did not follow chronologically; they reflected, rather, a Kantian legacy (a legacy that excluded Kant's own pre-emancipated view of music). The legacy loosely corresponded to his specification of the four moments of the pure aesthetic judgement, on the one hand, and to his determination that 'beauty is a symbol of morality', on the other. Adapting that double legacy, the formal step captured the inward move of musical meaning from external, referential meanings (now considered extra- and/or non-musical) to non-referential and structurally interior meanings. The transcendental step captured the upward move from concrete and empirical meaning to abstract and universal meaning. The formal step accommodated the work's desired unity of form and content; the transcendental step accommodated the noumenal or transcendental unity of the musical work and the non-musical world. I took Hanslick's work best to represent the formal step, Schopenhauer's work the transcendental. Each theorist gave the work its independence in objective and/or subjective terms. Both regarded music as pure. Hanslick spoke of the purely musical nature of purely instrumental music's empirical and objective content; Schopenhauer spoke of purely instrumental music's unmediated expression of the transcendentally subjective-objective Will. Putting the objective and subjective dimensions together rendered music both purely musical and thoroughly worlded. The phrase increasingly used to describe this worldedness was 'the purely human (*das Reinmenschliche*)'. As we shall see later, in its association with 'the purely musical', this phrase would sometimes give to music a quite ominous ideological significance.

Taking the formal and transcendental steps each as offering an independent account of the purely musical, the burden was obviously to choose between them. Many theorists and composers did, and out of that choice emerged two very different schools of musical aesthetics—one more empirical and gradually positivistic, the other more Romantic or metaphysical. I shall have more to say about this choice later. But there was also a way of conceiving these two steps, less as representing competing accounts than as representing the two different sides of the very same Romantic coin: one captured the specifically musical, or formal and empirical, dimension of music's significance, the other, its extramusical or transcendental dimension. (In this picture, 'the extramusical' again takes on the connotation of something 'beyond' or 'more' rather than 'non'.)

To match the complicated relation between the aesthetic and social, we might now think about our two steps as jointly representing a necessary but irreconcilable opposition. It will serve us well to introduce the term 'double' now, and to recommend *arguments of doubleness*, to recall, though not fully to endorse, the dialectical nature of so many claims within the Romantic and modern musical aesthetic. I find the term 'double' preferable to 'dialectical' because it stresses that the contradictions and conflicts in which elements or claims stand to one another are not always resolved (*a*) by picking one element at the expense of the other, (*b*) by reducing one element to a function of the other, or (*c*) as traditional dialectics dictates, by allowing a synthetic or higher third element to emerge according to a logic of historical development. In my view, the contradictions and conflicts cannot and should not always be resolved. Sometimes the elements or claims function in independence, sometimes in union, sometimes in resolution, but sometimes also in a desirable antagonistic relationship to one another. This antagonism, I shall later suggest, helps sustain a dynamic or open theory or practice advantaged by the presence not just of a plurality of claims, values, and ideals, but also by claims, values, and ideals that conflict with one another in progressive ways. However, recall-

ing Benjamin's famed dictum that '[t]here is no document of civilization which is not at the same time a document of barbarism', if
the conflicts can be progressive, they can also be regressive. Yet, I
shall maintain throughout this book that this possibility of regres-
sion is a risk we have to accommodate for the sake of a genuinely
open theory and practice.

Several conclusions follow from this general commitment to
doubleness. The most important in the present argument is that
music, or a musical work more specifically, is rendered discordant
in conception. Formally, a work may be a purely musical work
of art at the same time that, transcendentally, it can show the
(extramusical) world 'in its entirety'. Or, in critical terms, a work
might have the appearance of being a self-sufficient and harmonious whole, yet turn out to be what Adorno once described as a
profoundly non-harmonizing social 'cipher'. Such Janus-faced descriptions again reveal the deeply paradoxical or contradictory condition that has sustained a work's formalist claim to autonomy.
This condition has secured a work's aspiration towards freedom,
the aspiration to resist the social by bringing attention to society's
oppressive tendencies. This freedom is a freedom for a work to
show the power of its aesthetic form. Here is the essence of a
critical conception of the mimetic principle. A work does not copy
the world, it critically intervenes in it—and unnerves it—by claiming through aesthetic illusion that it has nothing to do with it. Here
is the essence also of a *critical formalism*. It is the sort of formalism
and autonomy that once motivated Eisler's 'philosophical' defence,
as well as (more or less directly) the three proclamations that
opened this chapter.

Following this critical line to its conclusion, we may also say that
it is by aspiring towards a purely aesthetic state that works have
played their social or political role. Less successfully, if at all, have
they played this role by functioning as merely social entities with
explicit or tendentious content. For, so the argument goes, in functioning this way, their resistance has been too quickly subsumed by
that which they resist. Censors who have sought to denounce
musical works have succeeded to the extent that they have been
able to reduce them to merely social entities or to music with
explicit messages. Clearly, the best defence against censors has
been to make that reductionism as difficult as possible. To produce
works of purely musical appearance has certainly been one way to

do this, because it has produced the illusion that the works are
'apolitical'. It is to be hoped that the censors have been taken in.
The musicians have known differently, however: the source of their
political or extramusical power has depended on their ability to
create illusions through aesthetic form. Schiller famously made the
point this way: 'In a truly beautiful work, the content should do
nothing, the form everything; for the wholeness of Man is affected
by form alone, and only individual powers by the content. . . .
Therefore the real artistic *secret* of the master consists in his annihilation of the material by means of the form' (my emphasis).[7]
Wagner made the point this way: Please do not think, he argued on
behalf of Beethoven's *Eroica*, that 'the idea of heroic strength
striving titanically for a noble cause' must be expressed though 'a
military account in music of the first Italian campaign'. No. All
these 'extraneous' or 'external' feelings and events have been
'transmuted' into the purely musical.[8] According to our general
argument, annihilation of material or transmutation of content is a
doubly deceptive but illuminating process of converting (perhaps
with intentional radical distortion) the non-musical into the purely
musical whereby the music will be purely formal in its musical
means and purely aesthetic in its effect.

Yet the formalist commitment to aesthetic illusion has proved
the censors' greatest frustration, for on which side of this con-
version resides the extramusical? How, in other words, could
censors ever tell whether composers were conveying something
extramusical to their publics through their purely musical works?
The ultimate teaching of the composers' great refusal is that the
censors have not been able to tell, a sad fact that has rendered their
judgements often arbitrary and their suspicions of pure music most
intense: 'if only', Grillparzer once mocked, 'the censors knew what
the musicians are thinking as they compose'.[9] However, the next
pressing philosophical question with which we are now faced is
whether any person has been able to tell.

What is the purely aesthetic, how can we know it, and what

[7] *On the Aesthetic Education of Man*, tr. R. Snell (New York, 1965), 105–6.
[8] 'A Happy Evening', in *Wagner Writes from Paris . . . Stories, Essays and Articles
by the Young Composer*, ed. and tr. R. L. Jacobs and G. Skelton (London, 1973),
185–6.
[9] From a letter by Grillparzer to Beethoven, quoted by Goldstein, *Political
Censorship of the Arts and the Press in Nineteenth-Century Europe*, 155; also by
Henry Raynor, *Music and Society since 1815* (London, 1976), 6.

justifies our equation of it with assertions of human freedom? Can we avoid giving a question-begging answer? Perhaps it looks as if we have so far rested our equation on a dichotomous argument of stipulation, i.e. as if we have merely stipulated that the musical or the autonomously aesthetic resists the unfree forms of the social. But we have not. If we focus our attention on themes such as aesthetic illusion, expression, and transmutation, our equation will soon lose its stipulative tone. However, what our equation will not lose is the breadth of its political and philosophical significance.

If, as I shall argue, we were to focus on the old and very obvious idea that expressing is something human beings individually and collectively do when they make music, we would soon see that music's aesthetic dimension of resistance less concerns an assertion of music's freedom *per se* than it does an assertion of a person's free and individual agency through the medium of music. If, furthermore, we were to take seriously the idea that music is composed by composers in order to be performed by performers and heard by audiences, we would soon move our interest away from a narrowly formalist concern with works and the question of their formed content and fix it more on the matter of people engaging with music as either an individual or social assertion of their freedom—their subjective freedom, as I shall often put it, to be musical. We might also then want to move our emphasis away from determining the borders of the musical domain to understanding the political power of communication through the expressive voice and performed act. Were we to do this, we could then also think about musical activity as a quest for the autonomous (musical) voice. This thinking would soon lead us to understand the great refusal of music and its musicians as a cultural reaction to the regressive tendencies of music's modern emancipation, to the tendencies on the part of musicians towards inexpression or disempowering disengagement, to the silencing of the autonomous voice. These tendencies would be found first in the actions of people and society, and then in the production of non-autonomous music as a consequence.

Finally, against the background of this way of thinking, we would also learn that there are two ways of articulating music's formalist claim to autonomy, one more progressive than the other. At its core, this book will explore these two ways, and the many transitions in our thinking about the relations between music, philosophy, and politics they demand.

2. 'Censorship is the mother of metaphor'[10]

... or as Barthes says: 'Perhaps a thing is valid only by its metaphoric power; perhaps that is the value of music, then: to be a good metaphor.'[11]

Let us return to the question whether we can know the aesthetic. I have already outlined some of the political and cultural background for making the aesthetic or the purely musical, as it were, unknowable. I want to pursue that explanation in another, though not unrelated, direction. This direction will allow us to see just how deeply our question about protecting music from censorship has been involved in nineteenth-century concerns with philosophical method.

My claim is this: that 'the purely musical', in tandem with 'the aesthetic', came to serve most explicitly in the context of German Romanticism as a repository for all that which could not be captured by a philosophical theory constrained solely by the authority of reason. 'The poetical' often played the same role, but my concern will exclusively be with 'the musical'. 'The purely musical', more specifically, served as a general metaphor symbolizing a repository for all that was unknowable by ordinary cognitive or logical means. It was not merely unknowable to censors looking for and at the wrong kinds of things. It was unknowable to all.

In terms that sound polemical, but should not be taken as such, music's (political) secrecy was sustained by its extraordinary (philosophical) silence. Purportedly meaningless in ordinary terms, music was rendered for the purposes of philosophy meaningful in extraordinary terms. It was under this condition of extraordinariness that it achieved its extramusicality or its metaphorical fullness of significance. Indeed, one might further say that music's purely musical meaning was already extramusical in the sense that music belonged to the extraordinary more than to the ordinary domain, though to give this new meaning to 'extramusical' renders

---

[10] Norman Manea quoting Borges in *On Clowns: The Dictator and the Artist* (New York, 1992), 30.

[11] 'Music, Voice, Language', in *The Responsibility of Forms: Critical Essays on Music, Art, and Representation*, tr. R. Howard (Berkeley, Calif., 1991), 285.

the term redundant. To say that music is extramusical is just to say that it is extraordinary. Yet this redundancy will prove in my argument a very happy one, because it will show how the concept of the purely musical can be interpreted to include the extramusical without compromising the formalist claim that music is, and is fundamentally about, its tonally moving forms. This interpretation I shall argue is consistent with a critical formalism. It is also consistent with what has recently and most pertinently been called an *enhanced* formalism, This is a formalism, as I shall read it, enhanced by an 'extra' or transcendental 'musical' moment.[12]

I first encountered the paradoxical idea of a silent repository for music when working on an essay on Schopenhauer's philosophy of music and its influence upon musicians. Wagner was one of those most influenced, but at that time I was interested in those who had influenced Schopenhauer. Most well known were Plato and Kant, with their domains of empirical appearance and transcendent(al) reality. But it seems less well known that Schopenhauer worked within an age-old tradition of German anagogic mysticism and philosophical anxiety that utilized claims of transcendence to find a sacred refuge for the individual, be it in God or in music. Attending to the medieval and Christian legacy in the Romantic musical aesthetic, theorists have noted the many fascinating institutional and behavioural parallels between the church, the museum, and the concert hall: the forms of silent contemplation, the shedding of worldly concerns, attitudes towards idolatry, and so on. They have less often acknowledged the influence of a certain medieval form of theological argument. At its core was the idea that one can show or point to what cannot be said or known by ordinary means by saying something that can be said or known by these means. The nature of the mediation was crucial, especially when it was a matter of reaching something perfect or divine. Showing one thing by saying another was the form exemplified in arguments of analogy. Like Augustine, but more explicitly like Aquinas, Schopenhauer demonstrated the use to which arguments of analogy (comparison, proportion, and especially negation) have to be put if philosophers are to say anything about that which, in the strictly philosophical

---

[12] Philip Alperson coined the term 'enhanced formalism' in response to Peter Kivy's work. However, Kivy explicitly rejects the sort of political and critical reading I am offering. See his recent *Philosophies of Arts: An Essay in Differences* (Ithaca, NY, 1997), ch. 7: 'The Liberation of Music'.

terms of rational explanation, cannot be spoken about. I argued that in this 'medieval' light Schopenhauer's descriptions of music were necessarily dependent upon an indirect, analogical narrative resting on a metaphysical aesthetic of inexpressibility.

Schopenhauer had begun his remarks by insisting that music stands apart from all other fine arts, because in music 'we do not recognize the copy . . . of any Idea of the inner nature of the World' (i. 256).[13] Familiar with claims about music's 'mimetic' failure to say anything determinate or particular about (the outer nature of) the world, he did not conclude, as others before him had, that music is therefore devoid of meaning or to be placed at the bottom in a taxonomy of the fine arts. 'Music', he judged, is 'a great and exceedingly fine art'. Indeed, it has so great an effect on 'man's innermost nature' and is 'so completely and profoundly understood by him in his innermost being' that 'we must attribute to [it] a [most] serious and profound significance'.

To differentiate music from the other arts, he wrote that the latter stimulate knowledge of (Platonic) Ideas. Ideas are the adequate representations of the (universal) Will. Music, by contrast, passes over the Ideas: it communicates no direct knowledge about them. Further, there is 'no [literal] resemblance between [music's] productions and the world as representation'. Music could exist even if there were no representation. Why? Because music is an immediate copy or manifestation of the Will itself. However, where there is Will there is representation, so music must be related to representation. But how?

Schopenhauer had realized immediately that the relation is 'abstract', 'very obscure', and 'essentially impossible to demonstrate', because to demonstrate it would be to establish 'a relation of music as a representation to that which . . . can never be representation'. 'In the explanation of this wonderful art', he wrote, the concept or explanation soon shows 'its inadequacy' and 'limits'. He then concluded with a sentiment that would later become identified more closely with Wittgenstein than with himself: if readers wish fully to understand these remarks, they should not try further to philosophize; they should just go and *listen* to music with the remarks in mind. ('Whereof one cannot speak . . .')

---

[13] All quotations of Schopenhauer are taken from *The World as Will and Representation*, tr. E. F. J. Payne (New York, 1969), vol. i, sect. 52, pp. 255–67 and vol. ii, ch. xxxix, pp. 447–57, unless stated otherwise. Page references are given in the text.

But what now could be the content of his subsequent musical remarks? He offered this answer: since we want to describe music but do not have a language that can 'unmask' or 'reveal' information about music as the manifestation of the Will directly, other than music itself, we can proceed only by drawing analogies to things we can describe, i.e. phenomena belonging to the world as representation. But 'we must never forget' that 'when referring to all these analogies . . . music has no direct relation to them, but only an indirect one; for [music] never expresses the phenomenon, but only the inner nature . . . of every phenomenon'. With this warning in mind, he proceeded to describe music indirectly, by analogy. For the remainder of this section, I shall provide a reading of Schopenhauer's view to motivate, first, the more general comments on philosophical method that will follow, and, after that, the interpretative framework within which I shall introduce the work of Richard Wagner.

Unlike other arts that communicate Ideas at a specific level of objectification, music, Schopenhauer writes, responds to every level. '[I recognize in] the whole of the ripienos that produce the harmony, between the bass and the leading voice singing the melody . . . the whole gradation of the Ideas in which the Will objectifies itself.' With the bass corresponding to the lower grades and the higher (tenor, alto, and soprano) voices to the plant, animal, and human worlds, Schopenhauer deliberately restores a view emanating as much out of ancient Western philosophy as from Eastern wisdom, that music is literally at one with the universe. Music is a universal language not because its meaning is available to everyone regardless of cultural difference. It is universal because it is a language that mirrors the Will without mediation. 'We could just as well call the world embodied music', he concludes, 'as embodied Will.'

As a universal language, music finds its profound meaning: it captures the entire endeavour of humankind, all 'the deepest secrets of human willing and feeling'. Our nature consists in the fact that our (individual) wills strive. After each striving is satisfied, our wills strive again. Our happiness (rarely achieved) consists in a constant transition from desire to satisfaction. The more normal condition of our having our desires frustrated leads to suffering. Our constant 'empty longing' for new desires results in languor and boredom. Music's patterns are structurally analogous to these patterns of desire, frustration, and fulfilment. '[T]he nature of melody is a constant digression and deviation from the keynote in a thousand ways, not only to the harmonious intervals, the third and the dominant, but to every tone, to the dissonant seventh, and the extreme intervals; yet there always follows a final return to the keynote' (i. 260). Melodies in different tempi and keys parallel the different forms and moments of our satisfactions or frustrations. 'The inexhaustibleness of possible melodies corresponds to the inexhaustibleness of nature in the difference of individuals, physiognomies, and courses of life.'

Schopenhauer recognizes that music expresses itself through activities of creation and reception, but only if these activities realize a transcendent form. Music is the product of genius; indeed, given its special status above the other arts, it requires more genius than they do. The dualism separating Will from representation, the universal from the particular, the metaphysical from the physical, music from the plastic and literary fine arts, also separates the composer-genius from the embodying (phenomenal) person. Composing music is far removed from all conscious intention or reflection; it is the pure product of inspiration and imagination. The composer 'expresses the profoundest wisdom in a language that his reasoning faculty does not understand'. In the composer, 'the man is distinct from the artist'.

What of music's expressive potential and understanding? Despite the apparent ease with which theorists have been able to attribute expressive or emotive qualities to music—happiness, sadness, gaiety, and sorrow—music fails to express the materiality or specificity of any given emotion. From the perspective of Will, it expresses *abstractly*, *universally*, and *essentially*. Music is pure temporal process, the dynamics of which directly correspond to the flow of the Will's emotional life. So if it expresses the different emotions at all, it expresses them 'in themselves' abstracted from any ordinary human motives or experiences that might generate their particularized instantiation. Emotions, Schopenhauer argues now by negation, are captured as 'mere form without the material, like a mere spirit world without matter'.

Correspondingly, music speaks to its listeners purely, through the non-conceptual activities of the imagination, unmediated by, and abstracted from, ordinary interests. At this level of disinterested contemplation, it speaks through the purely temporal and audible patterns of melody and harmony of an invisible spirit world and of the quintessence of life.

This purely aesthetic engagement with music is achieved by relatively few people. Schopenhauer criticizes composers and critics who try 'pathologically' to pull music down into the phenomenal world by subordinating it to the sentimental expression of an ordinary person's individual emotions, interests, and concerns; or by associating it with words (this attempt, he says, is the origin of song and later of opera); or by making music imitate in a programmatic manner (as Haydn had done in *The Seasons* and lesser so in his *Creation*). Against this, he claims that the most genuinely universal music is purely instrumental. '[I]f music tries to stick too closely to the words, and to mold itself according to the events [of the phenomenal world]', it is endeavouring to speak a language not its own. Only composers like Rossini (one of his favourite composers), who can keep 'free from this mistake', allow music to speak 'its *own* language . . . distinctly and purely'. So '[f]ar from being a mere aid to poetry, music is certainly an independent art; in fact, it is the most powerful of all the arts, and therefore attains its ends entirely from its own resources'.

Schopenhauer does not want to dismiss opera or song as altogether without value. Still, he can be very disparaging: 'Strictly speaking one could call opera an unmusical invention for the benefit of unmusical minds, in as much as music first has to be smuggled in through a medium foreign to it, for instance as the accompaniment to a long drawn out, insipid love story and its poetic pap.'[14] In so criticizing opera, he was dismissing only the operas that subordinate melody to words or actions. He dismissed the promise of Wagner's *Ring* cycle as such an example: Wagner 'should give up his music', he declared after reading the *Ring*'s libretto; 'he has more genius as a poet!' (Schopenhauer would never hear the complete score.) His point was comparative: only by giving priority to music, as Mozart and Rossini had, can we (the audience) encounter the most profound information expressed by the opera's words or dramatic actions, for music 'stands to the text and the action in the relation of universal and particular, of rule to example'. Music gives

---

[14] *Essays and Aphorisms*, tr. R. J. Hollingdale (Harmondsworth, 1970), 163.

opera its soul. True opera is essentially a genre of music and must be composed according to the principles of purely instrumental music. In this way, opera can also be absolute. Schopenhauer even suggests that, contrary to the traditional composition of song, the melody should be composed before the words, since that which expresses the interior Will should guide that which represents the exterior world. Such interiority is the source of music's freedom, whether or not the music is purely instrumental.

By being removed from the sphere of local human interests, and by being put into the transcendent aesthetic sphere, music does not lose its connection to what matters to human beings. On the contrary: for Schopenhauer, the really 'serious' side of life is that of the Will, and music traverses the course of that life.

Schopenhauer intends to show that music is 'rooted in the real nature of things and of man'; its autonomy does *not* deprive it of a metaphysical and moral involvement with the world. He corroborates this claim through his insistence that he is always offering a view of transcendence as existing not independently from the phenomenal world, but immanently within it. 'My philosophy', he once wrote, 'is never concerned with cloud-cuckoo-land but with *this* world.'[15] Despite the doubled description, there is only one world.

Schopenhauer conceives of the Will as a blind impulse that forever strives. It fails ever to achieve final satisfaction. Is our experience of music then comparably frustrating? Not according to Schopenhauer. The experience of music as the highest form of aesthetic experience is 'remote from pain' because it is without phenomenal reality. Unlike in our everyday existence, in music we experience the life of the Will without bearing the full pessimistic brunt of its associated frustrations. In becoming completely absorbed in the music, in the Will's pure expression, we become identified with the Will itself. In that identification, we are released from the servitude we experience to our individual wills. Music offers us, then, even if for just a brief moment, a release from our perpetual suffering.

In its purely metaphysical state, Schopenhauer next claims, music promises the true philosophy. First he defines philosophy as

---

[15] Quoted by Rudiger Safranski, *Schopenhauer and the Wild Years of Philosophy*, tr. E. Osels (Cambridge, Mass., 1990), 347.

nothing but a complete and accurate repetition and expression of the inner nature of the world in very general concepts, for only in these is it possible to obtain a view of that entire inner nature which is everywhere adequate and applicable. (i. 264)

Then he establishes the further claim:

Thus whoever has followed me and entered into my way of thinking will not find it so very paradoxical when I say that, supposing we succeeded in giving a perfectly accurate and complete explanation of music which goes into detail, and thus a detailed repetition in concepts of what it expresses, this would also be at once a sufficient repetition and explanation of the world in concepts, *or one wholly corresponding thereto*, and hence the true philosophy. (i. 264; my emphasis)

Parodying Leibniz's assertion that music is 'an unconscious exercise in arithmetic in which the mind does not know it is counting', he finally characterizes music as 'an unconscious exercise in metaphysics in which the mind does not know it is philosophizing'.

The hope that he might provide what he has just called a 'perfectly accurate and complete explanation of music' in general concepts is immediately thwarted. Could it be otherwise? Necessarily not, which is why he had to add that additional phrase 'or one wholly corresponding thereto' (emphasized above). Remember that, conceived as pure and unconscious philosophy, music must proceed in conceptual 'silence' (i.e. through its own medium of sound). If we must speak about music as philosophers, we must speak indirectly. Otherwise put, since music shows its meaning transcendentally through revelation and intuition, it cannot be translated into, or fully described by, a rational, conceptual, or empirical language. Anything, he writes at the very end of his treatise, which lies before or beyond the phenomenal world 'is open to no investigation'.

Either Schopenhauer can stop writing about music altogether or he can continue to write indirectly. He favours the latter, but only because it will further demonstrate the strength of indirect analogy between music and the phenomenal world. Since Will and representation are two perspectives taken on *the same* world, in some sense there must hold between them a perfect correspondence. Even so, the world of representation is also imperfect, and therein lies the paradox of true philosophical explanation.

Having established earlier in his treatise that moral human

beings cannot exist without the lower-order natural world, or that if the Will is objectified at one level it must be also at the other levels, he claims that melody (as the highest expression of the Will) cannot exist without complete harmony beneath it.

The high voice, singing the melody, is at the same time an integral part of the harmony, and in this is connected even with the deepest ground-bass. This may be regarded as the analogue of the fact that *the same* matter that in a human organism is the supporter of the Idea of man must nevertheless at the same time manifest and support the Ideas of gravity . . . hence the Ideas of the lowest grades of the [W]ill's objectification. (ii. 448)

Schopenhauer takes the point further. Just as one cannot find perfect harmony in the objectified world, just as there is unending conflict or inner contradictions between individuals at and between different levels of objectification, so comparable 'insoluble irrationalities' exist in music:

No scale can ever be computed within which every fifth would be related to the keynote as 2 to 3, every major third as 4 to 5, every minor third as 5 to 6. . . . For if the tones are correctly related to the keynote, they no longer are so to one another, because, for example, the fifth would have to be the minor third to the third, and so on. For the notes of the scale can be compared to actors, which have to play now one part, now another. (i. 266)

Now, he concludes, 'a perfectly correct music cannot even be conceived, much less worked out; and for this reason all actual music deviates from perfect purity'.

However, that any actual manifestation of music is imperfect does not detract from the redemptive quality of music's promised philosophical significance. As the Will's unmediated expression, music points to a true and profound knowledge of the world. But that this inner nature is also the source of our constant suffering should persuade us never to be convinced by optimistic visions of perfect harmony or happiness in our world. We are left only with the sublime (and, therefore, double-edged) knowledge of the unavoidable suffering of our insatiable wills but also of our desire and ability to escape this realization by any means possible, even if only temporarily. Temporary alleviation from the world does nothing to change its essential condition; it only hints at what the world would be like if our experience were different, if we had no illusions and no unfulfilled desires. The question remains whether this is merely an empty hint.

3. 'The rest is silence'

Schopenhauer revealed more about music through silence than through speech, more through what he could show indirectly—by analogy or in silence—than through what he was able to say literally in speech. Speech and silence, like saying and showing, are mutually dependent or correlative concepts. What cannot be said, what belongs to silent discourse, is revealed only by, or as a contrast to, what can be said. The limits of what can be said determine the limits of what can be shown; the world of speech delimits the boundaries the world of silence transgresses. Silence, a contemporary philosopher, Lie Kuen Tong, has written recently, should 'not be conceived as the mere absence of speech, but rather as its transcendence'.[16]

When Schopenhauer employed Shakespeare's expression 'the rest is silence' to mark the completion of his *Parerga and Paralipomena*, he was thinking about the finality of his life's project.[17] But he could also have been thinking about how the world as representation admits a form of description which the world as Will does not, and that when one reaches the limits of that description (which in a sense he had done) one enters the realm of extraordinariness or silence. What is useful about the phrase 'the rest is silence' is the relative and negating phrasing: it is not just that the two worlds are related—the one is known in its difference from the other. 'Behind our existence', Schopenhauer writes (i. 405), 'lies something else that becomes accessible to us only by our shaking off the world.' The point is that something has to be shaken off. The transcendent feature of the musical experience, in these terms, becomes a negating experience of that which must be transcended. Like the aesthetic, the musical experience refers to a human condition to be got beyond.

The sense of getting beyond a specific condition, the sense that one can reach for something that presently is not so or does not exist, sustains the strong connection in the nineteenth century between music, philosophy, and politics. This reaching suggests that individuals or societies strive to surpass the identity or the particular condition that currently defines them. They can see past who

---

[16] 'The Meaning of Philosophical Silence: Some Reflections on the Use of Language in Chinese Thought', *Journal of Chinese Philosophy*, 3 (1976), 169.
[17] Cf. B. Magee, *The Philosophy of Schopenhauer* (Oxford, 1983), 25.

they are to what they could (or should) be. 'While listening to great music,' Schopenhauer once wrote, 'everyone feels distinctly what his ultimate worth is, or, much more, what his worth could be.'[18] The notion of 'seeing past' suggests a positive power of vision, but it is a power that exceeds ordinary sight and ordinary words. It is a power described necessarily through metaphor. The metaphors chosen are typically those that have most challenged the terms of our ordinary or literal discourse. 'Silence' has served as our anti-dote to 'speaking', 'hearing' (usually conceived as an 'inner' hear-ing) our antidote to 'seeing'. That we have liked to think of our ordinary world as a barrage of 'chatter' and 'images' says some-thing revealing. That we say that it 'says something revealing' is exactly the philosophical device that interests me.

Philosophers have long conceived of the human condition dual-istically, and have generated a whole slew of binary oppositions to express that conception: subject–object, inner–outer, knowledge–opinion, fact–value, reason–passion, sacred–secular. These opposi-tions (like the purely musical—extramusical) have mostly suggested an evaluative lopsidedness: one side has been awarded more value than the other. Some theorists have employed one side to the exclusion of the other; others have worked doubly on both sides. Let me explain.

I think it generally agreed that any given philosophical theory or method both invokes ontological and/or epistemological limits and, in so doing, determines that of which the theory needs to take account. Theorists have differed on whether they regard those limits as including or as excluding. Those who have recognized the legitimacy of a theory governed by 'objective' principles of rational or logical coherence have treated those limits either as including or as excluding that with which they should be concerned. Those who have chosen the former have tended to ignore that which is ex-cluded as either nonsensical or functionally reducible to that which is included. Strictly speaking, for these theorists, there is nothing philosophical on the other side to be found because the limits determine all that is and could be the case. This attitude, we shall see later, is prevalent in the more empiricist version of the musical formalist's claim.

By contrast, theorists who have regarded limits as excluding

---

[18] Quoted by Friedrich von Hausegger in his *Die Musik als Ausdruck* (see E. Lippman, *A History of Western Musical Aesthetics* (Lincoln, Nebr., 1992), 290).

what is valuable have tended to treat limits critically or dialectically, rather than rejecting the method that generated the limits in
the first place. They have allowed that one can acknowledge, account for, or point to the value of that which is excluded through an
account of that which is included. Mostly, these theorists have
treated the excluded as more valuable than the included, in part
precisely because it resists subsumption under a theory of general
concepts or confinement by the theory's limits. The excluded terri-
tory has often been referred to in terms of the inexpressible,
unrepresentable, unsayable, or unknowable, in negating terms that
refer to all that remains once a philosophical theory, or philosophical speech less specifically, has reached its limits.

Theorists who have opted for this doubled discourse of speech
and silence, or expressing the inexpressible, have tended, by contrast, to see their philosophical method as enigmatic and paradoxical. Just as Schopenhauer's musical remarks are paradoxical
because they say what they cannot strictly speaking say, so argu-
ably is Socrates' claim about philosophical ignorance, or Confucius'
claim that, out of respect, knowledge should not be spoken aloud,
or Wittgenstein's modernist claim that truth and value lie at or
beyond the limits of the language of 'facts'.[19] Each claim renders
the valuable part of philosophy a silent discourse and, once this is
established, not subject to further investigation. Yet philosophy
continues: it does not cease to speak. Not only does philosophy
historically invoke an horizon between speech and silence; it also
situates itself above and below the horizon simultaneously.

Why, one may ask, have theorists supported a dualistic view if
it renders their method either overly constrained, on the one hand,
or paradoxical and enigmatic, on the other? There are many answers, but one jumps out immediately. There is that age-old, fundamental distrust of humanity, a distrust that reflects that anxious
impulse towards salvation, perfection, and purification I mentioned
earlier in the context of medieval theology, and a moment ago
when I spoke of the human desire to surpass one's 'all-too-human'
condition. A remarkable feature of nineteenth-century thought is
the extent to which theorists regarded human beings as essentially
ignorant and existentially deluded. Under this condition, human
beings live in, and are responsible for, an imperfect, disordered,

---

[19] I have borrowed these comparisons from Lie, 'The Meaning of Philosophical
Silence'.

and corrupt world, a world of barbarism described once by
Nietzsche as a world occupied by 'weeds, rubble and vermin'.[20]
Heine once described this world as 'a great cowshed which is not so
easy to clear out as the Augean stable because, while it is being
swept, the oxen stay inside and continually pile up more dung'.[21]
(Wagner would use the image to describe Paris.)

    These descriptions recall the gloomy distrust of the pessimistic
Schopenhauer, yet, quoted in isolation, they fail to capture the
hope expressed by an enigmatic music, or in metaphorical tandem,
by a paradoxical philosophy. But many theorists do express that
hope, for example Stendhal, in his biography of Rossini, to counter
the belief that reality 'is a plague'.

[F]ar from being concerned with *realism*, [art] has as its main function to
furnish sufficient *idealism* to purge the soul, as swiftly and as durably as
possible, of every taint of this dung-heap world.[22]

Hermann Hesse expresses the attitude more positively:

The human attitude of which classical music is the expression is always the
same; it is always based on the same kind of insight into life and strives for
the same kind of victory over blind chance. Classical music as gesture
signifies knowledge of the tragedy of the human condition, affirmation of
human destiny, courage, cheerful serenity.[23]

I am particularly intrigued by this antithetical solution to the de-
spair of imperfection, the positing of a musical world that provides
humanity with a metaphysical or existential escape—even if only a
temporary one—from 'base humanity'.

    Against this background, that Schopenhauer says so little about
music directly or literally becomes ever more significant. This mode
of description turns out to be a way of protecting music from a
reduction, translation, and corruption into the mundane. Describing music as the pure language of Will, or of free subjectivity, or of

---

[20] 'Schopenhauer as Educator', in *Untimely Meditations*, tr. R. J. Hollingdale
(Cambridge, 1983), 130.
[21] I first came across this quotation in Albrecht Betz, *Hanns Eisler, Political
Musician*, tr. B. Hopkins (Cambridge, 1982), 246.
[22] *The Life of Rossini*, tr. R. N. Coe (London, 1985), 266. Stendhal is satirizing the
view of 'Frenchmen concerned with taste'.
[23] *The Glass Bead Game (Magister Ludi)*, tr. R. and C. Winston (New York,
1969), 43–4. Hesse uses 'classical music' to refer to 18th-century compositions of
'classical form', but the claim has broader connotation.

pure feeling, spontaneity, and gesture protects music from the usual range of base concepts and feelings, common judgements, and desires. Not limited by the usual systematic or scientific laws of order and meaning, music succeeds in its own unspoken terms in revealing the spiritual meaning of the world. Its silence is not only revelatory and purifying, but also protective. A major claim in my overall argument may now be stated: music's silence, philosophically conceived, serves as the true Romantic expression of the musicians' great refusal; it serves as the esoteric philosophical basis of music's secret resistance to mundane censorious judgement.

However, it is not only music that has to be protected, but philosophy itself. The link between music and philosophy now becomes crucial. One way to protect philosophy in the nineteenth century was to connect it to its positivist aspirations to make itself into a pure, unadulterated science. Another was to take seriously philosophy's aspirations to achieve the status of pure music. Regarding the latter (the former is more familiar), the idea was that philosophy should aspire to the condition of pure music in becoming a mode of speech which, even if limited to a certain degree *by* the (empirical) bounds of sense, should none the less not be limited *to* them. As with music, so philosophy should give us access to what is ordinarily and otherwise unreachable. So far so good—until one notices the threatening circularity.

Music may serve as a model for philosophy if it is given a role or description that fits philosophy by extension or analogy. To ensure an easy transfer, theorists could make music essentially a philosophical metaphor to serve philosophy itself. But now they would be faced with an obvious circularity. With more circumspection, they could note shared properties between music and philosophy, draw a conclusion by analogy, and note at the same time the differences between the two. The differences would be crucial. In claiming that philosophy should aspire to the condition of music, they would have to know to which of music's properties it should aspire and to which not. Would this procedure shed their description of its circularity? I think not, because the circularity is far more pervasive than we have yet noted. It arises with any claim that philosophy should aspire to any ideal or condition, be it scientific or artistic, because that condition is already philosophically informed. The peculiar quality of the philosophical enterprise is that we are always already working within philosophy's domain, even when we are making claims about philosophy as deriving from another discipline. The use of the word 'another' here only obscures the point.

I shall not pursue the paradoxical or self-reflective quality of the philosophical enterprise further. It is well known. Suffice it to make explicit that philosophy was yet further turned in upon itself when, in the nineteenth century, it developed for itself a model based on a subject-matter (i.e. music) that paradoxically was, or metaphorically was claimed to be, more philosophical than philosophy itself. This paradox, I believe, accounts for the special and most peculiar quality of that century's philosophy of music, because it turned out really to be a thesis about 'the music of philosophy'. That is to say, 'the musical' functioned as a philosophical metaphor for a quality of philosophy to which philosophy was supposed to aspire.

Nietzsche once perfectly articulated this aspiration when he asked whether it had been noticed 'that music liberates the spirit? gives wings to thought? that one becomes more of a philosopher the more one becomes a musician?—The gray sky of abstraction rent as if by lightning: the light strong enough for the filigree of things: the great problems near enough to grasp; the world surveyed as from a mountain'.[24] The idea that a philosopher should become a musician was dependent upon seeing in music, or, rather, in the musician, the capacity to view the world at a distance. The assumption was that this distance offered a liberation and protection from the world's worldly constraints. The musician's freedom was an antagonistic ideal to which the philosopher should aspire. For (the early) Nietzsche, it was an ideal captured in the inexpressible expression of the human spirit. This expression would flow as an under- (or over-)current to challenge the rationalist limitations he found in the dominant philosophical method of his time. He sometimes identified these limitations with the 'rationalist Socrates', but by doing this he was deliberately putting aside his memory of the instruction Socrates had once been given in a dream that the philosopher should practise (*treiben*) music. 'Music' was the modern metaphor corresponding to what Socrates had termed

[24] *The Case of Wagner*, in *Basic Writings of Nietzsche*, tr. and ed. W. Kaufmann (New York, 1968), 614.

mousikē, and Socrates had used that term to refer to the practice of philosophy as a 'liberal art'. Nietzsche knew this:

The voice of the Socratic dream vision is the only sign of any misgivings about the limits of logic: Perhaps—this he [Socrates] must have asked himself—what is not intelligible to me is not necessarily unintelligent? Perhaps there is a realm of wisdom from which the logician is exiled? Perhaps art is even a necessary correlative of, and supplement for, science?[25]

When Nietzsche used 'the musical' as a metaphor to capture the spirit of free expression that was ideally to be found in philosophy, he had Schopenhauer in mind. But the question neither philosopher really dealt with was what was going to happen when, having satisfied this metaphysically musical ideal, philosophy turned itself round again to give an account of the actual practice of music? Could the music of philosophy really be reconciled with the philosophy of music? In my understanding, this question became one of the central concerns for the nineteenth-century theorists. It asked whether the more literal and formal concept of the musical serving music's emancipated practice could in any interesting way be related to the service the metaphysical metaphor of the musical was contemporaneously providing in the philosophical domain.

My research suggests that the literal and metaphorical services of the musical came into conflict at a particular historical juncture symbolized by Richard Wagner. Schopenhauer and Nietzsche remained mostly within philosophy's jurisdiction. Wagner tried to adjust the paradoxical demands of an essentially musical metaphysics—with its concomitant demands for silence and secrecy—to the demands of a dynamic and living practice of musical production. How, he effectively asked, do the creation, performance, and reception of works reveal the necessary failure of philosophy to speak its own meaning?[26] Even for Wagner, this question often remained one of philosophical method. But he revealed its broadest musical, philosophical, and political dimensions.

---

[25] *The Birth of Tragedy* (sect. 14), in *Basic Writings*, 93.
[26] Cf. Hartmut Reinhart's claim that Wagner saw the task of art (and his art) to be to represent Schopenhauer's philosophical insight ('Wagner and Schopenhauer', in U. Müller and P. Wapnewski (eds.), *Wagner Handbook*, tr. ed. J. Deathridge (Cambridge, Mass., 1992), 287).

4. Freed from Convention; Freed from Dogma[27]

Wagner understood the paradoxical position in which Schopenhauer had put the philosopher, and grasped immediately that its
most adequate solution lay with the composer and with music's
expression.

Though Schopenhauer propounds his theory of music as a paradox . . . [he]
also provides us the only serviceable material for a further demonstration
of the justice of his profound hypothesis; a demonstration which he did
not, however, pursue more closely, perhaps because he was not conversant
enough with music, or [perhaps] . . . because he [did] not base his knowledge on an understanding of the very musician whose works first laid
open to the world the deepest mystery (*das tiefste Geheimnis*) of
music . . . [namely] Beethoven.[28]

For Wagner, philosophy's demonstration operated ideally through
those works (and paradigmatically Beethoven's works) that express what philosophy or any other verbal language fails to express.
The essence of higher instrumental music consists in expressing
in tones something inexpressible in words. 'The orchestra indisput-
ably possesses a *faculty of speech*. . . . [W]e have plainly to call this
speaking faculty . . . the faculty of speaking the unspeakable.
. . . [T]he unspeakable is not something unspeakable *per se*, but
merely unspeakable through the organ of our understanding.'[29] In
contrast to speaking through the understanding, the orchestra
speaks the unspeakable through 'gesture' and 'feeling'. Through
these means, it reveals 'a schema of the world's phenomena quite
different from the ordinary logical scheme'. It 'thrusts home with
the most overwhelming conviction'. It 'guides our feeling with such
a sureness that our logic-mongering reason is completely . . .
disarmed'.[30] Music, he reiterated in devotedly Schopenhauerian
terms, speaks to us of 'the world outside us' and 'in terms intelligi-

---

[27] Adapted from Wagner's 'von aller Konvention losgelöste' ('A Communication
to my Friends' (1851), i. 364); 'frei von jeder dogmatischen Begriffsfiktion'
('Beethoven', v. 79). All quotations from Wagner are taken (unless specified otherwise) from *Richard Wagner's Prose Works*, tr. W. A. Ellis, 8 vols. (Lincoln, Nebr.,
1995). Unless context demands otherwise, references are given only to the English
translation and only for quotations that are longer than a phrase. I have sometimes
adapted Ellis's translations for the sake of accuracy and readability. I have also
consulted various editions of Wagner's *Gesammelte Schriften und Dichtungen*.

[28] 'Beethoven', v. 66.

[29] 'Opera and Drama', ii. 316–17.

[30] 'Zukunftsmusik', iii. 317–19.

ble beyond compare'. But it is intelligible to us not through logic, but because 'the message sounding in our ear is of the selfsame nature as the cry sent forth to it from the depths of our own inner heart'.[31]

Sometimes Wagner asserted the contrast between logical and musical intelligibility more vehemently: 'Science (*Wissenschaft*) has laid bare to us the organism of speech. She showed us a *defunct* organism. Only the poet's utmost want can bring [it] to life again . . . by healing up the wounds with which the anatomic scalpel has gashed the body of speech, and by breathing into it the breath that may animate it with living motion. This breath is—music'.[32]

Wagner typically accompanied his metaphysical claims with cultural judgements. Partly this was the response of a person experiencing political and cultural turmoil as a painful given of his daily life. More abstractly, he juxtaposed the literal and metaphorical concepts of the musical whenever he wanted to explain the failure of a given language to express the inexpressible. Sometimes he determined that a given language was metaphysically inappropriate for such an utterance, at other times, that a given language had, in a given case, been misused. Under the first, metaphysical determination, he followed Schopenhauer in asserting that the literal language of music—the language of tones—is the only language that expresses the inexpressible directly (*ohne Mittel*); it is the language *par excellence* of immediate feeling. Under the second, cultural determination, he adopted a critical stand against any language he thought had been put to death by a 'logic-mongering' formalism. He saw a defunct language to be one that had lost its spirit, breath, or expressiveness, or, in metaphorical terms, its music. Any language, he argued, including the literal language of music itself, must be animated by the spirit of the musical if it is to succeed either directly or indirectly in expressing the inexpressible.

That Wagner employed a metaphor of the musical—life, spirit, breath—as both a cultural and metaphysical standard to which all languages are supposed to aspire is an indispensable key to comprehending many aspects of his work: (*a*) his vehement attacks on the regressive tendencies in both musical and philosophical formalism; (*b*) his move away from the composition of instrumental music to that of opera; (*c*) his commitment to musical

[31] 'Beethoven', v. 70–1.   [32] 'Opera and Drama', ii. 265.

performance as an event in which politics is served only if the aesthetic of expression is also served; and finally, (*d*) his linkage between creativity, expression, and national identity. I shall pursue these themes in detail in the following chapters. Here I shall only sketch them in order to stay focused on the methodological argument. Consider the last theme first.

When Wagner argued that composers' creative potential, or the character of their works, is inextricably linked to the linguistic and national character of their countries, sometimes he meant exactly what the words suggest, that works can have, say, a German character, or that composers must be German to compose German music, and so on. At other times, he employed these terms metaphorically to suggest that for composers to compose works imbued with the musical spirit, they must express something that is 'purely human'. In these utterances, he equated 'the purely human' with the metaphorical concept of the purely musical or inexpressible. He then further confused the matter by employing a metaphor of 'being German' to signify the universal ideals and aspirations of the 'purely human' or 'musical' man. This was a quite common, cosmopolitan tactic in his period borrowed from French Revolutionary ideals. To sustain the metaphorical use, Wagner sometimes made the unmarked 'Man' (*Mensch*) stand for the androgynous man-woman to synthesize the purely human qualities of 'thought' and 'feeling'. At other times, he differentiated the unmarked 'German Man' from the equally unmarked 'modern' 'Frenchman' or 'Jew'.

Generally, in formulating his political theory in metaphysical terms, Wagner maintained that, in principle, any person can exhibit 'German' or 'purely human' qualities, even, literally speaking, Jews. (He mentioned Ludwig Börne as an example.) But when he transformed his political assertions or 'general ideas' into ideological weapons to bolster his cultural criticisms (generated, he said, by his 'sympathies'), he tended to fill in the ideal of the purely human with a determinate, Christian, nationalist, and racist content.[33] The 'cosmopolite', 'Frenchman', or 'Jew' could symbolize in Wagner's work either any person at all of whom he disapproved, or a particular person who was literally modern, cosmopolitan, or Jewish.

[33] Cf. Dieter Borchmeyer, 'The Question of Anti-Semitism', in Müller and Wapnewski (eds.), *Wagner Handbook*, 169.

Wagner sometimes rejected his own ideological positions. Sometimes he denied that national character should be defined by reference to a person's or community's outer, physical or racial properties. Rather, one should seek evidence of inner feelings emanating from their souls or characters—and, metaphysically speaking, any person (or community) may exhibit a 'purely human' soul. When he argued that way, he maintained a slightly more palatable conception of national character. When he argued otherwise, he trod a hazardous, ideological path. Decades after his death, 'the ideological Wagner' got a small come-uppance. Opening a wonderful novel entitled *Mendelssohn is on the Roof*, author Jiří Weil tells the story of two workmen who are instructed to help a would-be SS guard take down from the roof of the Prague concert hall the statue of Mendelssohn on the grounds of his being Jewish. Unable to locate the correct statue, the anxious guard recalls his education in 'racial science' and instructs the workmen to look for the face with the 'biggest nose'. Moments later, Wagner is toppling from his pedestal![34]

In the following chapters, I shall try to unravel Wagner's combined metaphysical and cultural judgements by isolating what I call a progressive, political model from its regressive, ideological counterpart. The idea governing my interpretative scheme and methodological argument will be that a practice (musical, political, or philosophical) is progressive when it is open, and it is open when it is regulated by suitable regulative or formal ideals that have neither been overdetermined nor closed by ideological content. Methodologically, I shall argue that such a practice demands that we take limits, doubleness, and explanatory gaps very seriously as techniques of philosophical theory. Interpreting Wagner, I shall argue that, in connecting the concept of purely human expression to the purely musical, he sometimes argued for a progressive model but sometimes for its dangerously close, regressive counterpart. Furthermore, I shall argue that Wagner himself sometimes used a comparable critical framework to mine when judging formalism from a transcendental or anti-systematic perspective.

Trying to account for Wagner's sometimes progressive and sometimes regressive thinking, I will suggest on the progressive side that a gap needs to be maintained in theory and practice, and

[34] Tr. Marie Winn (New York, 1991).

between the two, to capture the sense in which a practice is always *more than* any theory which either describes and/or prescribes it. Where a practice is taken to be fully determined by the theory, it loses its openness. So similarly with a theory itself. A political theory, say, is closed at the point at which it becomes fully determined by substantively ideological content. Faced with ideological saturation, individuals lose their expressive potential or autonomy, and the community within which they live becomes, to use Wagner's word, 'defunct'. To leave a theory limited and its corresponding practice underdetermined allows competing political ideals and conflicting expressions of those ideals to exist within a single practice. Here I use 'political' to refer to the formal nature of ideals and/or to the quality of underdetermination, and 'ideology' to the substantive or concrete content used to fill out those ideals and/or to the attempt to complete their determination. Under this stipulation, the distinction between the political and the ideological marks their mutually dependent and mutually exclusive aspects. The stipulation helps us to see the functional and critical interaction of these concepts in their jointly progressive and regressive modes.[35]

The idea of preserving a gap recalls what some theorists have described as a critical moment of non-identity or resistance. Another way to describe the gap is by appeal to a moment of excess, or to an intensification or enhancement of meaning that is not reducible to the meaning of which it is the intensification. In this sense, the gap is consistent with a transcendentalist account of something *extra*, and with a technique of doubleness that captures less, in this context, the twoness suggested by the term 'double' than the *more than* unified oneness. Consider the following. Donald Davidson has argued that a metaphor stands to its literal counterpart as offering a special and additional *use* of the literal meaning, but not an additional *meaning*.[36] I take metaphorical use

---

[35] 'Politics' and 'ideology' have numerous meanings and, even in my own argument, could be reversed. But given the derogatory connotations assumed recently by 'ideology', even more derogatory than 'politics', I have chosen to given the latter term the more neutral meaning. I have been influenced by Bernard Williams's distinction between 'ethical theory' and 'morality' (*Ethics and the Limits of Philosophy* (London, 1985)) to capture the dimension of ethical theory that remains neutral between substantive moral commitments.

[36] 'What Metaphors Mean', in S. Sacks (ed.), *On Metaphor* (Chicago, 1979), 29–45.

to accommodate the large domain of uses that surpasses the literal domain of meaning-use—the domain of gesture, artistic expression, etc. Davidson would not worry about this claim so long as it did not undermine his own concern to avoid confusing cognitive meaning and metaphorical use. But my concern is to describe how nineteenth-century theorists used metaphor to surpass the literal use of words in order to express the profound human desire to be more, different, or better than we are.[37] They used metaphor precisely to challenge the limits of literal use. Davidson warns against our taking this sort of rationale for the use of metaphor too seriously, especially if it commits the philosopher to the view that metaphors cannot successfully mean unless they carry 'cryptic' or 'coded' meanings. He suggests that philosophical theory is better served when metaphor is grounded not in metaphysical fancy but in literal meaning. However, nineteenth-century theorists, and Wagner especially, worried greatly about the limits or shortcomings of this philosophical sobriety. He expressed those worries clearly in his attacks on what he took to be an overly literalized formalism.

There is another way to capture the gap that less obviously pits the Romantic against the anti-Romantic, the transcendentalist against the formalist. (Davidson makes this suggestion himself in a different context.) This way attends to the claim that the conditions under which works are composed, or the rules of production prescribing their form and content, stand to those works as at best approximate causes or codifications, or as necessary but insufficient conditions. In virtue of their aesthetic character and concrete particularity, works are exemplary and as such are not reducible to the conditions or rules of their production. Contrary to suggestion, and following Kant, exemplars less exemplify or instantiate a predetermined theory or set of conditions. Instead they provide a standard or model by which to determine such a theory or set. To capture a work only in terms of its describable conditions (as Wagner thinks a formalist tends to do) always leaves something essential or extra out. 'For me,' Wagner once recalled, 'music was demoniacal, a mystically exalted enormity: everything concerned with rules seemed only to distance it'.

Supporting this claim of exemplarity, Wagner will argue that

[37] Note the original connotation in 'meta-pherein' of 'movement across' or 'transport', and in 'secernere' (secrecy) of 'dividing' or 'cutting off'.

where the conditions or rules for the production of a work are employed as fully determinative of a work, where they are taken as limits to be stayed within rather than surpassed, then the works produced as a result are metaphorically speaking unmusical. In philosophical terms, descriptive limits always suggest something beyond them. In musical or aesthetic terms, rules exist to be bent, broken, or ultimately left behind. The philosophical and aesthetic terms are connected: limits, Wagner will often say, are about aspirations and beginnings, not about confinements or endings.

More specifically, he will argue that a description of musicianship is a description of how we learn rules and technique, or how we learn to work within a set of conditions in order, at the moment of creative composition or performance, to go beyond that learning. Surpassing our learning in performance or playing musically is the way, in reversal, to keep rules and conditions alive. To sustain this argument, he follows Kant and Schopenhauer in asserting numerous paradoxes and forms of concealment. In one instance, he follows Kant's paradox of artifice and Schopenhauer's anagogic adaptation of Kant to suggest that the most successful way to explain the relation between something empirical or exoteric (rules or technology) and something transcendental, hidden, or esoteric (musicality) is by seeing one thing presented in the terms of another, or by something's being revealed by negating something else. Style or musicality, for example, resides in a perfected technique that is shown but then concealed to reveal the additional, but elusive, quality of musicality. The idea is that something concealed can be revealed only by paradoxically concealing that which can be directly revealed. As we shall see, the doubleness that is shown in this relation between the revealed and concealed will turn out to be a way of preserving the transcendental, critical, or enhanced dimension of formalism.

Concealment is an ontological matter; it is also methodological. Every time we make a statement about revealing our concealed musicality, we also comment upon our limited capacity to describe. Oscar Wilde once made the point marvellously in the quip that opens his play *The Importance of Being Earnest*:

ALGERNON. Did you hear what I was playing, Lane?
LANE (manservant). I didn't think it was polite to listen, sir.
ALGERNON. I'm sorry for that, for your sake. I don't play accurately—any

one can play accurately—but I play with wonderful expression. As far as the piano is concerned, sentiment is my forte. I keep science for Life.[38]

Musicianship, he was suggesting, demands scientific accuracy and technique, but not merely these things. It is the additional, inexpressible *extra* sentiment that 'science' fails to capture. (Again, what is musical is already extra.)

Wagner's methodological legacy is here comparable to Wilde's. Wagner will describe a musical formalism he takes to be in decline under the deadening constraints of scientific accuracy. It is not that accuracy is a bad thing; it only becomes regressive in a practice when it is taken as an end in itself, if the proper end of the practice is forgotten in its favour. Under this regressive condition, a formalized practice becomes 'dehumanized', 'loveless', or 'defunct'. His criticism will recall Goethe's *Faust*: the closed nature of practice is a reflection of the closed-mindedness or pedantry of its participants. A practice is closed when what could be a progressive ideal—and the formalist claim can be such—is used regressively to make rules and conditions sufficient in either ontological or explanatory terms.

One might think that endorsing a gap as a philosophical response to one's cultural fears of conformism postures an extreme confidence that allows one, as it apparently allowed Wagner, to judge progressive and regressive uses of philosophical method. But I think one should take from Wagner less his confidence than his Faustian warning that each of us, at every moment, is in danger of succumbing to closed-mindedness. 'The purely musical', serving as a metaphor for expression, is meant to capture this endless quest or aspiration towards large-mindedness.

Adorno once argued that '[m]usic is called upon to do nothing less than retract the historical tendency of language towards signification, by substituting for that tendency expressiveness'.[39] He recognized music's appeal in understanding philosophical method. He knew that music had historically been called upon to signify the 'other side' of philosophy. He knew that autonomous music had come to symbolize what lies beyond philosophy's limits of expression, both because it expresses what philosophy fails literally to

[38] *The Works of Oscar Wilde* (Leicester, 1993), 321.
[39] *In Search of Wagner*, tr. R. Livingstone (London, 1981), 99. I have slightly altered the translation.

express, and because it aspires to embody that indescribable quality that philosophy (representing the extreme condition of any
language) tends to lose in its academic rigidification. For Adorno,
autonomous music pricks a perennial thorn in the side of a
rigidified philosophy, precisely through its disharmonizing technique of expression.

To recognize that philosophical practice has a history in which its
progressive and regressive tendencies come or do not come to
fruition is to recognize both its historicity and its vulnerability as a
discipline. To recognize that vulnerability reflects the attempt to
overcome that regressive tendency of the Enlightenment to try to
control our practices through complete determination—the quest
for certainty. One might claim that the German and Romantic
response to the Enlightenment was precisely to try to pull out its
progressive tendency to maintain in our thinking that untouchable,
transcendent moment of autonomous human expression, or better,
perhaps, that moment of fundamental doubt. (The movement
of Modernism then tried to do that for Romanticism, as Post-
Modernism now tries for Modernism.) Once more, for Wagner, as
for so many others, that progressive tendency has been protected
and sustained by the metaphysical repository of music and the
inexpressible power of its aesthetic of expression. In the nineteenth
century, one might alternatively say, music was chosen to name
philosophy's failure to fulfil its Enlightenment project.

Wagner connected music's expression with human expression to
maintain a connection between aesthetics, politics, and philosophy.
He appealed to this tripartite connection whenever he attacked
what he took to be the overly separated academic disciplines and
their associated abstracted and alienated practices. He duly attacked communities and cultures according to their degree of
abstraction or, as he put it, their degree of 'bourgeois', 'cosmopolitan', or 'Jewish' estrangement. Because Wagner took this tripartite
connection seriously, I do so too, but in the following very specific
sense. At moments when I try to save the progressive side of
Wagner's view against its regressive articulation, I do not separate
his aesthetics from his politics, or the 'man from the music'. Instead, I separate, as far as one can, his politico-aesthetic model
from its crude, ideological determination, and in terms immediately relevant to my methodological argument.

Some recent commentators have tried to save Wagner from his ideological views by arguing that his aesthetic products—the works themselves—contradict or undermine his ideological posture. Slavoj Zizek argues that

[t]he possible way out of this deadlock is provided by the fact that Wagner's music dramas do not in themselves homogeneously realize his artistic program, but at the same time undermine it, and that the very artistic power of his work relies on this gap, of this inherent subversion of his ideological project.... Wagner is great not in spite of his protofascist, aesthetico-political vision, but for the way his very realization of that vision undermines it.[40]

Marc Weiner suggests that because the immanent content of Wagner's musical works fails to capture their transcendent meanings, the works cannot be read solely in terms of it.[41] David Levin recommends that we read Wagner's anti-Semitism in terms of aesthetic practices to avoid the temptation to separate out the aesthetic from the ideological.[42] I am sympathetic to these sorts of solution. However, I shall emphasize that Wagner's combined aesthetic and political principles contradict his ideological posture to the extent that the former endorse a progressive gap and the latter regressively fill it in. The contradiction I shall therefore highlight is between two Wagnerian *modes of argument*: one maintains an openness, the other does not. In other words, I shall not offer a resolution to the conflict between those parts of Wagner we want to admire and those we do not. That conflict probably cannot be resolved. I shall only offer a framework for understanding the conflict; again, my focus will be on method.

We may well recall one of Wagner's own attempts to express the progressive promise of his methodology in a letter to August Röckel written in 1854:

I believe I've managed ... to stave off the urge to make everything too obvious, because it has become clear to me that too overt a disclosure of one's intention may well disturb a correct understanding.... This,

[40] '"There is no sexual relationship": Wagner as a Lacanian', in David J. Levin (ed.), *Richard Wagner*, Special Issue, *New German Critique*, 69 (1996), 35.

[41] 'Reading the Ideal', Levin (ed.), *Richard Wagner*, 60.

[42] 'Reading Beckmesser Reading: Antisemitism and Aesthetic Practice in *The Mastersingers of Nuremberg*', Levin (ed.), *Richard Wagner*, 127 ff.

then, distinguishes my poetic material from the political [in my terms, ideological] material that seems to be the only kind of material known these days.[43]

Plausibly Wagner was expressing a desire to keep the poetical message secret to protect it from being misunderstood by its reduction to an ideological message. At the very end of his life he put the point this way:

[Being silent is the] only possible reconciliation of the seeing person [with the world]. . . . [T]here is not a decade which is not filled almost totally with the shame of the human race. . . . It seems very easy to talk about things of this world because everybody talks about them. But to portray them in such a way that they speak for themselves is only given to a few. [Only out of] silence [does] the power to portray what is seen develop. [Out of silence comes a drama that mirrors] the world reflected from our silent soul.[44]

The fact remains of course that Wagner increasingly forgot to 'speak' from silence, and lapsed unapologetically into 'everybody's' ideological obviousness. Nietzsche would accuse him of 'condescending' to the Germans and of becoming 'reichsdeutsch'.[45] 'Condescending' is just the right reductive word to capture the sense in which Wagner contributed, despite his words, to the 'shame of the human race'.

I have suggested that to endorse a gap in music, philosophy, or politics is to recognize an esoteric space in those domains for silence and for secrecy. Does this recognition necessarily entail a conservative commitment to something like an Invisible Hand or Natural Law? Have we, and this is more serious, aestheticized our politics and our philosophy? Have we had to put our faith in some kind of spiritual guidance or authority of tradition by taking our own human, rational, experiential, or epistemological limits too seriously? Dorothy Emmet once claimed that philosophical appeals to mystery are little more than avoidances of commitment and explanation. Perhaps some appeals are, but not all. Contrary to the many quietist moments of Romantic theory, I would like to understand a philosophy of limits as recommending the critical

---

[43] Quoted and trans. by Weiner, 'Reading the Ideal', 61.

[44] Quoted by Jürgen Kühnel, 'The Prose Writings', in Müller and Wapnewski (eds.), *Wagner Handbook*, 625.

[45] *Ecce Homo*, in *Basic Writings*, 704.

exposure of conflicts and problems in a practice that its authoritative determinations conceal. This philosophy does not 'leave everything as it is'. It does not depend on the authority of tradition to show us the 'right' direction. Rather, it tries to carve out a position in which it grants a fundamental primacy to the actions and products, to the exemplars, of a practice in which it none the less critically intervenes. This doubling position demands that theory constantly challenge practice and practice, theory—but, in either direction, with an underdetermining modesty. This modesty is reflected in how we choose to interpret philosophy's limits.

Seeing philosophy as having 'limits' suggests that there is something that is or cannot be expressed. However, that something 'on the other side' need not be interpreted as fixed or determinate in a *strong* realist, naturalistic, or transcendent sense. A formal rather than substantive commitment to something inexpressible allows that there be, at every moment, an horizon of differences or alternatives that cannot, under the current conditions of our practices, be expressed now. If this conclusion generates the fear that our philosophy will always be too historicized or contextualized, that is as it must be. To my mind, these qualities symbolize a positive aspiration to maintain in our theories, rather than religiously to ignore, that element of human doubt or scepticism regarding our capacities to capture everything in words. (One might say, if words sufficed, we wouldn't need melody.) The all-too-human risk that our underdetermined practices may not now go in the direction we desire is the risk we take, but, once more, it is a risk worth taking. The attempt to determine fully our philosophical theories, as we might our politics, is the attempt to provide a guarantee that will always prove deceptive.

The Romantic triplet of music, politics, and philosophy may be seen in one more of Wagner's projects. Following Goethe, Wagner argues that close attention be given to the expressive potential that lies behind the human deed. Whether that deed is musical, political, or philosophical, whatever its form or content, its value is given first and foremost by what motivates it. Mixing literal and metaphorical meanings, a musical deed may be musical or unmusical depending on its expressive import. In Wagner's view, music is not musical solely in virtue of its having the right sort of *content*, its being made up, say, of tonally moving forms; rather, it is musical when its content, be that content purely tonal or mixed with words, *expresses* something purely musical or, in his other terms, purely human.

Despite appearances to the contrary, this claim helps sustain Wagner's argument for moving away from the composition of symphonies to operas. His *Gesamtkunstwerk* is certainly about the synthesis of the modern, emancipated languages of the fine arts (the argument about content), but it is more fundamentally about the restoration of the expressive and autonomous voice of 'the musical' to modern musical practice (the argument about expression). The emphasis on expression connects Wagner's project, as I shall argue, to the ancient Socratic quest for *mousikē*—the cultivation of the soul, even granted that between their quests lies the momentous intervention of Christianity.

To conclude this chapter, suffice it to make two points. First, if any credence at all is to be given to the methodological claim that music promises the true philosophy, then it is also to the music—the works themselves—that we must turn. For otherwise our entire argument will reside, as Schopenhauer's argument mostly resided, only ever in the domain of the metaphorically musical. But are there, literally, works that can sustain this methodological claim? The first claim of the next chapter is that Wagner composed such a work. It is a work, I shall argue, that functions doubly as philosophical allegory and aesthetic exemplar. It also presents an argument against a threateningly regressive musical formalism.

Secondly, readers might already be objecting that by giving music so central a philosophical role, it has been made too *ernst*. Does the musical aesthetic of German Romanticism leave any room at all for music's playfulness or enjoyment? Must our singing always express something so profound about the human condition? Must our musical ideals always be tied to philosophical theses about human perfection and imperfection? The composer Ernest Bloch once complained that 'for the greatest number of German critics, [music] is but an excuse for long, diffuse philosophical theories; they use music as a springboard to launch *their* theories, *their* philosophies, *their universal panaceas* into the world, and forget that its true purpose is simply to be moving'.[46] In so far as my first concern in this chapter was with human freedom, it should not surprise anyone that I have stressed music's more 'serious' dimen-

---

[46] 'Gustav Mahler and the Second Symphony', *Ernest Bloch Society Bulletin*, 16 (1984), 6.

sions. More to the point, despite our ability just to enjoy or to be moved by music, it still seems to matter to us what music we make and which music moves us, and that mattering seems to be more than 'merely' musical.

The problem is this: when pressed to account for how and why music matters, we tend to resort to the most serious of terms. Yet those terms belong to the way we speak about music and not to music itself. This chapter showed that music itself, and the way we speak about it, are not the same. We might say that music sings the same truths in terms that are far lighter (*heiterer*) than those that pervade our philosophical speech. But if, one day, when listening to music we become tormented once again by its 'unbearable lightness' then we might find ourselves led back to philosophy's 'unbearable seriousness'. Perhaps the one experience always leads us to the other. It seems to have been this realization that inspired Claude Lévi-Strauss's words dedicated to his 'God, Richard Wagner'. I share less the dedication than his interest in the sentiment. '[M]usic is a language with some meaning at least for the immense majority of [hu]mankind, although only a tiny minority of people are capable of formulating a meaning in it . . . [I]t is the only language with the contradictory attributes of being at once intelligible and untranslatable. . . . [M]usic [is] . . . the supreme mystery of the science of [humanity].' It is a mystery, he concluded, that 'all the various disciplines' have come up against, and 'which holds a key to their progress'.[47] For the philosopher of music there are surely few thoughts more intriguing than that music's metaphorical silence and secrecy have historically held the key to philosophy's methodological progress.

[47] *The Raw and the Cooked: Mythologies*, i, tr. J. and D. Weightman (Chicago, 1983), 18.

2

Die Meistersinger: *Wagner's Exemplary Lesson*

1. 'He who is born a master among masters is in the worst position'[1]

> Soon after the tenor began the 'Prize Song,' I heard a quick drawn breath and turned to my aunt. Her eyes were closed, but the tears were glistening in her cheeks, and I think, in a moment more, they were in my eyes as well. It never really died, then—the soul which can suffer so excruciatingly and so interminably; it withers to the outward eye only; like the strange moss which can lie on a dusty shelf half a century and yet, if placed in water, grows green again.[2]

Philosophy, Socrates once said, is a training for death. It is a preparation of the soul rooted in the desire to know, and live in accordance with, the Good. It is a moral quest intended to protect the soul from the temptations of the body, worldly desire, and transitory satisfaction, from the corruption of power, opinion, and appearance. To practise philosophy was, for Socrates, to practise the highest *mousikē*.[3]

As I suggested in Chapter 1, there is an axis in the history of

[1] From the libretto of *Die Meistersinger* (Hans Sachs singing about Walther; II. iv). All quotations of the libretto are taken (and sometimes adapted or retranslated) from Susan Webb's translation, Metropolitan Opera Libretto Series, ed. P. Gruber (New York, 1992). Cf. Schopenhauer's statement: 'The person in whom genius is to be found suffers most of all' (*The World as Will and Representation*, i. 310).

[2] W. Cather, 'A Wagner Matinee', in *Youth and the Bright Medusa* (New York, 1975), 223–4.

[3] This opening paragraph is drawn from Plato's *Phaedo* 80e–81a: '. . . [the soul] is pure when it leaves the body and drags nothing bodily with it, as it has no willing association with the body in life, but avoided it and gathered itself together by itself and always practised this, which is no other than practising philosophy in the right way, in fact, training to die easily. Or is this not training for death?'; and 60e–61a: 'Tell him the truth, Cebes, [Socrates] said, that I did not do this with the idea of rivalling him or his poems, for I knew that would not be easy, but I tried to find out

musicological thought, culminating in German Romanticism, that adopts the ancient notion of *mousikē* and combines it with principles of Christian teaching to produce for music an aesthetic that, alongside philosophy, advocates an ideal of perfection, purification, or cultivation. Creativity, performance, and contemplation *practised correctly* by individuals protect their souls from the temptations of fame, fashion, and false judgement. Practices that share an end may work with different means, so whereas philosophy is considered the exemplary practice of reason, music comes increasingly to be considered the exemplary practice of 'immediate feeling'. In the nineteenth century these two practices are intimately connected as two sides of a coin. Correct feeling, or intuition, like correct faith, is taken to be a route to truth working alongside, though sometimes surpassing, reason's achievements.

Central to this account of music as a practice of cultivating the soul is a dialectical drama of negative acts directed towards perfectionist ends. The general idea here is that when we engage in practices such as that of music—and the Romantic thought is that musical practice is exemplary—we perform negative acts of putting matters aside, behind, or below as a way to demonstrate our aspiration to achieve a purified or transfigured condition within an impure world. Our aim is to achieve a condition of freedom or negation *within* as opposed to a freedom *without*. The latter is found dramatically in denying the world through death; the former, and it is this condition upon which I shall focus, is found in life. Freedom within is a distancing and doubling condition. It is a condition of living in a world we strive to transcend, where the point of this transcendence is to make the world we live in better, or, more pessimistically, at least the life we live in the world.

In this chapter, I shall argue that Wagner's opera *Die Meistersinger von Nürnberg* claims a (worldly) aesthetic of negation with perfectionist ends. However, it claims this aesthetic, not initially in the way we would expect of a work of art, by its embodying or showing it; rather, it presents it by means of its libretto in the

the meaning of certain dreams and to satisfy my conscience in case it was this kind of art they were frequently bidding me to practise. The dreams were something like this . . . "Socrates," it said, "practise and cultivate the arts (*mousikē*)." In the past I imagined that it was instructing . . . me to do what I was doing . . . to practise the art of philosophy, this being the highest kind of art, and I was doing that . . . but . . .'. Socrates goes on to discuss the possibility of his having been instructed to write verse/poetry (tr. G. M. A. Grube (Indianapolis, 1981)).

form of an explicit argument. It thus stands to this aesthetic in the first instance as a philosophical or allegorical text. However, if we end up accepting the argument the libretto promotes—which Wagner presumably wants us to do—then eventually we have to conclude that the opera also embodies this aesthetic.

Despite the opera's having been composed, as Wagner explained, to counter debt, to give his singers non-taxing parts, to receive untroubled performances of his music, and to find a more accepting audience, its appearance as a traditional grand, three-act comic opera proves deceptive. These stated motivations are revealed as concealing his genuine ones by the opera itself, because its libretto argues in favour of correct motivations for creativity and against its corruption by false ones. Genuine works of art result from correct motivation, and examples of these are supposed to be Wagner's other operas. Those operas (most notably *Tristan und Isolde*) are intended to demonstrate an aesthetic of freedom that *Die Meistersinger*'s argument demands. This argument demands that we put something aside to reveal another thing. Dramatically, in *Tristan*, life is put aside in favour of eternal and redemptive love; musicologically, the conventions of grand opera are put aside to make way for a new kind of modern music. As allegorical text, *Die Meistersinger* argues for the freedom to create a new art, the art of *Tristan*; as work of art, it sings a drama of 'secret suffering'. I shall eventually argue that the philosophical saying and the secret singing are closely related.

Wagner conceptualized *Die Meistersinger* over more than a quarter-century as an accompaniment to the composition of his other works, partially, I suggest, to serve as their justification. In a strong sense, the opera is Wagner's *opus absolutum et perfectum*, an exemplar of his life's work and argument. 'It will be the finest product of my genius,' he wrote on one occasion, but added that he would 'say no more'.[4] Of course he did, and one thing he once said was that 'music indeed has nothing to do with the common seriousness of life . . . its character, on the contrary, is sublime and grief-assuaging radiance; yes, it smiles on us, but it never makes us laugh'.[5] This statement will eventually help us unlock the opera's melancholy secret.

[4] Letter to Peter Cornelius, *The Letters of Richard Wagner*, ed. and tr. W. Altmann (London, 1927), vol. ii, no. 512.
[5] 'On Poetry and Composition', vi. 143.

I shall interpret *Die Meistersinger* through four interconnected arguments. Wagner did not explicitly formulate them as such; I have extrapolated them from his extensive prose and musical work to make the best sense I can of the argument he did formulate in the opera. I shall name them, respectively, historical, musical-aesthetic, political, and philosophical. Methodologically, each invokes at least one dimension of doubleness, but usually several. Each is described so as to show both its progressive and its regressive tendencies.

2. The Historical Argument

The historical argument addresses the anachronism that arises in Wagner's attempt to transform criteria for the correctness of musical production specified by the mastersingers' guild set up during the Reformation into criteria appropriate to a Romantic aesthetic. However, the anachronistic doubleness is justified by a transformation of criteria that requires not the replacement of one thing by another, but the continuation of that thing under a modern guise. To borrow Eric Hobsbawm's words, Wagner's idea is to invent a tradition that is grafted onto an old one. The transformation he urges us to accept asks us to see music no longer as serving religion as a means, but as embodying its own religious or aesthetic end— as having become, the Romantics would say, religion itself, and for Wagner 'the last true religion'. He accordingly transforms the positive criteria for music conceived as a means into negative criteria for music conceived as an end.

In an increasingly quoted essay, Hobsbawm describes the most significant features of 'invented traditions'.[6] These traditions may look more or less emergent or deliberately invented and may be 'quite recent in origin', despite their appearance or claim of age. Each tradition is ritualistically and symbolically governed by an overtly or tacitly accepted set of rules that receives its authority by its suggested continuity with the past. This past must be adequate to the function of the tradition, and demands, therefore, a suitable interpretation. The peculiar feature of invented traditions is that, though they respond to novel or contemporary situations, they do so by referring to factitious or suitably interpreted old situations. Such responses create the illusion of repetition of what a

---

[6] 'Introduction', in E. Hobsbawm and T. Ranger (eds.), *The Invention of Tradition* (Cambridge, 1983), 1–14.

'traditional' response would have been. In cases where an invented tradition is grafted onto an old one, the past presumably takes on a double character: it functions with both its traditional and its invented interpretation.

Wagner's engagement with tradition in *Die Meistersinger* operates on two levels that together suggest significant acts of Hobsbawmian 'invention'. First, a central part of the opera's subject-matter is about the invention of a German and a Romantic tradition of art that uses a three-centuries-old Lutheran tradition of mastersinging to serve as its authoritative past. The story is set in the sixteenth century; the argument belongs to the nineteenth. Secondly, the opera itself contributes to the actual invention of what Wagner claims is a newly emergent German tradition of art, by virtue of the relation in which the opera stands to a tradition of historical treatments of the mastersingers and so by association with Germany's actual Lutheran past. Both within and without the opera he asserts the newness of the tradition of German art so that he may identify with it as its most inventive figure. This invention engages him in critical acts of invective and commendation. He looks to the past for both its regressive and progressive tendencies: he describes how a tradition can deteriorate, but describes that tradition simultaneously in the light of its potential to serve as 'an invented past' for a new one. Together, his critical use of the past sanctions his transformation of a Protestant musical tradition into a past that will stand as the authentic past for his Romantic musical aesthetic. He characterizes this transformation through an anachronistic identification of the Romantic spirit of music with the Nürnbergian spirit of the Lutheran reform in religion. Presumably, in inventing traditions, such anachronism is bound to occur.

Wagner's sources for the composition of *Die Meistersinger* were many. There were personal sources and literary ones produced by, among others, Jakob Grimm, Georg Gottfried Gervinus, and E. T. A. Hoffmann. They have all been explored at length in the literature. I will not repeat the breadth of that exploration here, but will focus on what is certainly one of the most significant sources, Johann Christoph Wagenseil's 1697 chronicle *Buch von Der Meister-Singer Holdseligen Kunst. Anfang, Fortübung, Nutzbarkeiten, und Lehr-Sätzen.*[7] As the title indicates, Wagenseil

---

[7] I have borrowed some factual details from Herbert Thompson's *Wagner and Wagenseil: A Source of Wagner's Opera* Die Meistersinger (London, 1927).

records the original functions of the mastersingers, and shows how their tradition was codified by strict rules. Soon we shall see that it is precisely the issue of rule-following that focuses Wagner's identification of both progressive and regressive tendencies in the mastersingers' tradition.

There are two pertinent stories told about the mastersingers of the Middle Ages. In 962 a group of masters at the University of Paris attacked the clergy for evil and corrupt living, and when forced by Pope Leo VIII to defend themselves against heresy, responded successfully by offering a detailed codification of their values. Apocryphal or not, the story was called upon to rationalize the mastersingers' codification designed to uphold and preserve the true value of song in the service of religion.[8] The second story (which Wagner uses as background in *Tannhäuser* and explicitly in *Parsifal*) tells of how the black art and magic practised by the corrupted master Klingsohr was overpowered by a young and pious knight.

The masters would never relinquish their claim to embody piety. Assembled as a guild of lower- and middle-class professional craftsmen, their 'solemn brotherhood' became identified with the Lutheran movement of pious reform, and with Nürnberg, where Wagenseil was born in 1633 and which Wagner, during his lifetime, increasingly idealized as one of the few remaining, if not the last, idyllic, free, and morally upright German cities. 'I am directing attention more and more to Nuremberg,' he wrote to Hans von Bülow in 1866, and continued quite ominously:

It is remarkably significant that this very genuine and unique 'German' art centre, Protestant Nuremberg, should have come to the Bavarian Crown and consequently into the domain of my ardently Catholic royal friend. It is *there* that the future 'German Academy' belongs, as do all those other things which can never flourish in the superannuated un-German capital of our little Louis Quatorze. There is the place for the spirit of a united Germany to flourish. There, too, is the place for our school, around which there must ultimately grow up a general School of Art and Science, German and non-Jewish. I should like the King to give me a lodge of the castle of Bayreuth for my retreat—Nuremberg near by—all Germany

---

[8] Susan Webb identifies a direct reference to this story in *Die Meistersinger*. When Walther asks who 'created the rules which stand now in such high renown?', Hans Sachs answers: 'They were Masters, greatly in need, spirits oppressed by the troubles of life: in the wilderness of their difficulties, they created an image for themselves which remained within them . . .' (Libretto, 191). She also notes that the University of Paris did not exist in 962.

about me—Only for heaven's sake don't let a word of this get abroad.
Even the King would not [yet] understand it. . . . [T]o the world as well—
I must convey the idea empirically, and little by little. 'Hans Sachs' belongs
to Nuremberg—yes, then for the present not another word. The rest—will
make itself understood.[9]

For Wagenseil, as for Wagner, certain historical suppositions
about the mastersingers legitimized their long-standing authority.
Though Wagenseil tries to, but finds he cannot, sustain the ortho-
dox view that their singing originated with the gypsies, who in turn
borrowed from the early Jews of German extraction, for him, as for
Wagner, it proves more imperative to find origins that are 'truly
German'. And though he speaks of the connection between the
masters and the more secular and vernacular productions of the
Minnesänger and *Spruchsprecher*, again it is a matter of asserting
the 'Christian' superiority of the former. With the connection between true Germanic history and true religion established, the
identification of the spirit of music follows. Wagenseil traces the
origins of mastersinging to the ancient 'Bards', who, according to
Herbert Thompson, shared with the Druids and Prophets the task
of ministering religion among 'the ancient Gauls and Teutons'. The
Bards were the source of the 'Bar', the masters' song subjected to
intense scrutiny in Wagner's opera. For both Wagenseil and
Wagner, the tradition of mastersinging secures the triadic unity of
the 'Christian', 'German', and 'musical' spirits. 'Strictly speaking,'
Wagner writes, music is 'the only art that fully corresponds to' and
'is the exclusive product of' Christianity.[10]

The figure Wagner employs in *Die Meistersinger* to symbolize
this 'holy trinity' is King David of Israel. In the opening scene this
famed harpist is first represented 'with a long beard' on the masters' shield,[11] and then as 'the one whose pebble brought down
Goliath, his sword in his belt, his sling in his hand'. We are then told
about the David of courageous youth, represented in a painting
by Nürnberg artist Dürer, kneeling with harp in hand, in an act of
religious reconstruction, 'before the Lord Christ who hangs upon

[9] *Letters*, vol. ii, no. 614.

[10] 'Religion and Art', vi. 223.

[11] The image on the shield is referred to again in Act iii, as being 'greeted' by the
Volk as they congregate for the singing contest. Cf. Moshe Barasch's description of
the shield based on Ps. 26 ('How the Hidden Becomes Visible', in H. G. Kippenberg
and G. G. Strousma (eds.), *Secrecy and Concealment: Studies in the History of
Mediterranean and Near Eastern Religions* (Leiden, 1995), 381–2).

the cross'.[12] We then see David in the face of a young knight and poet Walther von Stolzing, who has arrived in Nürnberg (it turns out[13]) for both the 'love of art' and the 'art of love' and stands in St Catherine's Church as an onlooker to the service taking place.[14] David is seen in Walther's face through the instantaneously loving eyes of the esteemed master Pogner's daughter, Eva (of Paradise). She establishes the initial connection between Walther and the Holy Spirit ('heil'ger Mut') of Music. She also allows herself to be betrothed by her father in the form of a 'prize' to the singer who will offer the best master song in the singing contest to take place the next day on the feast of St John. Needless to say, Walther will win the prize.

But it will take the entire course of the opera for him to do so. On the way Wagner will teach him that, if he is to express King David's musical and 'manly' spirit successfully, he must be correctly guided by the aged Nürnbergian patriarch of the masters, the cobbler-poet Hans Sachs. Serving a double role as historical personage and dramatic character, Sachs represents what mastersinging has always ideally stood for and what it may stand for again in Wagner's renewed form. Sachs is described progressively, as a dreamer and as out of sync with his fellow masters. And just as Wagner will put Walther into the honest hands of Sachs, so he will also teach him to resist the regressive history of the mastersingers' tradition, and the contemporary threat of such, represented most extremely by Sixtus Beckmesser. Beckmesser is the aged town clerk and censorious 'marker' who desires to win the contest himself, but finds he can only act on this desire corruptly. It is also the 'group of twelve' mastersingers who will symbolize the atrophying tendencies

---

[12] This is Wagenseil's description. Thompson (*Wagner and Wagenseil*, 18) remarks that the image probably corresponds to a painting hanging in the Germanic Museum at Nürnberg, and to a woodcut described by Emil Naumann in his *History of Music* as also by H. E. Krehbiel, as we read here, in his *Studies in Wagnerian Drama* (1891):

> It is a small affair of wood, with two doors, and was painted by a Franz Hein in 1581. On the doors are portraits of four distinguished members of the Guild. Two pictures occupy the middle panel, the upper, with a charmingly naïve disregard of chronology, showing King David praying before a Crucifix; the lower, a meeting of Master-singers, with a singer perched in a box-like pulpit. Over the heads of the assemblage is a representation of the chain and medallion with which the victor in a singing contest used to be decorated.

[13] Initially, there is some ambiguity in the reasons stated for his arrival.

[14] Scholars note that Wagner's use of this church is historically inaccurate.

of their tradition. Bearing, like Sachs, their historical names in character,[15] they doubly represent the past: they express what their tradition once was and what it has become. They also represent that dangerous unwillingness often associated with the aged or established to embrace the challenge and need of the new. In the libretto's terms, each year, for regenerative purposes, spring must follow winter and youth must infiltrate age.

I have emphasized how the masters stood for Christian piety in the spirit of their songs. I have not yet mentioned how Wagenseil describes their production in the traditional terms of crafts and liberal arts. Thus he describes how the masters attained perfection in their trade through untiring industry, and the levels of schooling and conditions of apprenticeship appropriate to this industry. Those masters who attain perfection (and he singles out the historical Sachs) have reached the highest stage of learning: the mastery of practice and theory. Against this familiar conception of craft, the mastersingers' detailed *Tabulatura* secures its authority. As Wagenseil records, and as Wagner reiterates almost verbatim, there are rules for every conceivable aspect of the craft determining what singers must and must not do. Indeed, when we think about crafts, we are able to think about the conditions of correctness and error appropriate to their every aspect, and we see those conditions as being justified by the quality of the products that result: either the shoes fit or they do not. Further, a rule-based conception of a craft is quite appropriate for a practice that serves specific religious ends. Strict control over the rectitude or moral strength of the practitioners and their craft—rules for 'prosodical rectitude', the correct naming of songs, performance appropriate to religious and secular ceremonies, and social manners and attitudes—are, for the masters, entirely in order.

Yet in these rules lies the problem. Lutheran reform had criticized the Catholic Church for concentrating on public, complex, and elaborate ritual at the expense of simple, private, individual faith. Could a comparable criticism not be marshalled against the masters? With their activities so highly ritualized, with so many rules regulating every aspect of their craft, was there any room left for individual expressions of faith and moral character? Apparently, Wagenseil was not troubled by this question. Perhaps he saw

---

[15] Walther is linked to the historical 'Walther von der Vogelweide', whom the character refers to as his Master.

religion's ritual as inevitable or necessary—even in Lutheranism. Perhaps he recognized that Luther had separated the need for rules from the need for ritual and, though Luther had rejected the latter, he had not rejected the former. Or perhaps he was thinking about the ideals of a liberal arts education and, in accordance with his times, was content to believe that singers who followed the rules 'to the letter' were, contrary to the extreme Pauline dictum,[16] not precluded from following rules also 'in their spirit'. With the correct understanding of these rules, each singer could produce faithful and morally appropriate songs.[17]

Wagner found the question deeply disturbing. Tackling it, his anachronism set in. He effectively 'invented' for his mastersingers a history informed by a contemporary conception of art. This conception rejected a critical tenet of the traditional view of craft, namely, that there is *no gap* between following rules and producing products. He projected a Romantic conception back into the mastersingers' art so that the products could be seen as ends in themselves, as non-rule-bound, unmediated embodiments of the 'Christian', 'German', and 'Romantic' spirit.[18] His characters each then played their metaphysical part in demonstrating the need for this gap.

Walther is the estranged and individual artist who contributes to the mastersingers' art by virtue not of his obeying the rules, but, rather, of his either breaking or reinterpreting them as his love— doubly for woman and art—dictates. Great art, Wagner tells us in his libretto, is 'rarely achieved from ordinary things (*gemeinen Dingen*), and never, without a little madness (*Wahn*)' (III. i). Walther is the inspired artist who works through subjective sentiment and the inspiration of pre-willed dreams, and is able, after a

---

[16] 2 Cor. 3: 6: 'The letter kills, while the spirit gives life.'

[17] Wagenseil represents the correct and proper aspects of mastersinging. Yet modern scholars remind us that the historical Sachs was known also for the naturalness of his singing and for the light-heartedness of his songs (e.g. John Warrack, in 'Sachs, Beckmesser, and Mastersong', in Warrack (ed.), *Die Meistersinger von Nürnberg*, Cambridge Opera Handbooks (Cambridge, 1994), 53–4). Warrack also reminds us that rules for mastersinging helped maintain a standard from one city to another, a standard designed to prevent the invasion of colloquialism. Another reason given for the codification of mastersinging was to 'elude unwanted foreigners'. The development of the masters' *deutliche Kunst* was linked to the development of *Hoch deutsch* and *deutsche Politik* (see Wagner, 'Shall we Hope?', vi. 123–4).

[18] Volker Mertens argues comparably for Wagner's backward projection of a 19th-century social system ('Wagner's Middle Ages', in Müller and Wapnewski (eds.), *Wagner Handbook*, 267).

quick but intense education, to produce a song worthy of a master. He also manifests an essential quality of genius: though dramatically a foreigner to the Nürnberg masters in birth and class, his estrangement symbolizes the universal, free, and anti-bourgeois subject to whom, in matters of creativity, it is inappropriate to attach empirical or 'prejudicial' attributes.

Hans Sachs is the sobering teacher who recognizes the Romantic difference between art and craft, but understands the sorts of constraint to which art must nevertheless remain subject. In his doubling guise as 'cobbler-poet', he argues for the relation between rules and inspiration, between the public and private dimensions of artistic practice, or between the practice of art that demands an objective or communicable basis and an individual's subjective or spontaneous contributions.

Beckmesser is the regressive pedant, a 'rhyme-bound sticker and paster', conceptually confined by his craft view either to follow rules and produce good (rather than beautiful) songs, or to break rules and make a fool of himself.[19] Now into the metaphysical drama enters another David, a young and uninspired, but 'model', apprentice. This David, like Beckmesser, prefers to abide by what he has been told the rules mean. He lacks the courage to acknowledge their interpretative openness; he refuses to challenge the limits of their immediate heritage. It is through this David, in his opening conversation with Walther, that Wagner first marks his transition from a craft view of song to his Romantic view. David tells Walther proudly that he has learnt '[s]hoemaking and poetry-making' as 'one and the same'. So when David then asks Walther how far his (David's) art of song has got him given all that he has learnt as a scholar, Walther is able consistently but mockingly to reply, 'as far as a pair of very good shoes'.

Wagner consummated his invented tradition of mastersinging by transfiguring the spirits of the historically pious but reforming Christians Martin Luther and Hans Sachs into the combined Romantic spirit of his two characters 'Sachs-the-wise' and 'Walther-the-rebellious', and then into his own self. With this transfiguration accomplished, he invented his theological past and the grounds for

---

[19] Cf. his words in Act II, scene vi: 'I know all the rules well, keep good measure and count; but of course digressions and oversights sometimes do take place, when the head, altogether full of fears, intends to venture to court for a young maiden's hand.'

its critique by imposing upon it a contemporary conception. What became his famous parody of pedantry in the opera was possible only because he saw the rules of mastersinging in their regressive mode as threatening his conception of the inspired creation of the true musical art, a form of creation, as he saw it, that demanded both wisdom and rebellion.

When, finally, Wagner constructed the memory of his having been inspired to compose *Die Meistersinger* after seeing Titian's painting *The Assumption of the Virgin Mary*, he fashioned his supreme gesture of invention. This inspiration united a Christian with a Romantic aesthetic impulse and gave to Wagner's opera the quality he prized most—the appearance of historical inevitability.[20] In Wagner's mind, his opera could now serve as a historically legitimized standard by which to judge the subsequent creation of a modern German art.

3. The Musical-Aesthetic Argument

This second argument attends to Wagner's use of traditional musical form, format, and style as a way to argue for their outmodedness and the need for their modern development. This argument depends upon a transformation of Classical into Romantic principles of form (the doubleness of the old and new). The transformation is then integrated into a larger debate over the aesthetic thesis of formalism, translated in *Die Meistersinger* into a debate over the correct and incorrect employment of rules. Describing this debate enables us to identify the disagreement that arises specifically in this opera between Wagner and his most ardent critic, Eduard Hanslick.

There is much musically at work in *Die Meistersinger* that thickens Wagner's invention. Most evident, as many scholars have noted, is the mixing of archaic and modern musical forms. But this mixing is conceptually complicated because it serves different aims. In accordance with his general argument, Wagner must demonstrate the outmodedness of the archaic and the historical inevitability of the modern, but the modern he supports is not the 'fashionable' modern of his day, but his purportedly non-corrupted alternative. So, the first thing he must make clear in musical

[20] For Wagner's recollection, see his *My Life*, tr. A. Gray, ed. M. Whittall (Cambridge, 1983), 667.

terms is that his favoured modern does not *sound like* the actual modern.

Secondly, if it is true that *Die Meistersinger* contains an argument for a type of art that we hear fully developed in his other operas, but not directly in this opera, then one would think that this opera's musical language, like its text, would suggest more than is literally heard. It would not satisfy Wagner to argue for something in words that could not also be shown in tones.

Thirdly, for Wagner's suggested modern to bear the quality of historical inevitability, it must convey the feeling that it emerges naturally out of the past in a way the present 'corrupted' and 'artificial' modern does not. In other words, the archaic forms employed in the opera must show their progressive musical potential. Adapting words sung by Sachs, for the 'music of the future' to emerge out of the 'true' German past the music must 'seem so old yet sound so new'.

Finally, because *Die Meistersinger* contains within it a singing competition, then, if the winning song is actually to *sound* worthy of winning, it must immediately please contemporary ears at the same time that its philosophical message challenges them. These ears, after all, are intended to be Wagner's own public symbolized in the masters' ears, and the latter have to hear the 'Prize Song' of the contest as breaking new ground. 'We must take the era by the ears,' Wagner writes in one of his earliest essays, 'and honestly try to cultivate its modern forms.'[21]

Given these diverse aims, what we actually hear in the opera are Protestant (Lutheran) chorales and diatonic songs in forms recalling even if not complying with sixteenth-century style. We hear and see arias, duets, quintets, and crowd scenes as we would in contemporary French and Italian opera, but whose musical style, as Dahlhaus has shown, is always more dissonant than chromatic. Such dissonance is set discursively into a developing argument that suggests a Romantic's restless striving towards the infinite. Wagner's musical intention is to persuade listeners of the transformation of Classical into Romantic principles. In doubling mode, this transformation does not mean the rejection of Classical principles of form into Romantic principles of formlessness. It means,

---

[21] 'On German Opera', viii. 58. In the rest of the sentence, Wagner refers to the 'modern' as transcending national identity, even, in this case, German identity.

rather, the invention or incorporation of the former into the latter, so that we hear form in formlessness or formlessness in form.

Metaphysically, and still in doubling mode, Wagner wants the Romantic tension between form and formlessness both to be expressed musically and to help sustain the dramatic tension between order and disorder. That tension begins in Act II with a night-time riot among the young apprentices. The riot expresses the chaos that emerges from a single action of a guild member that breaks a rule. Beckmesser sings a song to a woman he believes is Eva (but who is in fact Eva's attendant and the young David's lover, Magdalene), hoping he will win her heart before the singing contest takes place. The riot is later brought to both its philosophical and dramatic resolution by Sachs, who, in the light or reason of the following day—his name-day it turns out—ponders calmly on the nature of *Wahn*. Why, he asks, 'do people torment and torture themselves to the quick in futile, crazy rage?' And how, he wonders, will he bring about a noble and ordered end out of this madness and disorder?

Wagner now complicates the aesthetic significance of his mixture of musical forms by importing into it his critique of rule-following. First, he equates the spirit of classicism with unthinking conformity to the masters' *Tabulatura* so that he can move easily from claims about the limits of rule-following to claims about the outmodedness of Classical form. Then, from these claims, he jumps a step higher to attack the emerging formalism on the grounds that it smacks of a pedantic classicism and represents a denial of all that his 'music of the future' stands for. More than that, he then makes formalism stand for everything in contemporary culture he deems corrupt. That he is able to move seemingly so easily between these four critiques—of rule-following, classicism, formalism, and contemporary culture—might seem overly blithe. Yet it was consistent with the way theoretical positions were being staked out in his time. Hanslick, parodied by Wagner in the rule-bound character of Beckmesser, was, in Wagner's day, the most significant proponent of formalism and the defender of nineteenth-century classicism. He was the high critic of Vienna, serving as the composers' gatekeeper. So venerable and feared[22] was he that Wagner found he could use him as a symbol to which the attributes associated with pedantry

---

[22] Wagner refers to him as 'that most fearsome critic', (*My Life*, 644).

and aged censoriousness could be attached, as also those attributes Wagner associated with what he called the modern tyranny of the French, the Viennese, the fashionable, the petit bourgeois, and the Jews. Though justifiably defensive on personal grounds, even Hanslick noticed Wagner's tendency to turn everything he touched into a metaphysical symbol for his inflated world-view. He recalled:

I have often been asked by those disposed to think of all criticism as personal, what it is that I have 'against Wagner.' Nothing at all! That he should have been so cool as a result of my review of *Lohengrin* was to be expected. . . . I was even less offended later, in 1869, when [he] smuggled me into his [essay] *The Jew in Music*. Wagner couldn't stand a Jew, and consequently he developed the habit of regarding as a Jew anyone he didn't like.[23]

We should keep in mind my reference to an 'inflated world-view' if we want to determine the disagreement between Wagner and Hanslick that is expressed specifically in *Die Meistersinger*. Recall, first, Hanslick's most well-known claim that the 'musically beautiful' resides not in feelings aroused by music but in music's tonally moving forms. The substance of this claim is not the immediate object of Wagner's critique. Certainly Wagner objected to one implication of that claim, namely, that the musically beautiful is more adequately embodied in purely instrumental or absolute music than in opera, but this was not the objection he articulated in *Die Meistersinger*. He focused his concern elsewhere. He seemed to associate Hanslick's claim about the musically beautiful with an argument for maintaining conventional melody against what Hanslick called 'vague melodization'. (Wagner preferred 'endless melody'.) He then took this argument to corroborate an argument for closed or fixed musical form, which in turn corroborated one in favour of strictly rule-bounded form. It was this last argument, I

---

[23] *Music Criticisms, 1846–99*, tr. H. Pleasants (Baltimore, 1950), from translator's preface, 11–12. Hanslick denies the Jewish family origins Wagner 'accuses' him of (at least on his father's side; he does not mention that his mother was Jewish), and denies that his treatise *On the Musically Beautiful* plays into Jewish hands, as Wagner claims it did. Wagner notes in *My Life* (704) that his friends had informed him of Hanslick's being offended upon hearing a reading of the *Meistersinger* libretto to which he had been invited 'as a friend': 'My friends all concluded that Hanslick had interpreted the entire libretto as a pasquinade directed at him and our invitation to the reading as an insult. And the critic's attitude toward me indeed underwent a highly noticeable change from that evening forward and turned unto bitter enmity, the results of which we were soon to see.' Wagner neither affirms nor denies that Hanslick was correct in his interpretation of the events.

suggest, that inspired the composer of *Die Meistersinger*'s deepest dissatisfaction.

When Hanslick reviewed *Die Meistersinger* he picked up immediately on Wagner's portrayal of pedantic characters to set up his own criticisms. 'A fussy apprentice,' he called David, 'with devastating thoroughness, he instructs [Walther] in the rules and regulations of the "Singers' Court" and the poetic rules and regulations of the *Tabulatura*, enumerating forty to fifty different "tones and tunes." It sounds like an extract from a volume by Wagenseil set to music.' Of Beckmesser, he wrote: 'the town clerk, a mischievous old fool, has the office of censor; he sits behind a curtain and chalks up the singer's mistakes. But first the rules are read to the singer, a procedure which the audience, satiated already with learned explanations, might be spared.'[24] Could this be true—had Hanslick, in a return gesture of *tu quoque*, found pedantry in Wagner's operatic critique of pedantry? Was Hanslick just getting back at Wagner's depiction of himself as a critic who was dry, narrow, and old-fashioned in his tastes (which he perhaps sometimes was)?[25] Was this all their fight was about—two musicians each self-servingly calling his opponent a pedant? I do not think so. Despite their increasing hostility, both acknowledged that Hanslick had once reviewed Wagner's operas in rather accepting and friendly terms: Hanslick even stated his considerable liking for *Die Meistersinger*.[26] Their opposition was not therefore entirely personal. Rather, each criticized the other symbolically, as representing certain tendencies of their age. In Hanslick's mind, Wagner stood for an overly radical rejection of classicism. In Wagner's mind, Hanslick stood for the 'deplorable state of criticism'. But even if this is a correct description of their antagonism, it still does not fully answer our question: what exactly was the composer of *Die Meistersinger* seeing of Beckmesser-like pedantry in Hanslick that Hanslick apparently did not see?

I think the answer lies in their respective attitudes towards

---

[24] '*Die Meistersinger*', in *Music Criticisms*, 113.

[25] Cf. Peter Gay, 'For Beckmesser: Eduard Hanslick, Victim and Prophet', in *Freud, Jews, and Other Germans: Masters and Victims in Modernist Culture* (Oxford, 1978), 257–77.

[26] He liked the theatrical spectacle most of all. But he did not like the argument for the opera's 'music of the future': 'Brought up on the school rules of the singers' guild, and suddenly enlightened by Walther's "free poetry" [Sachs] is a kind of converted Mozartian who dares to deliver a special vote on behalf of the "music of the future"' (*Music Criticisms*, 118).

aesthetic theory. In terms I outlined in Chapter 1, Hanslick's position is metaphysically constrained, Wagner's metaphysically inflated. Hanslick devotes himself to producing an objective and scientific account of the musically beautiful that falls entirely within the empirical bounds of sense. Wagner, by contrast, permits transcendental claims about musical meaning that are unverifiable precisely because they transcend those bounds and, hence, the purview of the empirically expressible. Hanslick takes music to have a significance that can be formulated by reference solely to music's tonally moving forms. Anything else we might want to say about music is expressible only through metaphor, and metaphor has no proper place in a scientific treatise. Wagner wants to capture the way music expresses what empirical theory fails to express, namely the dimension that transcends the empirical quality of music or, in Schopenhauerian mode, the empirical world in its entirety. However, whereas Hanslick is not denying absolutely that music can 'convey' transcendent or extramusical significances (they just play no part in a scientific account of the 'purely aesthetic' as he conceives it), so Wagner is not denying that the beautiful is expressed in and by a work's empirical content. He is just denying that the beautiful (or, perhaps better, the sublime) is reducible to that empirical means. Music as the 'purely aesthetic' language of the inexpressible (as he conceives it) always means something *extra* to its scientific expression.

Wagner finds in Hanslick's approach to theory a respect for theoretical limits that smacks of academicism and dryness. Wagner refers to it as 'rationalistic pettifogging'. Hanslick refers to it as the 'straitjacket of scholarship'. The irony is that Wagner's 'masterly' pedantry in *Die Meistersinger* is purposeful, and though Hanslick is quick to pick up on the pedantry, he apparently does not see it as intentional, and even if he does, he still finds it pedantic.[27] In Wagner's view, whereas intentional pedantry can demonstrate the limits of rational scholarship, unintentional

---

[27] Surely Act I is intentionally pedantic. Walther's lack of pedantry stands out as exceptional. We are relieved every time he sings; it breaks the monotony of David's listing the rules. In later acts, Hans Sachs symbolizes the anti-pedantic strain, as Wagner explains: 'I took Hans Sachs as the last manifestation of the art-productive spirit of the *Volksgeist*, and set him . . . in contrast to the pettifogging bombast of the other Meistersingers; to whose absurd pendanticism . . . I gave a concrete personal expression in the figure of the "marker"' ('A Communication to my Friends', i. 329).

pedantry takes these limits too seriously. Hanslick, in Wagner's eyes, exemplifies just such a serious or small-world academic. It is Hanslick's pedantry in theoretical attitude that mirrors the musical, small-world attitude of Beckmesser. In philosophy and in music, a pedant is what Wagner loathingly calls a 'semi-man', in contrast to the artist, who is a 'demi-god'.[28] The pedant interprets anything that falls outside the boundaries of form and the limits imposed by rules as being insignificant: he soon forgets that there is anything on the other side; he only sees the one sharply circumscribed side.[29] 'Here', sings Beckmesser, 'one is admitted only by the rules.'

Of course, there is a danger here in thinking that anyone who follows rules is a pedant. This is not what Wagner is saying. Wagner has nothing against rules. He only wants to use Sachs to teach that to know how to follow rules in the practical sphere is to know how to follow them in order to transcend them, and, in the theoretical sphere, to recognize the limits of claims or conditions for what they are—limits on what we can know and say, but not on what there is or on what can be shown.

What Wagner ultimately adopts in his joint parody of Hanslick and Beckmesser is a larger-world, but deeply bitter, stand against what he sees to be the regressive 'scientistic' tendencies increasingly dominating the practice of both philosophy and music. The dominant mentality in universities, he argues in one of his many Faust-inspired essays, renders the spirit of genius too radical and throws it out. Too many ways of knowing are dismissed. The academic establishment rejects any form of knowing not explained in terms of logic or the method of science. Theology is relegated to, and is dismissed as emanating from, the *Volk*. Philosophy is reduced to method and only in this reduction belongs to the academy.[30]

We may now read Wagner's criticisms of the modern music of Classical form in terms of its having become increasingly stifled and lifeless in his century, as having become out of date and, to

---

[28] 'Ferdinand Hiller', iv. 261.

[29] Cf. Wagner's more specific comment regarding Lessing that 'artificial art' (*künstliche Kunst*) produces its effect by the most exact observance of boundaries and limits (*Grenzen und Schranken*), since she must ever be on her watch to guard the unlimited force of imagination (*unbegrenzte Einbildungskraft*) ('The Play and the Nature of Dramatic Poetry', ii. 119).

[30] From 'Public and Popularity', vi, esp. 74 ff.

introduce a new term, as having become unnatural. All that now sustains the Classical form is artifice and technique, and these have become falsely employed as they have come to serve as ends and not as means for the Classical expression of art. Hanslick certainly criticized unformed melody and favoured Classical form, but in his mind this did not automatically translate into a means–ends confusion over rules. Wagner ignored this point (which he should not have) and went on: all traditions atrophy when a confusion of ends and means occurs. Artifice and technique shape a living tradition only when they are employed as vehicles or means for their own negations and not as ends in themselves. In their negation, they generate the semblance of 'naturalness' and 'art'. Wagner's so-called formlessness is also constructed as artifice and bears all the hallmarks of technique—it is not random—but it is intended to appear as entirely natural, spontaneous, and inspired. Naturalness should always be the end of art; artifice should only ever be the means by which that end is expressed.

Invoking this paradoxical relation between artifice and nature, and between technique and art, takes us to our two final arguments. Both reveal how necessary this paradoxical relation is for maintaining through music the freedom of the human subject, whilst recognizing, simultaneously, the need for art's public (objective) codification. It is this relation that Wagner had suggested musically in his antagonistic play between the constraint and freedom respectively of Classical and Romantic form in their nineteenth-century exemplifications.

4. The Political Argument

The political argument attends to how Wagner uses the artist and *das Volk* as sources of correctness and naturalness to counter what he takes to be the incorrectness and mere artifice imposed by the 'civilizing tendencies' and 'foreign domination' prevalent in contemporary cultural institutions (the doubleness of nature and artifice). The centrality of a 'sense of rightness' in this argument for true German community appears to put Wagner firmly in the arena of what today we call political conservatism. At moments his descriptions extend past conservatism and become quite sinister. It cannot be denied that Wagner encouraged explicitly ideological views, offered many self-serving opinions, and showed too great a readiness to blame the predictable suspects of his time.[31] But *Die Meistersinger* also presents a political argument of sufficient metaphysical generality that it does not immediately pre-establish a clear ideological commitment. At this level of generality, the argument shows more continuity than disparity between his descriptions of German community and those of a free art. It also accords with an aspiration Wagner once articulated in these terms:

[A]s an artist, [I] am contributing to the creative destruction of the modern world. So, if you ask, what you are to understand by what I am, I reply: I am neither a republican, nor a democrat, nor a socialist, nor a communist, but—an artist being; and, as such, everywhere that my gaze and my will extend, an out-and-out revolutionary, a destroyer of the old and builder of the new by the creation of the new.[32]

On the other hand, a political argument that does not pre-establish a singular ideological commitment also leaves it open for us to place any one of several into it. At times, Wagner certainly suggested ways of filling it in.

The political argument concerns the *spirit* of music and the *practice* of art in their relation to society. Wagner develops this argument as he seeks the connections among music, art, and human freedom. The connections are suggested in *Die Meistersinger* in its references to the expressive qualities of naturalness, spontaneity, and immediacy, to moral qualities of courage, honour, self-sacrifice, and to the general quality of common sense. Wagner identifies two sources for these qualities: the individual artist and the metaphysical *Volk*. They share the function of keeping society open: the artist creates only in so far as he expresses the artistic spirit of the *Volk*.[33] The artist contributes free

[31] Wagner recalled that he once tried to have a performance of his opera in Nürnberg, 'governed by the idea of offering the German public a picture of its own true nature'. He said he 'had the hope of winning from the nobler, stouter class of German burghers a hearty counter-greeting', but his hopes 'were disappointed'. He said he had been willing 'to donate his honorarium to the statue the Nürnbergeans were erecting of Hans Sachs', but recalled the 'sumptuous synagogue of purest Oriental style' built opposite the statue. To justify his failure in Nürnberg, he concludes: 'These were my experiences of the German burgher-world' ('Shall we Hope?', vi. 114–15).

[32] Quoted in Paul Lawrence Rose, *Wagner: Race and Revolution* (New Haven, 1992), 103.

[33] 'Sketches and Fragments', viii. 349. My reading of the political argument most closely concurs with that of Arthur Groos as offered in his 'Constructing Nuremberg: Typological and Proleptic Communities in *Die Meistersinger*', *19th-Century Music*, 16/1 (Summer 1992), 18–34. For Wagner's own comments on the different meanings of 'Volk', see 'The Art-Work of the Future', i. 74–7.

expressions of art; the *Volk* contribute their common sense. These contributions are codified within conventions and institutions; these rational codifications are necessarily artificial and imperfect. They function progressively, in Wagner's view, when they work in accordance with the original, natural contributions and regressively when they break the bond. Modern and civilized institutions have broken the bond; they have become self-enclosed totalities.[34] What Wagner consequently sees in modern society is the domination of the merely ornamental and trivial, the 'alien' or 'artificial' conventions of 'the foreign' and 'French' in 'their full-bottomed wigs', and the 'rootlessness' of 'the bourgeois Jews'. 'Hail Winckelmann and Lessing,' he proclaims against this 'invasion', 'ye who, beyond the centuries of native German majesty, found the German's ur-kinsmen in the divine Hellenes, and laid bare the pure ideal of human beauty to the powder-bleared eyes of French-civilised mankind!'[35] Because individuals live in social formations—as souls live in bodies—they are potentially imprisoned or cut off from their 'natural' springs. Society conceived as the completion of nature can go right or wrong, depending on whether progressive or regressive human impulses dominate.

For Wagner it is the function of art, and most especially of music, to cut the chains of this imprisonment by promoting the negating aesthetic experience. 'Nothing today is free but the artwork, which in itself fulfils the beautiful and the strong as semblance.'[36] In this light, Walther's song at the end of the opera is a master song not just because it conforms to a desired form and content, but also because of the experience it affords the mastersingers, who are guided by the judgements of the *Volk*. Only for dramatic purposes are the *Volk* separated from the mastersingers; they are *Volk* themselves—they simply have to be reminded of that fact. Furthermore, it is the masters who, in listening to Walther's song, are reminded of what their rules stand for. The song is a master song used to educate or re-educate masters through the experience of art. Music, Wagner writes to generalize the lesson, has an enno-

---

[34] Cf. Wagner's claim that art is not 'an artificial product', nor an 'arbitrary issue', but 'an inbred craving of the natural, genuine, and uncorrupted man' ('The Art-Work of the Future', i. 89).

[35] 'German Art and German Policy', iv. 43.

[36] 'Sketches and Fragments', viii. 369.

bling effect: its geniuses reveal to us what is genuine (*echt*) about ourselves.[37]

This interpretation is endorsed by Beckmesser's failure to sing the song he steals from Sachs's desk (III. iii). Beckmesser steals only the words that Sachs writes down on hearing Walther's morning-dream song. Discovering his theft, Sachs warns him to memorize the words well and to find for them their appropriate melody (*Weise*). But Beckmesser's subsequent failure to perform what he steals shows that Wagner also demands in a master's performance a quality approaching moral integrity. Sachs advises Beckmesser: 'study the song carefully; its rendition is not easy; even if you succeed with the melody, and arrive at the tune!' The 'even' is crucial: ontologically, the song is its words and its melody, but morally, only a singer in touch with the artistic spirit, living in freedom or in love (or, thinking of Sachs, a person of courage and generosity) can sing the correct melody in the right way as a correct accompaniment to the words. 'What a difference the proper (*recht*) word and delivery make!', proclaim the *Volk*, on hearing Walther sing. 'Yes, indeed', reply the masters; 'I realize it's another matter, if one sings badly (*falsch*) or well (*richtig*).' So, just as Wagner teaches that it does not suffice for an artist to create merely according to the rules he has memorized, he teaches a parallel lesson to the singer of songs: one cannot musically perform a song simply by memorizing the words and singing the correct notes. A singer must sing the song in the right way—with inspiration and understanding. Wagner dramatically parodies Beckmesser's failure with this lesson in mind; even when Beckmesser thinks that he is singing the words he has stolen, the words he sings are heard as garbled nonsense. Beckmesser, Sachs concludes, has wasted the understanding he must once have had (III. iii).

It is part of Wagner's argument to acknowledge that, though the experience of art is limited by its transitory nature, still it may produce an intimation of what society could be like, or what it might once authentically have been. His argument is always future-directed, even though it calls upon an (idealized) past. He writes: 'Through the most intimate understanding of antiquity the German spirit has acquired the ability to imitate the purely human in all its original freedom, which it does, not by using classical forms to

[37] Cf. 'Introduction to the Year 1880', vi. 34–5, yet another attack on pedantry in the academy.

depict a particular subject, but by using the classical view of the world to produce the new and necessary form.'[38] When he speaks through Sachs of the importance of preserving the masters' tradition, he endorses two views: first, that the tradition carries the natural spirit of music and the authentic (German) spirit of the *Volk* despite any regressive appearance; secondly, that mastersinging is a public affair that leaves space for the creative freedom of individuals, but ultimately is an activity *for* the community protected by an ideally wise elite. The masters' tradition, codified albeit imperfectly in terms of rules and exemplified by master songs, provides a public and communicable basis for future masters to understand what would otherwise remain a private affair. As Sachs tells the young Walther: in composing a master song it is not sufficient merely to have the creative inspiration, nor even to retain a personal memory of such; it is necessary also that the song be communicable. A real master is one who can express his private inspiration through codifiable technique; a real master is one who can express the spirit of music in a publicly accessible (poetic) form. 'Man is in a twofold way a poet,' writes Wagner elsewhere, 'in his *beholding*, and in his *imparting*. His *natural* poetic gift is the faculty of condensing into an inner image the phenomena presented to his senses from outside; his *artistic*, that of projecting the image outwards.'[39] When Walther 'scarcely dares' to think about the inspiration he has just dreamt, Sachs responds that '[d]reams and poetry [must] willingly help each other' for it is the 'poet's job exactly, to observe and interpret his dreams'. 'Believe me, the truest illusion (*wahrster Wahn*) of man becomes revealed to him in dreams: the whole art of writing and poetry-making is nothing but the true interpretation of dreams' (III. ii).

Wagner's use of the past has a further function: to see, in the tradition of mastersinging, evolutionary development. Aware of its historicity, the masters are constantly reminded that their tradition is a living tradition and should continue ideally to 'regenerate' itself or be 'reborn' in accordance with the spirit or magic (*Zauberspruch*) of music. Remember that Wagner's argument has depended all along upon seeing a tradition's codification in rules as

---

[38] 'What is German?', iv. 155–6. I have used Stewart Spencer's translation given in Müller's 'Wagner and Antiquity', in Müller and Wapnewski (eds.), *Wagner Handbook*, 235.

[39] 'The Play and the Nature of Dramatic Poetry', ii. 152.

doubly imperfect: first, rules are limited in so far as they do not descriptively exhaust the spirit of music that guides the tradition; secondly, they become purely artificial when they break the bond with their natural originating spirit. Wagner now adds a third claim: rules must constantly be renewed, but since they are not self-renewing, they must await the musical and moral input of the artist and 'his beautiful song'.

In a more general context Wagner argues that whereas 'nature supplies the model for aesthetic creation (*Nachbildung*)', '[c]ulture (*Kultur*) by itself never yields more than mechanical imitation (*Nachahmung*)'.[40] In *Die Meistersinger*, he gives detail to this distinction. Sachs begins the argument by defining 'a master':

In the favored time of youth, when in the grip of powerful urges toward happy first loves our breasts are expanded to the fullest; then many may succeed in singing a beautiful song: spring did the singing for them. Come summer, autumn, and winter time, much misery and worry in life, much married happiness as well—baptism of children, business affairs, dissension and conflict—the one who still wants to succeed in singing a beautiful song, see: he is called a master!

Walther now asks Sachs: but how will 'a master, from whom spring has . . . faded, recapture it in an image?' Sachs answers: young artists will come along with new songs; they will freshen the rules. The refreshed rules will remind the masters of their own youthful inspirations, and that will help preserve (*bewahren*) the spirit of their youth. So 'learn the master-rules in good time', Sachs warns Walther, while you are young. In time, that learning will serve you well.

Sachs realizes that the artist cannot refresh the rules by himself; he must work alongside, and in the spirit of, the *Volk*. So he adds a new instruction: in a singing contest 'let the people be the judge' (and in this particular case, the loving Eva). Wagner's artistic and political lesson is complete: a tradition of art, like society as a whole, must constantly keep in touch with the natural spirit of the *Volk* or its 'free' individuals to avoid its becoming overly artificed.

Each year, Sachs summarizes, the masters' rules must be tested outside the academic establishment, in a natural, festive environment, by persons who are not already acquainted with them. Given that the young artist and the *Volk* are still on 'the true track of

---

[40] 'German Art and German Policy', iv. 84.

nature', they should guide the test. But be careful, Sachs warns; do not equate their natural innocence or 'untrained ears' with a civilized ignorance. Wagner is explicit: his *Volk* do not represent the tastes of fashion; they embody, by contrast, music's natural and rural spirit. Comparably, an artist will never win a prize 'by flattery'. 'Downfall and disgrace constantly threaten art that runs after the people's favor,' sings master Kothner in concurrence. Even the artist and the *Volk* must work to preserve their integrity to avoid falling into mediocrity (*die Mittelmässigkeit*). By this term, Wagner writes, 'we usually mean something that issues no new and unknown thing, but something already known of pleasing and insinuating form. In the best sense, it would be the product of talent—if we agree with Schopenhauer that talent hits a mark we see but cannot reach. Genius, by contrast . . . attains a goal we cannot even see.'[41]

Beckmesser's early confrontation with Walther dramatizes the difference. Beckmesser dismisses Sachs's lesson on the natural revisability of rules. He has become so cut off from change that he believes the past of his tradition is represented perfectly and entirely in its present. Nothing new to him is ever appropriate. When Walther defends his singing as being in accord with the original, nature-inspired rules of the 'good master' Walther von der Vogelweide—the defence is expressed in his 'Trial Song'— Beckmesser dismisses this defence with the closed-minded claim that those rules no longer apply because they are not the rules *he* knows. Beckmesser's dismissal disregards Wagner's claim that, because a tradition is forever evolving, its participants should always be on the lookout for signs of atrophy. Walther's appeal to a natural, originating spirit in birdsong is supported in the opera as entirely appropriate.

But is it appropriate under all conditions? Consider the warning Adorno once issued against identifying the origins of music in birdsong. He might have been addressing Wagner directly:

The anamnesis of freedom in natural beauty deceives because it seeks freedom in the old unfreedom. Natural beauty is myth transposed into the imagination and thus, perhaps, requited. The song of birds is found beautiful by everyone; no feeling person in whom something of the European tradition survives fails to be moved by the sound of a robin after a rain

---

[41] 'Public and Popularity', vi. 56.

shower. Yet something frightening lurks in the song of birds precisely because it is not a song but obeys the spell in which it is enmeshed.[42]

According to this view, a bird cannot escape 'nature's fate'. But is this true also of the singer who aspires to sing like a bird? The argument would certainly be regressive if the answer were yes. Does it have to be?

Recall the principle that natural expressions necessarily appear through social conventions or through the medium of artifice. Presumably, if the 'naturalness' is to be experienced as such, a negation is required: the artifice must be left behind. The aesthetic experience is Wagner's paradigm for this act of negation. Wagner follows Schopenhauer: 'The musician', Wagner writes, 'looks quite away from the incidents of ordinary life; [he] entirely upheaves its details and its accidentals, and sublimates whatever lies within it to its quintessence of emotional content—to which alone music can give a voice, and music only.'[43] When music gives its voice, so nature, according to Wagner, also gives its voice.

Alternatively put, the relation in which nature stands to artifice demands failure. Only when artifice is recognized as failing to be natural does it serve its proper function. Recognized as such, it reveals what it would otherwise conceal. Wagner writes: 'By leading forth his artwork in continuous organic growth, and making ourselves organic helpers in that growth, the poet frees his creation from all traces of his handiwork.' This statement closely recalls Kant's, regarding art's aim to appear *as if* it were natural.[44]

But do acts of negation actually reveal the natural? I do not think so. When artifice is seen through, the natural is not given to us as such; it is constructed at another level of appearance. Acts of negation, such as we find in aesthetic experience or creation, do not strip appearances away; they add them. This is all Wagner really needs for his argument. He does not need to speak of a return to the natural; he only needs to say that aesthetic experience opens up

[42] *Aesthetic Theory*, tr. R. Hullot-Kentor (Minneapolis, 1997), 66.

[43] 'On Liszt's Symphonic Poems', iii. 249.

[44] 'The Arts of Poetry and Tone in the Drama of the Future', ii. 337. I am referring to Kant's account of genius and the negative moments (disinterest and purposiveness without purpose) and publicizing conditions (necessity and universality) of the pure aesthetic judgement. Each moment or condition contains a negating *ohne* (something without something): 'ein Wohlgefallen ohne alles Interesse'; 'was ohne Begriffe allgemein gefällt'; 'ohne Vorstellung eines Zwecks'; 'ohne Begriff als Gegenstand'.

a world of appearance (illusion) that allows us to see through the artifice. If this is right, the aesthetic aspiration to sing like a bird, or to hear human song as bird song, is sufficient, despite the paradoxical formulation, to protect human art from being reduced to the unfreedom either of nature, on the one side, or of artifice, on the other.

5. The Philosophical Argument

The philosophical argument ties the previous ones together. It has three interconnected themes: rules, limits, and concealment. It reveals the full impact of *Die Meistersinger*'s lesson. This lesson is about the protection of integrity of the individual and the community against the constant threat of prejudice, pedantry, corruption, and unsound judgement. It is about the way music as the language of escape provides a justification for life, in so far as it is able, in Wagner words, to break 'forth from the chaos of modern civilization'. But to recall the Socrates of the *Meno*, it also turns out to be about the concealment involved in teaching; it is about teachers or masters who paradoxically teach by not teaching.

Wagner's lesson begins by recalling the traditional view that an education in a given practice demands that we attain not only technical or theoretical knowledge, but also practical knowledge. The former knowledge is associated with learning rules; the latter demands that we know the products themselves, the so-called exemplars or exemplary instances of that practice. When Aristotle spoke about teaching virtue, his first instruction was that students should seek examples of virtuous men. When late Enlightenment and early Romantic theorists pulled apart two concepts of imitation—'copying' or 'rule-following' from 'following in the example of'—they changed the way we thought about a practice's practical knowledge and its corresponding theoretical knowledge.

Recall Winckelmann's paradoxical prescription that the only way for Germans to become great lies in the *Nachahmung* of the *unnachahmlich* works of the Greeks. How can one imitate inimitable art?[45] Kant answered the question more explicitly than

---

[45] *Reflections on the Imitation of Greek Works in Painting and Sculpture*, tr. E. Heyer and R. C. Norton (La Salle, Ill., 1987).

Winckelmann: '*Following* by reference to a precedent, rather than . . . [copying], is the right term for any influence that products of an exemplary author may have on others; and this means no more than drawing on the same sources from which the predecessor himself drew, and learning from him only how to go about doing so.'[46] For Kant, works are exemplary for others; others learn from them. They learn neither by merely mastering explicit and determinate rules nor by copying masterpieces to produce what nowadays we might call works 'in the school or style of'. Rather, they try to acquire an understanding of the aesthetic ideals and understanding that artists have exemplified through their works. For Winckelmann and Kant, the significance of exemplary works (or works by exemplary artists) lies in the way these works express ideals.

Composers, performers, audiences, and critics are granted access to these ideals in a rite of aesthetic passage. They are required to move beyond their daily or ordinary cares, and to suspend their normal use of conceptual and cognitive skills. Employing sentiment, imagination, and free subjectivity, they enter an unsullied world of pure aesthetic experience. Theorists who have described this passage have not been content, however, to let pure subjectivity render experiences that are merely private or personal, so they have specified the normative conditions under which these experiences can be communicated or universalized. In his essay 'Of the Standard of Taste' Hume argued for these conditions in terms of a standard which would have the advantage of reconciling the different sentiments of men, but would not determine what those sentiments should thereafter and forever be.[47] It was important for Hume, as it would become essential for Burke and Kant, that a standard by which aesthetic judgement could claim a normative universality should not serve thereafter as a substitute for subjective experience; it should only ever serve as the guide by which to produce the public judgement. The standard would both acknowledge the subjective freedom that conditioned creativity and aesthetic experience, and serve normatively to communicate that freedom to others. The standard depended upon a certain relation holding between subjective experience and the object of that

[46] *Critique of Judgment*, I/32, tr. W. S. Pluhar (Indianapolis, 1987), 146–7.
[47] *Essays: Moral, Political, and Literary*, ed. E. F. Miller (Indianapolis, 1987), 226–49.

experience—the work of art itself. The relation was something like a harmonious sympathy between sentiment and form, or a jarring of that sympathy if the work was ugly or if the sentiment was sullied by prejudice.

For present purposes, the most important aspect of the standard of taste was that it was recommended as a theoretical response to the failure of earlier theorists to account for the agreed objective beauty of works of art—their aesthetic value and corresponding judgement—in terms of objective properties. An account of objectivity given entirely in objective (empirical and conceptual) terms was the theoretical way to strip from the aesthetic its aesthetic significance. Such an account bore all the marks of what I shall call *Beckmesser's Complaint*: it reduced inspiration to a determinate set of rules, nature to artifice, beauty to a determinate set of empirical properties, and subjective freedom to communicable convention. Theorists therefore developed non-reductive accounts to balance the demand in aesthetics for free and subjective experience with the demand for objective judgement. They found this balance in a standard which no rules could supply. The standard, once more, was the only way to keep a public practice of artistic production and aesthetic judgement open enough to accommodate both the innovations of genius and the 'guiding and guardian spirit' of free expression, without that practice succumbing to the arbitrary input of subjective whim.

The notion of exemplarity proved crucial in these accounts. Theorists found that conceiving of works of art as exemplary preserved their essential particularity, immediacy, and non-reducibility. In their aesthetic dimension, works of genius would never quite fit any existing description given in terms of a set of properties. Only conceived as formed content might these works receive a commonplace, empirical account. It was this lack of fit between the aesthetic and the empirical that I earlier described in terms of a *gap* between the rules of a practice and its products. In present terms, the gap could be maintained only by a standard of taste that never presumed to *set* the standard for creativity, but only to *condition* the standard of judgement. In the practice of aesthetics and the arts, the products always came first. Kant wrote: '[T]hough understanding is capable of being instructed, and of being equipped with rules, judgement is a peculiar talent which can be practised only, and cannot be taught. It is the specific quality of so-called mother-wit; and its lack no school can make good.'[48]

The appeal to exemplarity suited a theory that recognized that epistemological limits differentiated a world or domain that could be known empirically from one only transcendentally (pre)supposed, the 'the domain of transcendental law'. Kant wrote: '[I]t is precisely in knowing its limits that philosophy consists.'[49] Yet this appeal to the limits of theory and to exemplarity had strong theological origins that Schopenhauer would make far more explicit than Kant, and it was the theologically rooted metaphysics that Wagner would use to generate the negatively formulated claims of his musical aesthetic. I shall list some of those claims now in the form of seven fragments.

1. The 'history of music = Christian expression': 'where the word can no farther, there music begins'.[50]
2. We should take Kant's view of spatio-temporal limits seriously, and see that we are subject to a law 'concealed from eyes historical, ordaining the mysterious sequence of a spiritual life whose acts are guided by denial of the world and all its history'.[51]
3. 'It is reserved for music alone, to reveal the primal elements of this marvelous nature; in her mysterious charm our soul is shown this great, unutterable secret.'[52]
4. '[U]nder no conditions would I pretend to teach how men should make, but merely to guide them to a knowledge of how the made and the created should be rightly understood.'[53]
5. 'Only by examples, examples, and again examples, is anything to be made clear, and eventually something learnt.'[54]
6. 'Technique is the accumulating property of every artist . . . it can be accepted, learnt and acquired. That which is to be portrayed by means of technique is in nowise to be learnt, and of it therefore we do not speak.'[55]

---

[48] A133, in book II of the Transcendental Analytic, *Critique of Pure Reason*, tr. N. Kemp Smith (1929; New York, 1965), 177.

[49] Ibid. A727, p. 585.

[50] 'Sketches and Fragments', viii. 362. I attend to the rest of this fragment in the next chapter.

[51] 'The Public in Time and Space', vi. 86.

[52] 'Halévy and "La Reine de Chypre"', viii. 179.

[53] 'On Operatic Poetry and Composition', vi. 172.

[54] Ibid.   [55] 'Sketches and Fragments', viii. 373–4.

7. Regarding Jesus: 'Therefore I speak to them in parables, because with eyes to see they see not, and with ears to hear they
hear not, for they do not understand. I will open my mouth in
parables, and will utter things secret from the beginning of the
world.'[56]

Consider Wagner's argument, first, for the aesthetic of exemplarity and the priority of products, and, secondly, for concealment understood in terms of paradoxes—of one thing being
presented in terms of another, or of something's being revealed by
negating something else. These forms of concealment are developed in the content and the form of Wagner's argument. They
are developed through the complex interaction of saying and
showing.

For example, Walther's three songs serve an exemplary function:
they are well learned from only when they are understood. Sachs
reveals the progressive potential of Walther's songs against
Beckmesser's regressive misreadings. 'If you want to measure by
rules that which doesn't run by [your] rules,' Sachs tells the masters
on hearing the 'Trial Song', 'leave behind *your* treasured rules, and
look instead for *its* rules!' (my emphasis). To each song Wagner
attaches three readings: the naive (Walther's), the pedantic
(Beckmesser's), and the wise (Sachs's), and in each case the wise
draws on the naive and pedantic to remove the error from both.
But the three songs also serve a single exemplary function: they
function in developmental relation to one another within an overall
context of pedagogy. This is shown in the way that what is revealed
as having potentially been in the 'Trial Song' is a quality that is
explained (through saying) in the production of the 'Morning
Song', and finally exemplified (through showing) in the 'Master
Song'. That quality is the paradoxical marriage of natural inspiration and artificial rules. The 'Trial Song' is the demonstration of
natural innocence, the 'Morning Song' the song of learning, and the
'Master' or 'Prize Song', the exhibition of a lesson learnt. Together
the songs reveal the full evolutionary force of a paradox that
demands among both the verses of a single song and the three
songs themselves, that the last of the three be the 'love-child' of the
first two.

The songs also show another paradox, that involved in the very

---

[56] 'Jesus of Nazareth', viii. 330.

teaching of the lesson.[57] When Wagner equates the ability to sing songs with an innate, natural ability, it becomes apparent that Walther, in a certain sense, never really needed the lesson at all. When Sachs rhetorically asks (after the 'Trial Song'), whether, 'if true art is innate in him . . . what does it matter who taught it to him?' he undermines the role he immediately adopts as teacher. What Walther learns over the course of the opera he has always known, even if, in his youthfulness, he shows no signs of being able to say what he knows. For the young Walther, it is enough that he can sing what the 'miraculous power of the poet's song' has made accessible to him 'in secret', without explanation. Walther's life as reflective knower—as master—is ahead of him. Only the aged Sachs makes the lesson explicit. 'But how might I claim to measure what seems immeasurable to me?', he asks on recalling the 'Trial Song':

No rule seemed to fit there—and yet there was no error in it. It sounded so old—and yet was so new—like bird-song in sweet May! Whoever hears it and, beguiled by illusion (*wahnbetört*), imitates the bird's singing, to him it might bring mockery and disgrace: the command of spring, sweet necessity, laid it in his bosom: then he sang, as he had to; and since he had to, he was able to. [II. iii]

The transition from youthful or naive innocence to reflective wisdom is not the transition from not knowing to knowing rules, but to making implicit rules explicit to oneself as one's own. It is a transition from singing to saying. This is a transition of doubleness: the singing is not subsumed or replaced by the saying. Saying, one might say, without singing is artistically empty, as singing without saying, however beautiful, is blind.

6. Concealed and Revealed Conclusions

In *The Complete Operas of Richard Wagner*, Charles Osborne dismisses the 'secret suffering' demonstrated in Sachs's *Wahn* monologue.[58] This monologue, he writes, 'is an aesthetic error in its intrusion of a tragic view of the world into what its composer

---

[57] It has been argued (and rejected) that the Socrates of the *Symposium* is 'the prototype' of Sachs (see Ulrich Müller, 'Wagner and Antiquity', in Müller and Wapnewski (eds.), *Wagner Handbook*, 233). I am suggesting a connection be made between Sachs and the Socrates of the *Meno*.

[58] (London, 1990), 174.

intended to be a comedy about the course of true love in medieval Nuremburg'. Osborne attributes this error to Wagner's intermittent Schopenhauerian moodiness.

Dahlhaus takes this moodiness seriously.[59] He argues that '[t]he philosophy of art informing *Die Meistersinger* is . . . more complex than it at first appears to be, particularly in the relationship between what is explicit and what remains unsaid'. He claims, and there is no disputing this, that the opera is about *Wahn*, the conception of art as illusion and escape from the mundane seriousness of life. He then argues that the dramatic conflict between the characters Beckmesser, on the one hand, and Hans Sachs and Walther, on the other, is almost irrelevant to what he calls the 'crucial issues', which he soon identifies in the singular as an 'unacknowledged, subversive and secret idea'. Though secret, this idea is none the less revealed by Walther's 'Trial Song' of Act I, but its revelation, according to Dahlhaus, is an 'act of betrayal'. He explains:

The idea of Walther's 'natural genius' is an illusion, revealed as sham by the Trial Song itself, for its line and rhyme schemes are so complicated that the ability to compose a song to them as immaculately as Walther does presupposes the most intense effort and application. The paradox is not, of course, an accidental oversight . . . rather it encapsulates the esoteric artistic philosophy of *Die Meistersinger*, as opposed to the exoteric philosophy represented by Sachs. . . . Wagner's fundamental aesthetic conviction, which he shared with Kant, was that art, in order to be art, must conceal itself and appear in the guise of nature. The means and expedients must not be allowed to be visible, reflection must be transformed into spontaneity, immediacy must be recreated and still be immediacy, and every trace of effort must be expunged. The paradox is that it takes technique to deny technique.[60]

I disagree with Osborne's position. I disagree with Dahlhaus's only in matters of detail. First, I disagree that the 'Trial Song' reveals Walther's 'natural genius' to be a sham. I disagree that it reveals the paradox of technique. I grant only that this song initiates our thinking about this paradox. I have argued that only the 'Master Song' reveals the paradox fully and that a significant part of Wagner's lesson was to show why the 'Trial Song', in failing fully to reveal this paradox, had to fail the first judgement of the masters. The first song stands to the master song as *Tristan* stands to *Die*

[59] *Richard Wagner's Music Dramas*, tr. M. Whittall (Cambridge, 1979), 65–79.
[60] Ibid. 69–70.

Meistersinger, as a desired deed (first song) stands to a plea for its acceptance (third song).

Secondly, if by Sachs's 'exoteric philosophy' Dahlhaus is referring to the final political monologue on the preservation of German traditions, I disagree that this lesson is sharply opposed to the so-called esoteric secret regarding the paradox of technique.

Thirdly, Dahlhaus leaves it unclear how the sober paradox involving the hiding of technique to give the appearance of naturalness leads to, or illustrates, his larger, less sober thesis that the opera contains an 'unacknowledged, subversive, and secret' idea. If there is a secret idea in the opera, surely it is more than the idea Kant was content to acknowledge quite openly. What is it about the paradox that its revelation is also its betrayal?

Sachs sings a monologue glorifying Germany, her people, and her art. The monologue is intentionally harmonious and affirmative in its ideological promise.[61] It also suggests deep fearfulness as it warns of the potential for corruption in a community ruled by foreigners. Scholars mostly interpret this monologue as unapologetically ideological and as disturbing the opera's otherwise aesthetic argument. Some have even concluded that there are two 'unrelated' dramas in the opera: the aesthetic and the political.

There are reasons to reject this last conclusion, and not just because scholars have discovered that it was Wagner's wife, Cosima, who persuaded him to end on an upbeat note with a 'daylight . . . vision of a lovely reality'.[62] Apparently, Wagner once thought of ending with Walther's 'Prize Song'—presumably at the song's end. Yet consider the consequences: we would never have known whether the masters judged the song correctly, whether Eva accepted Walther as the winner, or whether Walther accepted his other prize, the mastership. Yet is not the last piece of information crucial? Some scholars have suggested that Walther ultimately did not learn Sachs's lesson very well, because he seemed far more content to win the girl than to accept the position of master.[63]

---

[61] Wagner writes of the ending as intentionally having an 'inspiriting effect' ('About Conducting', iv. 358).

[62] *Cosima Wagner's Diaries*, An Abridgement, ed. G. Skelton (New Haven, 1994), 402.

[63] Cf. Cosima's remark to King Ludwig, that 'Walther's refusal of official honours was very much part of his character' (quoted by Peter Wapnewski in 'The Operas as Literary Works', in Müller and Wapnewski (eds.), *Wagner Handbook*, 79).

Because Walther is still youthful and selfish, Sachs has to lecture him (and his audience) on the importance of Walther's having sung not just a *prize* song, but also a *master* song—a song that has made him worthy of joining their elite community. This is also the subject of Sachs's final monologue. Reading it as a pedagogical correction to Walther's youthful error allows us to reject the two-drama view and to see the monologue's aesthetic lesson as overriding, and perhaps even as cancelling out, its suspicious ideological content. Barry Millington finds a suitable precursor in Schiller for the priority Wagner gives the aesthetic: 'Separated from the political, the German has established for himself his own worth, and even if the Empire were to be destroyed, German excellence (in art) would remain undisputed.'[64] Dahlhaus and Deathridge conclude, comparably, that the words of Sachs's speech 'are not chauvinist: they plead the cause of art and testify to indifference towards the state'. Wagner's idea, they say, is to subvert the audience and society for the sake of art. Sachs's last monologue, they conclude, is about art not politics.

   This last conclusion is misleading. It is hard to believe that when scholars speak of Wagner's prioritizing the aesthetic, they really think that the aesthetic and political are, in Wagner's view, separable, and the latter somehow dispensable. They may be motivated to speak this way given perhaps their desire to defend 'the real Wagner'—the musical genius—from the ideological man. But given the evidence Wagner himself provides, it is hard to read his aesthetic views as not being as much about social and political expression as they are about musical expression. Perhaps one would want to separate, as far as one can, the political model from the ideological content, but that separation is very different from separating aesthetics from politics. In this chapter, I have tried to demonstrate the latter inseparability by attending to how Wagner's description of the paradox of technique (the paradox of artifice and nature) is inextricably connected to his interest in locating the source of human freedom within a regulated community. I think it would be better to conclude that there is one drama in *Die Meistersinger* that has an intricately woven aesthetic and political expression. To conclude this way is not to forgive Wagner his

---

[64] *Wagner* (Princeton, 1984), 254.

ideological views. It only protects the formal and non-reductive relation holding between Wagner's aesthetics and politics from the temptation to reduce either to an overriding claim about ideological content.

How, finally, should we handle Dahlhaus's claim that there is a tension between the exoteric, political message and the esoteric, aesthetic message? Given Wagner's apparent proclivity for concealment, plausibly his conclusion contains a negative gesture, a gesture of 'night' to counter Cosima. Perhaps another ending can be read between Sachs's final lines. Perhaps Sachs should have ended by repeating the substance of his other great monologue on madness and disorder. Would that have rendered the conclusion too disordered? Wagner had to end on a note of order. Sachs had promised in his *Wahn* monologue that he would show how disorder can work for a noble and ordered end, and when he had fulfilled his promise, the opera could end. But did Sachs mean to imply that, a point of order having been found, disorder no longer exists? No. Order, he had argued throughout the opera, stands to disorder as either its healthy or its unhealthy expression. Disorder, rightly channelled, has its historical moment, as does disorder wrongly channelled. Reading his two major monologues in tandem, it is plausible to read the opera's ending as signalling a single historical moment, a temporary moment of order.

So imagine, if you will, what happened in the coming weeks and years after this temporary moment had past. Walther and Eva are happily married and Walther has taught the masters something they perhaps have forgotten. Time goes by and Walther loses his youthful enthusiasms. What happens next? Does Walther turn out to be a successor to Sachs or to Beckmesser?[65] You might think we cannot answer this question because 'we just don't know', but remember that Wagner used a lot of sources for his opera and not all authors who told the story ended at the same point. There is one version that might have given Wagner a conclusion perfectly consistent with his argument, but which seems, in a particular sense, to be better left concealed. The version is offered by the early Romanticists Wackenroder and Tieck as the conclusion to their own book

---

[65] The usual assumption is that the apprentice David will succeed Beckmesser and Walther will succeed Sachs. I am suggesting that there is nothing to guarantee that conclusion. Both David and Walther might end up acting like Beckmesser.

Outpourings of an Art-Loving Friar, and tells the sad 'musical tale of Joseph Berlinger'. (Wherever you hear the name Joseph think of Walther *in old age*.)[66]

My compressed version of the story goes like this: There once was a young boy named Joseph who was profoundly inspired by music. Whenever he heard the spirit of King David he became completely enraptured; he felt 'nobler and purer'. He was forever contemplating his 'marvelous gift of music, which affects us the more powerfully and stirs all our vital forces the more deeply, the vaguer and more mysterious its language is'. He decided that he would descend from his 'sublime poetic ecstasy', to make his whole life 'an endless melody'. Leaving his beloved father at home, he went in search of musicians with the hope of entering their world. It was his beginning and his end.

Many years later Joseph is an old man reflecting back upon his life. 'What a lamentable life,' he cries; 'how cruel even my first years of musical instruction were! How disillusioned I felt when I peeped behind the curtain of mystery! . . . To think that instead of flying unrestrained I first had to learn to climb around on the clumsy scaffolding and prison bars of artistic rules and regulations! What torment I had to endure in order first to produce a regularly constructed work by means of vulgar mechanical scientific reasoning before I could even contemplate expressing my feelings in music! What a tedious expenditure of mechanical effort! And yet, what of it? I still possessed youthful energy and was full of hope for a glorious future! And now? Now my glorious future has become a piteous present.' Joseph continues to recall his loneliness and abandonment 'amidst', he says, 'the discord of so many unharmonious souls around him'. Still questioning the meaning of his life as an artist, he finally draws his sad conclusion: 'An artist must create for himself alone . . . and for only one or two others who understand him.' With this he dies.

---

[66] Wagner certainly knew their book. His idyllic view of Nürnberg closely matches theirs: 'Nürnberg! You once famous city! How I loved to wander through your winding streets! With what childlike devotion did I behold your old German houses and churches, which so clearly bear the stamp of our national art! How deeply I love the works of that past time, those works which speak such a sturdy, powerful, and truthful language!' The passage goes on to describe the creative spirits of Dürer and Sachs (*Outpourings of an Art-Loving Friar*, tr. E. Mornin (New York, 1975), 40–50). Borchmeyer also makes this connection (*Richard Wagner: Theory and Theatre*, tr. S. Spencer (Oxford, 1991), 252).

The voices of Wackenroder and Tieck take over. They say they do not entirely disagree with Joseph's conclusion but remain uncertain:

Alas! What a bitter irony of fate that it was [Joseph's] very strength, his sublime fantasy, which wrought his destruction! Should [we] say that he was perhaps born to enjoy art rather than to practice it? Are those men perhaps of happier constitution in whom art works silently and secretly like a veiled spirit, never disrupting their everyday affairs? Or must the man of unfailing inspiration perhaps anchor his exalted visions boldly and firmly in this everyday life if he is to become a genuine artist? Is not this unfathomable power to create perhaps something quite different from— and it seems to me now—something still more wonderful and more divine than the power of the imagination?

Wackenroder and Tieck answer their questions with a classic proclamation of concealment:

The artistic spirit is and must ever remain a mystery for man, and his head swims when he tries to plumb its depths. But it is, too, an object of the highest wonderment, as must be said of all that is sublime on earth.

With this, they appropriately conclude that they can 'write no more'—whereof one cannot speak . . .

Walther might have died an unhappy man or, like Sachs, the resigned hero of forbidden celebration, to use Catherine Clément's well-chosen description.[67] Or he might have died a corrupted man like Beckmesser, having forgotten the spirit of King David amidst all his worldly success. The fact that there is a choice here is the major point because Wagner, I believe, was warning us that anyone, at any moment, can become afflicted by *Beckmesser's Complaint*. 'The hour of weakness comes for all of us,' sings Sachs. Here is potentially a more profound source of the fear expressed in Sachs's seemingly ordered final monologue. Behind order lie the progressive promise and the regressive threat of disorder. The progressive promise, however, hardly dares reveal itself for fear of its regressive counterpart. Its revelation is too often its betrayal. '[H]uman life,' Schopenhauer once wrote, 'like all inferior goods, is covered on the outside with a false glitter: what suffers always conceals itself.'[68] In this century Willa Cather expressed a comparable

---

[67] *Opera, or the Undoing of Women*, tr. B. Wing (Minneapolis, 1988), 130–1.

[68] *The World as Will and Representation*, i. 325. Quoted also by Adorno in *In Search of Wagner*, 82.

point, but attached to it a certain confidence. The artist's secret is passion, she wrote: 'That is all. It is an open secret, and perfectly safe. Like heroism, it is inimitable in cheap materials.'[69]

Wagner might have been confident, but apparently he was not laughing. He wrote to King Ludwig in 1868: 'It is impossible that you should not have sensed, under the opera's quaint superficies of popular humour, the profound melancholy, the lament, the cry of distress of poetry in chains, and its reincarnation, its new birth, its irresistible magic power achieving mastery over the common and the base.'[70] But did Wagner hide his melancholy because he thought that to reveal it would betray it? Only in part. Perhaps he did reveal it, but in what he had argued to be the only way, in showing not in saying, in artistic or musical expression, and not directly in words. To sustain this conclusion, recall my first claim about *Die Meistersinger*, that it has a strange double nature: as philosophical allegory it teaches a lesson about an aesthetics of negation with perfectionist ends. Yet this is a lesson whose conclusion has ultimately to be shown in the opera's status as a work of art. It is the conclusion that is shown not said. Schopenhauer helps us here again when he writes that the 'close relation that music has to the true nature of all things, explain[s] the fact that, when music suitable to any scene, action, event, or environment is played, it seems to disclose to us its most secret meaning, and appears to be the most accurate and distinct commentary on it.'[71] Suffice it to say that when the action or environment that music accompanies is about music itself, as *Die Meistersinger* is, then its secret or inexpressible meaning engages with the aspirations of *mousikē*—the cultivation of the soul—in a way nothing that merely speaks can.

If this is true, then perhaps it is also true that Wagner rendered impotent *Die Meistersinger*'s lovely vision of daylight by expressing

[69] *The Song of the Lark* (Lincoln, Nebr., 1978), 477. Cf. Schoenberg's comment on compositional know-how: a 'secret science is not what an alchemist would have refused to teach you; it is a science which cannot be taught at all. It is inborn or it is not there. This is also the reason why Thomas Mann's Adrian Leverkühn does not know the essentials of composing with twelve tones. All he knows has been told him by Mr. Adorno, who knows only the little I was able to tell my pupils. The real fact will probably remain secret science until there is one who inherits it by virtue of an unsolicited gift' ('The Blessing of the Dressing', in *Style and Idea: Selected Writings of Arnold Schoenberg*, ed. L. Stein, tr. L. Black (Berkeley, Calif., 1975), 386).

[70] Quoted by Ernest Newman, *The Wagner Operas* (New York, 1949), 280.

[71] *The World as Will and Representation.*, i. 261–2.

it through the melancholy medium of song. After reading Schopenhauer, Wagner said that he became increasingly convinced that he should abandon his revolutionary plans to transfigure society by direct political means. Thereafter, he devoted himself to producing aesthetic spectacles that sang a claim to freedom through complex negations of phenomenal reality. *Die Meistersinger* showed the necessary deceptiveness of appearance in the creation of artworks; its exemplary lesson showed that a second-order deceptiveness was also required, an aesthetic deception that hid a philosophical pessimism behind a political optimism. It was his pessimism regarding the fulfilment of the promise of freedom for both society and the individual that Wagner concealed in the aesthetic 'secrecy and silence' of his song. It was a pessimism that was entirely consistent with his opera read also as philosophical allegory.

3

The Quest for Voice: Resituating Musical Autonomy

Music is feeling, then, not sound . . .

(Wallace Stevens[1])

Heard melodies are sweet, but those unheard
Are sweeter; therefore, ye soft pipes, play on;
Not to the sensual ear, but, more endear'd,
Pipe to the spirit ditties of no tone.

(Keats[2])

Music does not exist for the purpose of emphasizing . . .
something which happens outside its own sphere. Musical
expression only begins to be significant where words and action reach their utmost limits of expression. . . . It is only that
which cannot be expressed otherwise that is worth expressing
in music.

(Delius[3])

1. Introduction

Wagner established for *Die Meistersinger* its intertwined aesthetic
and political lesson by making the subject of the opera be about
the medium in which it was written.[4] Singing in song about song
gave the opera an aesthetic condition of immediacy as well as a

[1] 'Peter Quince at the Clavier', v. 2, in *The Collected Poems of Wallace Stevens*
(New York, 1955), 90.
[2] 'Ode on a Grecian Urn', v. 2.
[3] 'At the Crossroads' (1920), in S. Morgenstern (ed.), *Composers on Music: An
Anthology of Composers' Writings from Palestrina to Copland* (New York, 1956),
321.
[4] I have borrowed part of a sentence from Lucy Beckett that says that *Die
Meistersinger* is 'about the medium in which it is written, namely, song' ('*Die
Meistersinger*: Naïve or Sentimental Art?', in Warrack (ed.), *Die Meistersinger von
Nürnberg*, 98).

reflective political significance. The opera asked its audience to listen to the singing of songs sung and to what the songs were saying about singing. However, contrary to expectation, the opera's intertwined thesis was established not simply because song contains the double language of words and melody, but also because when singers sing, they use their voice to a fundamental human purpose. Singing, to put Wagner's attitude into a single claim, is a fundamental act of human expression of shared aesthetic and political significance.

In this chapter, I shall investigate this single claim. I shall not focus again on *Die Meistersinger*, though you will hear that opera's arguments in the background. Neither shall I focus exclusively on Wagner, though he will still play the central role. I shall set the claim within a broader spectrum of literature ranging from the mid-eighteenth century to the present. The reason for enlarging the scope is to broaden the possibilities of what, in Chapter 1, I called a critical view of formalism and musical autonomy. That view rejected the idea that music finds its freedom in separation from the life of society and endorsed the idea that music finds its freedom *within* that life when it expresses itself independently at a critical distance. To give further substance to this idea, I want to look at the promise of a Rousseauian view to which so many theorists since Rousseau have offered their revisions—Wagner included. At its core, this view identifies singing or vocal expression as the shared source of human community, on the one hand, and of music's significance, on the other. It says that the inexpressible moral or passional basis of expression that inspires acts of singing is commensurate with the inspiration behind public speaking within which lies the potential for human freedom.

This view has been supported far less in the positivist or Enlightenment aspect of German musicological thought than in its highly Romantic, metaphysical, and significantly French-inspired aspect. In this century's writings of, for example, Lévi-Strauss, Barthes, and Derrida, a project has emerged to keep the aesthetic and political connected via passion-inspired acts of voiced and embodied expression. This project has found support in recent French and French-inspired feminist and musicological thinking about the repressed political voice, thinking that finds in embodied, and often in artistic, expression the source and site for the liberation of that otherwise silent voice.[5] In the nineteenth century, as more recently, this 'connected' way of thinking challenged a purportedly 'artificial' way of thinking that was believed to keep the different art forms too separated from each other and from all other kinds of human activity. Wagner, in particular, reacted strongly in this regard. By asserting too often that music was only about its notes, formalists, he said, were severing musical meaning from its expressive potential, rendering the meaning of music's notes effectively 'null and void'.

What older and more contemporary arguments apparently share is a powerful misgiving that 'modern' institutions have severed, or at least overly concealed, their connection to the full range or potential of human expression. Attempts to restore the connection have covered the entire spectrum of ideological positions, again more or less conservative or liberal, optimistic or pessimistic, essentialist or anti-essentialist, naturalistic or socially constructed. As I argued in the previous chapter (at the end of the political argument), I favour viewing the connection between work and expression, or act and expression, as doubled, or paradoxical, to avoid a potentially regressive commitment to origins. However, of this more later. For most of this chapter I want to focus on one crucial part of the argument for musical autonomy, the part that shifts our emphasis away from music's *formed content*[6] (should music be made up of instrumentalized sound-patterns alone?) to its literal and metaphorical *use* of the human voice.

Shifting the priority from content to use enables us to think about autonomy as an attribute first of persons and their acts and, secondarily, of their products. This thought highlights what is shared between the arts that are otherwise separated by reference to their content or medium, and between artistic acts and other acts of human expression. This commonality recalls a pre-modern, indeed ancient, conception of an expressive act and the conditions under which that act is regarded as free. In this historical linkage the following rule emerges. In its quick rendition, the rule says that

---

[5] Cf. Richard Leppert, *The Sight of Sound: Music, Representation, and the History of the Body* (Berkeley, Calif., 1993), Thomas S. Grey, *Wagner's Musical Prose: Texts and Contexts* (Cambridge, 1995), Philippe Lacoue-Labarthe, *Musica Ficta (Figures of Wagner)*, tr. F. McCarren (Stanford, Calif., 1994), and, more specifically, Carolyn Abbate's description of female operatic characters singing out against their repressed condition (*Unsung Voices: Opera and Musical Narrative in the Nineteenth Century* (Princeton, 1991)).

[6] I shall use the term 'content' mostly to mean music's formed content.

music is expressive because and when human beings are expressive. More carefully, it says that the content or product of music—the work—is properly autonomous when it draws on the autonomy of the voice that performs it, and for this to happen the *relation* between product and voice (work and performance) must be preserved. Where and when the relation (or doubleness of content and expression) is severed, the claimed autonomy of the product is a false one.

In formulating this argument, I shall appeal again to limits, concealment, and paradoxes. Consider claims such as 'song is the essence of instrumental music', or 'the essence of the expressible is the inexpressible'. They depend for their sense on our mixing metaphysical and empirical uses of the terms. Such mixing, as I argued in Chapter 1, has a special history recalling the Romantically conceived relation between music and philosophy. One Romantic purpose of intermingling music and philosophy was to give to philosophy and to music their metaphysical fullness, their metaphorical voice. This was a politically motivated restoration in the Wagnerian spirit, for Wagner desired that the *gesamt* of his *Gesamtkunstwerk* restore to modern culture the original and idealized (Greek) aesthetic and synthesizing impulse behind philosophy, music, and, not irrelevantly, gymnastics. With this restoration in mind, he aimed to give a meaning to music's modern emancipation quite different from the emancipation he thought the formalists were supporting. He challenged them with this question: what was really in most need of emancipation in 1800, music as a language of tones or music as a language of human expression?

2. Autonomy Understood and Misunderstood

Wagner challenged his opponents at every opportunity. His targets were philosophers, critics, professors, and musicians. He often named his opponents or their views as absolutist, although he was not against all forms of absolutism. He used this and other related terms negatively when they were linked to an 'emancipated metaphysics'. By this he meant an absolutist view of music that treated music's meaning as merely musical or as residing solely in music's sounding content. He used the terms positively when music's sounding content was connected to 'purely human' manifestations of a 'unifying' or 'absolute' principle of expression. These manifestations indicated the purely human 'motives', 'feelings', or 'virtues' of an individual or community.[7] He also attacked composers who were producing works of purely instrumental music, but, again, not because he was entirely against it. He referred to its production negatively when it was associated with negative uses of absolutism, and positively when it was not so. He was waging 'war to the death', he said, against music conceived 'as an absolute separate art',[8] because, so conceived, music failed essentially to be 'musical'.

Wagner's opponents fought back, especially Hanslick, who liked to oppose the 'Wagner–Liszt household' with their 'nonsensical' theories 'cooked up for the domestic requirements' whenever he could.[9] Where he read Wagner's linkage of the purely musical with the purely human as implying a replacement of the former by the latter, he criticized him for failing to capture what was specifically musical in music. Thinking about music in terms of a metaphysical or political idea says nothing unique about music's 'specifically musical' form, content, or beauty. 'The tragedy', he generally complained, 'is that most of our younger composers think in a foreign language (philosophy, poetry, painting) and then translate the thought into the mother tongue (music).'[10]

As this debate settled into an academic mode, it looked as if the various theorists involved would henceforth align themselves entirely according to whether music should be produced with or without words, programmes, and metaphysical ideas.[11] For the formalists: (*a*) the presence of words threatened music's autonomy, where 'autonomy' is defined as being separated from any other medium: music has independent ontological status; (*b*) the presence of a programme threatened music's semantic autonomy: the language of music can convey the meaning it wants without any help from an outside source; and (*c*) the presence of metaphysical

[7] As suggested in Ch. 1, Wagner's use of 'the purely human' is not unique to him; the idea and/or phrase is employed with similar connotation by Goethe, Schiller, Kant, Schopenhauer, Fichte, and Feuerbach to capture their varying conceptions of persons as moral and free. Recall, also, that it was Wagner who coined the term 'absolute music'.

[8] 'On Musical Criticism', iii. 69.

[9] *Music Criticisms*, 158.

[10] Ibid. 292.

[11] Theorists include A. B. Marx, Ambros, Zimmermann, Kretzschmar, and Hostinský. See B. Bujić (ed.), *Music in European Thought, 1851–1912* (Cambridge, 1988) and Lippman, *A History of Western Musical Aesthetics*, chs. 10 and 11, for excerpts and summaries of their views.

ideas undermined their bid to describe music's autonomous status and significance in purely empirical, objective, or scientific terms. By contrast, for the transcendentalists (or, more disparagingly, 'the Wagnerites'),[12] the presence of words, suggestion of programmes, and links to metaphysical ideas maintained in music its poetic and dramatic aim without at all compromising the freedom of musical expression. For the formalists, music achieves its beautiful form in the radical separation of its language of tones from any outside element; for the transcendentalists, the language of tones achieves its sublime expression in its profound metaphysical connection to everything else.

As the debate further took on the confidence of academic design, technical problems arose. For the separatists, there were the problems of demarcating the proper barrier between the different arts, of delimiting the scope of the purely musical and of justifying their empirical approach, however prosaic the results. For the connectionists, the corresponding problems arose of settling the priority given to the different arts, of determining the proper place of the purely musical within the scope of the purely human, and of justifying their use of metaphysical principles, whatever the cost to theoretical plausibility.

Describing the debate in these academic terms stresses the theoretical difference. But there is another way to describe it, in terms of the two sides reminding each other of the dangers and limitations of their respective positions. This way has the advantage of demonstrating the extent to which the theorists of the period were involved in a shared project guided as much by their deep fears of purported cultural decline as by the demands of academic accuracy. It could not have been academic interests alone that would justify a war 'fought to the death'. Many claims about music's 'proper content' were motivated from the standpoint of cultural criticism. This was most especially true of Wagner's and Hanslick's attacks upon each other.

When Wagner judged the 'emancipated aesthetes' as encouraging a 'loveless' 'divorce from life', and absolute music as lacking

---

[12] Cf. Hanslick's attack on the 'Wagnerites' in his *Aus Meinem Leben* (Basel, 1987), in which he expresses as much disapproval of Wagner's followers as of Wagner himself. He describes the followers as 'pedantic' in their uncritical worship of Wagner (see also translation by H. Pleasants, in Hanslick, *Vienna's Golden Years of Music, 1850–1900* (New York, 1950), 330–5).

'moral will' because it had 'failed to become deed', these were all judgements made within the larger context of his critique of 'Judaism in music.' For the often obsessive Wagner, remember, 'Judaism' could stand for modern 'rootlessness' or 'dehumanized expression' in nearly every conceivable form. But when Hanslick criticized Wagner for 'absolutizing the intellect', and for having 'perverted basic musical laws' by composing music in a style 'contrary to the nature of human hearing and feeling' or as lacking 'a human element', he, too, was making judgements about the corruption, as he saw it, of the modern musical soul. Only his targets and solutions were different. When Wagner argued that music's future lay in opera, Hanslick balked at this absolutist judgement and at the failure of Wagner's own operas to prove the claim. He declared: 'It is unthinkable that his method shall be . . . the only valid opera style from now on, the absolute "work of the future". When an art arrives at a period of utmost luxury, it is already on the decline. Wagner's opera style recognizes only superlatives; but a superlative has no future. It is the end, not the beginning.'[13]

Generally, when musicians feared that something corrupt was happening in musical practice, and criticized their colleagues for encouraging that corruption, they pretended (as we nowadays sometimes pretend) that they were acting on theoretical reasons alone. They tended to transform evaluative claims into theoretically motivated descriptive claims about music's true nature, thereby masking their cultural motivation. This made the descriptive claims seem all the stronger and the academic differences all the greater. But the academic version of the debate also masked the desire to restore to the type of music they were criticizing its true musical potential, and this intention united, not separated, them. There was clearly a tension between the opposed and shared parts of their academic and cultural projects.

When Wagner criticized composers of instrumental music for playing down to the sentimental reactions of their audiences and failing to fulfil the proper purpose of human cultivation, Hanslick sympathized, even though academically Wagner was equating Hanslick's approach with precisely that failure, and Hanslick vice versa. When Hanslick made comparisons of the sort in which he rejected Strauss's impure, programmatic poem *Don Juan* and de-

---

[13] *Music Criticisms*, 152.

fended Brahms's pure First Symphony, because the former 'stupefied' its audience with 'pleasure gas' whereas the latter 'convinced' by its 'moral element',[14] Wagner was happy with the type of judgement, just not with its application. Again, both theorists were applying the same kind of judgement; in the opinion of each, the other was just applying it to the wrong example.[15]

In sum, their cultural criticism tended to be focused on the type of judgement, the academic debate on the examples. The latter focus tended to split the preference for so-called absolute or purely instrumental music from its programmatic or dramatic opposition. It was this split that made the debate look as if its sole concern was with music's proper content. Otakar Hostinský wrote as much in 1877:

Hanslick starts by trying to distinguish as clearly as possible the power of music from that of poetry, in order to render each of the two arts its due. Hanslick, however, ceases where Wagner . . . begin[s]—with the search for . . . an alliance between the two arts, terms which are conditioned by their limitations and the barriers dividing them. If a composer strives for perfect expression of a poetic idea by means of instrumental music, Hanslick and Wagner are at one in believing him doomed to fail. But whereas Hanslick would advise him to abandon the whole thing, Wagner would urge him to seek the assistance of the human voice. . . . At this point . . . the[y] go in different directions.[16]

As Hostinský well knew, Wagner and Hanslick were united in their recognition that music had been liberated from its 'servitude' to poetry in the Beethoven symphony. They disagreed, however, over the meaning of that liberation for music's future. 'It is one of those spiritual watersheds', Hanslick recognized, 'which interpose themselves insuperably between opposing currents of conviction.' Hanslick took Beethoven's contribution to the art of purely instrumental music to be the final releasing of the art of tone from its servitude to poetry, word, idea, programme, religious occasion, and philosophical idea. Wagner thought that servitude should be transformed, as Beethoven had transformed it, into a relation not of severance but of independent and unifying partnership. Wagner criticized the symphonists for believing that aiming to write

---

[14] Ibid. 127.

[15] Wagner criticizes Hanslick's examples most obviously in 'Judaism in Music' (iii. 104 ff.).

[16] See Bujić (ed.), *Music in European Thought*, 147.

Beethoven's Tenth Symphony[17] was the correct way to do justice to Beethoven's legacy. Hanslick celebrated these symphonic achievements as sustaining music's liberation. 'There is much that is new,' he wrote of Brahms's Second Symphony,

and yet nothing of the unfortunate contemporary tendency to emphasize novelty in the sense of the unprecedented. Nor are there any furtive glances in the direction of foreign artistic fields, nor any begging from poetry or painting. It is all purely musical in conception and structure, and purely musical in effect. It provides irrefutable proof that one (not everyone, to be sure) can still write symphonies . . . in the old forms and on the old foundations.[18]

For our purposes, the most significant aspect of Hanslick's defence of the symphonists was his conviction that he was *thereby* defending music's autonomy, and that Wagner's operas and Liszt's programmatic works were not. He even urged that the term 'musical' no longer be used when speaking of such. The 'mystico-allegoric tendency' he perceived in Wagner's *Ring* reminded him of Goethe's *Faust*, he complained, whose 'poetic effect is diminished' by its indulging in '"hidden inner meanings" which torture the reader as riddles. Whether a given composition derives from the depths of musical sensibility or from the result of imaginative contrivance cannot . . . be proved scientifically.'[19] For Hanslick, only the 'scientifically provable' could constitute the specifically musical content of the purely musical work as an autonomous (self-sufficient and self-meaning) product. The 'union with poetry' might extend 'the power of music', he could concede, 'but not its boundaries'.[20]

But could Hanslick not have acknowledged that Wagner was employing a different and broader conception of autonomy that was deliberately unbounded by the scientifically provable? As we shall soon see, Wagner was conceiving of music's autonomy in terms of an expressive quality that connected music's production of works to its practice. He wanted to know what it meant for people to speak, sing, or act freely within any practice, how that autonomy determined a freedom of musical expression, and how that concep-

---

[17] 'Shall we Hope?', vi. 121. Apparently the reference to Beethoven's 'Tenth' came from Hans von Bülow's description of Brahms's First Symphony.
[18] *Music Criticisms*, 157.
[19] Ibid. 143.
[20] *On the Musically Beautiful*, 15.

tion then dictated an appropriate form and content for the works themselves.[21] Could Hanslick, in a moment less constrained by methodological commitment, not have taken on board this larger conception without its compromising the substance of his formalist claim? Was he not already hinting that he could when he conceded that music's power transcended music's specifically musical borders? Had he not already demonstrated that he could in his less constrained and abundant production of music criticism? Could he not have seen that Wagner was trying to accommodate the formalist's desire to capture what is specifically musical about the empirical language or art of tones within a larger cultural project to understand the purely musical in its 'inspired', 'expanded', or 'extra' connection to autonomous human community? Perhaps Hanslick could not see all this, or at least had good methodological reasons not to allow himself to.[22] However, with the advantage of hindsight we can. And, I suggest, we should, not least because, by enlarging our concept of autonomy in this Wagnerian direction, we will restore to what has become an overly academic debate a cultural principle that can be shared by formalists and transcendentalists alike.

Wagner's project had its many acknowledged and unacknowledged precursors. He worked closely with the writings of Herder, Goethe, Schiller, Feuerbach, and Schopenhauer, but the ever-present though unacknowledged shadow behind his German canonic line was the French influence of Rousseau.

---

[21] Wagner used the terms *Freiheit* and *Ausdruck* to capture this broader conception of autonomy. Dahlhaus claims that 'the concept of the purely musical did not exist for Wagner' ('The Music', in Müller and Wapnewski (eds.), *Wagner Handbook*, 307). I am suggesting that it did, but that it captured music's content in relation to its purely human expression.

[22] Bujić has discovered that Hanslick deliberately omitted the following words from the final version of his aesthetic treatise that would have significantly 'enhanced' his formalism in a Schopenhauerian direction.

[Music is] created by the human spirit from material that lends itself to working by the imagination. In the mind of the listener this spiritual content connects beauty in music with all other great and beautiful ideas. For him music acts not merely and exclusively through its own beauty, but also as a tonal representation of the great movement in the cosmos. Through deep and innermost connections in nature the meaning in music is raised high above itself and allows us to feel at the same time the infinity in the work of the individual human talent. Thus the elements of music: sound, notes, rhythm, strength, frailty, are to be found in the whole universe, and thus man finds the entire universe in music. (*Music in European Thought*, 39)

3. Rousseau's Contribution

My comments on Rousseau are limited to his *Essay on the Origin of Languages, in which Something is said about Melody and Musical Imitation.*[23] They are also selective. I am concerned only with what he has to say about (*a*) the centrality of the human voice in comprehending the expressive potential of human beings, and how that expressive potential motivates a conception of autonomy that is equally musical and political; (*b*) how his view of expression motivates us to seek autonomy initially in a performative utterance and then, by extension, in its content; and finally, (*c*) how the link between expression and autonomy accommodates the substance of, yet resists reduction to, a purely empirical account.

Almost at the essay's end, he writes: 'I maintain that any language in which it is not possible to make oneself understood by the people assembled is a servile language; it is impossible for a people to remain free and speak that language' (xx. 3).[24] Rousseau argued that a language is servile or its speakers unfree when their mode of communication is severed from its origin. What did he mean by 'origin'?

Though he described the geographical and physical conditions under which languages first came into existence, he was not mainly concerned with this sort of 'origin'. He was less interested in describing the presence or absence of language in man's pre-political state, than in highlighting the special connection between the development of language and society under a 'conventional' or 'moral' state. This connection distinguished humans from animals because it distinguished the moral need for vocal communication from the pre-political adequacy of bodily gesture. There could have been vocal utterances in the pre-political state, but the necessity for them sprang from social attachment, from moral need, from sympathetic passions of pity and care. 'The [physical] needs dictated the first gestures, and the passions wrung the first utterings' (ii. 1). The connection between voice and passion tied the voice most directly to the 'origin' of language with which Rousseau was con-

---

[23] *Rousseau: The Discourses and Other Early Political Writings,* tr. and ed. V. Gourevitch (Cambridge, 1997). See also Gourevitch's essay 'The Political Argument of Rousseau's *Essay on the Origin of Languages*', in T. Cohen, P. Guyer, and H. Putnam (eds.), *Pursuits of Reason: Essays in Honor of Stanley Cavell* (Lubbock, Tex., 1993), 21–35.

[24] References to Rousseau's *Essay* are to chapter and paragraph.

cerned. We might well call this origin the 'moral' or 'passional' origin of language.

His view that language originated in our moral needs led Rousseau to claim that the first language would have been 'figurative' or 'allegorical' rather than literal, corresponding as it does to our passions rather than to our ideas. 'At first men spoke only poetry; only much later did it occur to anyone to reason' (iii. 1). This is why the first languages were 'songlike and passionate before they were simple and methodical' (ii. 3). Furthermore, as the 'signs' of language achieved literal meanings by being attached to 'ideas', the original figurative meanings were increasingly relegated to the domain of the metaphorical. A strict relegation would eventually prove ruinous to the language.

Rousseau mostly referred to 'languages' in the plural. He wanted to show that languages differentiate 'one nation from another' (i. 1) and that this differentiation has moral import. Languages differ according to physical conditions of climate and population. These differences affect the kinds of passions people have. Languages that are fully connected to the moral origin differ from those that either have no such origin (say, a purely formal language) or have become detached from it. Languages also differ according to their place in a historical development, i.e. whether they are in their primitive or domestic state, their genuine or popular state, or in their state of rationalization. The first corresponds to the pre-political state, the third to the declining condition of writing and standardization, a state Rousseau mostly identified with contemporary European languages. The middle state corresponds to a time in which the moral 'way of life' was best exemplified. He found (or idealized) this time in the Athens of the fifth century BCE.

Genuine languages existed in a public polis in which individuals fully participated in the life of that community through civic acts of oratory and expression. The language was alive, invigorated by the people's passions. The participation demanded full presence: people communicated fully in mind and in body. How they spoke and what they said together moved the 'hearts and minds' of those who listened. Fully engaged, language was inseparable from their 'way of life'. Under this condition, Rousseau wrote, it was morally suasive and 'conducive to liberty' (xx. 3).

A language so connected to society required a certain kind of content. To illustrate this requirement, Rousseau turned to music.

Under a broad conception of 'music' (or at a time when 'music' had its full figurative meaning and had not yet been literalized), to say that language was moral was to say also that it was musical. Music was just the vocal expression of passion. 'Verse, song, speech have a common origin' (xii. 1). He did not mean merely that the language of speech and the language of music have the same source, although he thought it true to say that they do; rather, the language of speech just was the language of music. Words were uttered with melodic inflection, accent, rhythm, and that inflection was part of the word's meaning. It was not then a matter of setting words to music; words or utterances had inherent musicality or 'settled musical accent' (vii. 5). Rousseau would later mark the decline of languages by their need to be set to music; the need itself suggested that they had lost their inherent melody. He was all the time recalling Plato and the Greek language: Athenians sang their laws; when they changed their melody (their tune), it was evidence of their having changed their morals. In this broadest sense of 'musical', he suggested, as Plato before him, that when the state is harmonious, the state is in good order and its language and people are free.

Much of Rousseau's argument was typical of, although not unique to, the eighteenth century inasmuch as he looked to Athens as a point of reference by which to assess the purported decline of Enlightenment society and philosophy. Although he regarded the development of languages as 'entirely natural', he did not regard it as necessarily symbolizing moral progress (despite his using the term 'progress'). His criticisms were threefold. He criticized (*a*) the impact of rationalization and literalization on language; (*b*) the dominant trend, represented by Rameau, to reduce music to the empirical science of harmony; and (*c*) the dominant trend, represented by Du Bos,[25] to turn an aesthetic appropriate to the ear into one appropriate to the eye. Taken together, he argued, music and speech have become severed from their performative or expressive import.

Rationalization in the academic age of science marked a separation of 'heart and mind'; it tended towards the dissociation of sensibility. The meanings of words, the language as a whole, had

---

[25] Gourevitch discusses the connection between Du Bos and Rousseau in some detail ('The Political Argument of Rousseau's *Essay on the Origin of Languages*').

become so standardized that they no longer stamped the moral character of society.

[B]y a natural progress all lettered languages must change character and lose vigor as they gain in clarity . . . in proportion to the effort to perfect grammar and logic, this progress is accelerated, and . . . in order to cause a language to grow rapidly frigid and monotonous one need only establish academies among the people who speak it. (vii. 7)

So long as academies gave languages their significance, they failed to be morally suasive. They no longer *served* passion; they became *servile* to reason.[26]

In proportion as needs increase . . . as enlightenment spreads, the character of language changes; it becomes more precise and less passionate; it substitutes ideas for sentiments; it no longer speaks to the heart but to the reason. As a result accent dies out and articulation becomes more pervasive; language becomes more exact and clear, but more sluggish, subdued, and cold. (v. 1)

In terms that are now metaphorical but once were not, 'sluggish, subdued, and cold' languages are languages that have lost their melody or forgotten their moral voice.

But where had melody gone? One answer is that it had been given exclusively by the eighteenth century to the independent art of 'music alone'.[27] This answer has some truth, but needs qualification. Rousseau argued that in the process of separating instrumental music from song, melody from word, both sides, metaphorically speaking, had lost their melody. It was not the separation *per se* that was responsible (there had always been words and melodies uttered in separation, even in ancient Athens); it was only the kind of separation that followed upon a language's having become self-sufficient and formalized.

Music had become such a language under the influence of Rameau's science of vibrations. 'Note how everything constantly brings us back to the moral effects,' Rousseau wrote a little unfairly to explain Rameau's error,

and how far the musicians who account for the impact of sounds solely in terms of the action of the air and the excitation of [nerve] fibers are from understanding wherein the power of this art consists. The more closely

---

[26] This is my distinction, not Rousseau's.
[27] Cf. Gourevitch's note on this phrase (xix. 2n.) in which he refers to the 'fall' that occurred when music was disunited from poetry.

they assimilate it to purely physical impressions, the farther they remove it from its origin, and the more they also deprive it of its primitive energy. By abandoning the accents of speech and adhering exclusively to the rules of harmony, music becomes noisier to the ear and less pleasing to the heart. It has already ceased to speak; soon it will no longer sing, and once that happens it will no longer . . . have any effect on us. (xvii. 1)[28]

Rameau's error, according to Rousseau, was to substitute harmony for melody. In this substitution, singing became 'an art entirely separate from speech'. Since 'the harmonic aspects of sounds caused the inflections of the voice to be forgotten', he explained, and since music was 'restricted to the exclusively physical effect of combinations of vibrations', music was deprived of the moral effects it produced when it was 'doubly' melody and speech, and as such 'the voice of nature' (xix. 9). Rousseau did not illustrate his criticism by offering examples of unmusical or unnatural musical works; his target remained focused on the science of harmony:

[H]armony deprives [melody] of energy and expressiveness, it eliminates the passionate accent in favor of intervals, it restricts to only two modes songs that should have as many modes as there are tones of voice, and it eradicates and destroys a great many sounds or intervals that do not fit into its system; in a word, it separates song and speech to such an extent that these two languages contend, thwart one another, deprive one another of any truth, and cannot be united in the treatment of a passionate subject without appearing absurd. (xiv. 6)

The scientific principle had in fact deprived 'all modern European languages' of their moral melody; they are all 'more or less in the same situation', Rousseau declared; 'I do not even exclude Italian. Italian is no more a musical language than is French. The difference is simply that one lends itself to music and the other does not' (viii. 6). Having to 'lend itself' to music was already a mark of a language's decline.

Rousseau held writing largely responsible for the decline. 'The art of writing', he argued, 'does not . . . depend on that of speaking. It depends on needs of a different nature.'

Writing, which might be expected to fix [or to stabilize] language, is precisely what alters it; it changes not its words but its genius; it substitutes precision for expressiveness. One conveys one's sentiments in speaking, and one's ideas in writing. In writing one is compelled to use every word in conformity with common usage; but a speaker alters meaning by his tone

---

[28] A nice defence of Rameau is offered by Enrico Fubini in his *A History of Music Aesthetics*, tr. M. Hatwell (London, 1990), 210–11.

of voice, determining them as he wishes; since he is less constrained to be clear, he stresses forcefulness more; and a language that is written cannot possibly retain for long the liveliness of one that is only spoken. What gets written down are words . . . not sounds. (v. 13)[29]

To preserve the vigour of language, he determined, we should try to read as we speak, not speak as we read.

Rousseau justified the priority he gave to the voice and ear over the visual sign and eye in terms of imitation. Both hearing and seeing are equally immediate forms of communication, but they differ in their modes of imitation. There is imitation of nature and imitation of the soul. The former consists in producing a picture or copy of the object world; the latter consists in expressing the subject world. The focus on imitation shifted the emphasis in the discussion away from the language's content or signs—are the signs visual, auditory, or both?—towards its mimetic employment. 'Just as the sentiments which painting arouses in us are not due to colors, the power which music exercises over our souls is not the product of sounds. . . . [I]t is the passions which they express that succeed in arousing our own, [or in the case of painting] the objects which they represent that succeed in affecting us' (xiii. 1). In so shifting the emphasis Rousseau did not dispense with content; only in reference solely to itself would content fail to provide the whole explanation. It must always be connected to its underlying expression or imitation. If in the arts of painting or music it were simply a matter of combining colours or sounds in a way pleasing to the ear or eye, neither art would be a fine art, but a natural science. Imitation (expression) alone raises them to the rank of a fine art, even though the arts of painting and music imitate differently through their use of the different senses (xiii. 8).

Rousseau distinguished the two types of imitation largely to challenge the attempt by contemporary aestheticians to see the developing art of music as being imitative in the same way that the visual arts are imitative, and to challenge the long-standing priority the eye has been given over the ear.[30] Both challenges were

---

[29] See Gourevitch's note about ii. 1 regarding the different meanings of 'voix'.

[30] Recently the eye and visual gaze have again become the dominant means by which theorists formulate their idea of a critical consciousness and resistant voice. Cf. Terese Brennan and Martin Jay (eds.), *Vision in Context: Historical and Contemporary Perspectives on Sight* (New York, 1996), esp. ' "Authentic Tidings of Invisible Things": Vision and the Invisible in the Later Nineteenth Century' (83–98), in which author Gillian Beer describes the subordination of the visible *sight* to invisible *insight*.

supposed to show that the language of voice is the most human art because it least depends upon the copying of nature. Rousseau employed a concept of distance to explain the difference between painting and music. Communication through sight is always distanced or detached in so far as the image produced belongs to the object or spatial world. Communication through the ear is immediate and connected; it turns our attention inward. Being a strictly 'sympathetic' language, music 'enflames' and 'moves' the passions of the heart. The voice, he concluded, is an organ of the soul (xvi. 7).

For Rousseau it was the strain of melody (the figurative 'song') that connected the voice directly to the heart.

By imitating the inflections of the voice, melody expresses plaints, cries of suffering or of joy, threats, moans; all the vocal signs of the passions fall within its province. It imitates the accents of [various] languages as well as the idiomatic expressions commonly associated in each one of them with given movements of the soul; it not only imitates, it speaks; and its language, though inarticulate, is lively, ardent, passionate, and a hundred times more vigorous than speech itself. This is where musical imitation acquires its power, and song its hold on sensitive hearts. (xiv. 6)

With this view established, Rousseau found opportunity again to attack the academic establishment:

I believe that if these ideas had been explored more adequately, much foolish speculation about ancient music could have been avoided. But in this century, when every effort is made to materialize all the operations of the soul and to deprive human sentiments of all morality, I should be greatly surprised if the new philosophy did not prove as fatal to good taste as it does to virtue. (xv. 6)

His attack quickly acquired sufficient detail to strike the academic establishment, Rameau, and Du Bos with one blow:

Physical observations have occasioned every kind of absurdity in discussions of the fine arts. The analysis of sound has revealed the same relations as has the analysis of light. Straightway the analogy was seized upon, without regard for experience or reason. The systematizing spirit has jumbled everything and, since it proved impossible to paint for the ears, it was decided to sing to the eyes. I have seen the famous clavichord on which music was supposedly produced with colors; what a gross misunderstanding of how nature operates it was, not to see that the effect of colors is due to their permanence and that of sounds to their succession. (xvi. 1)[31]

Rousseau attacked the Enlightenment inclination to turn aesthetics into a purely empirical or scientific matter of sensory experience, on the one hand, or of pure intellection, on the other. Neither development paid attention to the fact that passion was being expressed, even though, in Rousseau's view, expression provided the connection between music and political community. Theorists who were putting faith solely in reason and rights to secure a just political community were having difficulties accounting for music's role, especially given music's definition as the pure art of tone. Apparently, it was easier to render music apolitical than to render the art of tone political in the rationalists' terms. Rousseau saw these developments as jointly threatening music and our moral welfare. A dispassionate language suggests dispassionate speakers; dispassionate speakers suggest a dispassionate society. Such a society is a one in which people no longer sing. Recalling Plato, music only serves *mousikē* when it expresses the melody of the soul.

Rousseau illustrated music's curative potential with a humorous story about its medicinal powers. To cure a person who has been stung by an insect, an Italian would require Italian tunes,

a Turk would require Turkish tunes. One is affected only by accents that are familiar; the nerves respond to them only insofar as the mind inclines them to it; one has to understand the language in which one is being addressed if one is to be moved by what one is told. Bernier's Cantatas are said to have cured a French musician of the fever; they would have given one to a musician of any other nation. (xv. 3)

Rousseau was also invoking a larger, figurative sense of 'health'. Although he had little faith in modern languages, his view still allowed that it is not so much the content of the Italian language (words, tunes) that cures the Italian soul, as something more fundamental, namely, a people's freedom to express its particular passions. Of course this freedom is expressed through words, melodies, popular songs, but these songs only express what they are meant to express if the society and language are working together in connection to their moral origin.

[31] Cf. Leppert's remarks on painted musical instruments and of their treatment as furniture in *The Sight of Sound*, ch. 6.

Towards the end of his essay, Rousseau gave this connectedness to moral origin a proto-Romantic motif. In musical expression, he argued, is found something silent and something inexpressible.

One of the great advantages the musician enjoys is that he can paint things that cannot be heard, whereas the Painter cannot represent things that cannot be seen; and the greatest wonder of an art that acts solely through movement is that it can fashion it even into an image of repose. Sleep, the quiet of night, solitude, and silence itself have a place in the spectacles of music. It is known that noise can produce the effect of silence and silence the effect of noise, as when one falls asleep while being read to in an even and monotonous voice and wakes up the moment the reading stops. But the effect of music on us is more profound, in that it excites in us through one of the senses, affects similar to those that can be aroused through another, and since that relation is perceptible only if the impression is strong, painting, which lacks the requisite strength, cannot imitate music as music imitates it. Though the whole of nature be asleep, he who contemplates it is not asleep; and the musician's art consists in substituting for the imperceptible image of the object, that of the [e]motions which that object's presence excites in the beholder's heart. It will not only churn up the sea, fan the flames of a conflagration, cause rivers to run, rain to fall, and streams to swell, but will also depict desolation of dreadful deserts, dusk the walls ... appease the storm. ... It will not represent these things directly, but it will excite in the soul the very same sentiments which one experiences upon seeing them. (xvi. 8)

4. Between Rousseau and Wagner Stands Beethoven

Rousseau was cognizant of the separation of melody from speech, but he did not experience it with the largeness of consequence that Wagner did. Whereas he could still use vocal music as the paradigm for musical composition, Wagner could not. Wagner had to take stock of Beethoven's symphonies and the emancipation of instrumental music they had come to symbolize. Wagner took stock in strikingly Rousseauian terms, but he transfigured those terms in typically nineteenth-century ways. Consequently, there is as much discontinuity as continuity between their views. Stressing the continuity, Wagner showed that his aim was not so much to give music back its speech by reuniting the now separated arts but, more fundamentally, to give music back its expressive voice—*whatever* music's content. Though he would compose operas rather than symphonies, though he would argue for the reuniting of melody and speech, and for the uniting of those two elements to produce drama, his paradoxical-sounding aim to reunite the arts within the musical work was dependent upon this claim about expression. It was this claim that would give his view of autonomy its shared musical and political significance.

To recall Rousseau's terms, Wagner saw music's emancipation as a process of abstraction in which a literal concept of music was gradually abstracted out of an ancient metaphor of songlike expression. If the process of literalization begins when a metaphor begins its life, then we can say that there has always been a tension between the metaphor and the ever-sharpening literalization of music's concept. However, what occurred around 1800 was not just an increasing of tension but an attempt to do away with the tension altogether. Though the attempt was marked by the final narrowing down of the content of music to the empirical art of tone, so that 'music' was severed from 'poetry'—this is why we think the issue is about content—it was more fundamentally marked by an act of total literalization in which the residue of the metaphorically musical, with all its poetic, dramatic, figurative, moral, political, and metaphysical significance, was relegated to the domain of the extra- or non-musical. Whereas this relegation left the formalists proud, it left others worried that the literal concept of music in liberating itself from its metaphor had rendered it in all important respects meaninglessly modern.

When Wagner announced that his intention was to restore to the concept of music its metaphysical fullness, what he therefore meant was that he intended to reconnect its literal meaning to its formerly metaphorical, and now extramusical, meaning.

We have accustomed ourselves to limiting our idea of 'music' to the mere art, and now at last to the mere artifice, of *Tone*. That this is an arbitrary restriction we know very well, for *that* which people invented the name '*music*' included not only *the arts of poetry and tone*, but also several artistic displays of the inner man insofar as he has expressively communicated his feelings and intuitions in [their] most persuasive materialization through the agency of the language of sounds.[32]

To succeed in this restoration Wagner had to play with the current duality between music's now literal and metaphorical meanings. This play often made his claims look paradoxical: we

---

[32] 'On Musical Criticism', iii. 68.

must give to purely instrumental music its song, to poetry its melody. The reconnection also gave him the opportunity to forge ahead. But to reconnect literal and metaphorical meanings, one could not just redefine the literal to include the metaphor (that would likely turn the argument into one solely about music's content). Rather, one had to take the modern, literal meaning and transfigure it dialectically against its traditional, and now antithetical, metaphor. Wagner offered three arguments for this transfiguration. He argued that 'the genuine drama' (as he sometimes named his full conception of the musical work) should be properly rather than improperly 'erected on the basis of absolute Music'.[33] He argued that the purely musical should be reconnected to the purely human. He argued that the empirical dimensions of the art of tone should be accommodated within a metaphysical argument for the expressive origin of melody in passion. For each argument he used Beethoven's Ninth Symphony as exemplar.

Wagner told a story, as was then quite normal, of the history of the arts. It showed them in unity and in separation achieving at different times their expressive potential. He told a story about music's history that revealed music's full metaphysical meaning or 'poetical mystical message' in Greek drama, and of the rebirth of such under ('true') Christianity. In the development of the arts, he saw the gradual separation of genres (drama from opera, poetry from music, poetry from drama, drama from theatre) and of performance modes (speaking from singing, singing from acting, speaking from acting, playing from singing). However, he was bothered less by the separation *per se*, than by the inclination it demonstrated to sever meaning from expression (or 'expression' from 'true expression'). To recall Rousseau's 'literalization' argument again, as a language approaches formalization, it tends to function in abstraction from its expressive basis. As part of his critique of 'empty formalism', Wagner accordingly traced the increasing impoverishment of musical meaning directly in proportion to its being cut off from its true dramatic and poetic aim. Formalism connected to this aim was permissible; formalism for its own sake was not. In the previous chapter I named the false security given by this academic severance *Beckmesser's Complaint*.

Wagner described the negative impact of the emancipation of

[33] 'Opera and Drama', ii. 20.

instrumental music through attacks both on theoretical proponents of formalism and on the composers he deemed conceptually under their sway. Though he tended to criticize composers of modern symphonies and those of modern operas separately, the attacks on the latter often derived from those on the former. The arguments were more tortured than confused. He attacked composers of modern operas for composing operas as they would symphonies, and though he often expressed his objections as if it were instrumental music he objected to, his real target was that which instrumental music had come to symbolize. In the symphony and modern orchestra he saw all the dangers of modern alienation. He criticized Rossini, whom he otherwise regarded as a 'genius', for making absolute melody the main content of the opera, thus 'wresting' it from its drama. He criticized his otherwise beloved Weber for hacking opera into 'petty pieces'. He criticized his once friend Meyerbeer for turning opera into an explicitly nationalistic play of 'historical Characteristique'.[34]

His criticism was here partly influenced by his judgement on the potential of different national musics:

[T]he *German* alone possesses a language whose daily usage still hangs directly and conspicuously together with its roots. Italians and Frenchmen speak a tongue whose genuine meaning can be brought home to them only by a study of older, so-called dead languages: one might say that their language . . . speaks for them, but not that *they* speak in their language.[35]

His terms quickly became harsher:

As a Jew, [Meyerbeer] owned no mother tongue. No speech inextricably entwined among the sinews of his inmost being. He spoke with precisely the same interest in any modern tongue, and *set it* to music with no sympathy for its idiosyncrasies. He was interested only in how far it could be used as a compliant server of Absolute Music.[36]

In conceding to this modernist aura, he continued, Meyerbeer symbolized opera's so-called 'Jewish' turn into 'Beckmesserish nonsense'—the turn of opera into a 'monstrous piebald, historico-

---

[34] Ibid. ii. 42 and 81 ff.

[35] Ibid. ii. 357–8. I find these words comparable to Rousseau's, though it must also be said that this sort of view was uniquely held neither by Rousseau in his century nor by Wagner in his.

[36] Ibid. ii. 87; my emphasis. Wagner once praised Meyerbeer for the (unrooted) cosmopolitan and universal qualities he gave to his *Les Huguenots* (cf. Curt von Westernhagen's *Wagner: A Biography*, tr. M. Whittall (Cambridge, 1978), 50).

Romantic, diabolico-religious, fanatico-libidinous, sacro-frivolous, mysterio-criminal, autolyco-sentimental dramatic hotch-potch'.[37] 'Meyerbeer is a very close friend of mine,' he wrote to Hanslick in 1847, '[b]ut if I were to . . . sum up . . . what . . . I find so offensive about the lack of inner concentration and the outer effortfulness of the opera industry today, I would lump it all together under the heading "Meyerbeer".'[38]

Wagner's play of literal and metaphorical description was pervasive in his writings. By identifying 'Meyerbeer' now with all that was wrong with the modern, 'German' opera industry, he effectively separated 'Meyerbeer' from the sort of French and Italian operas of which he sometimes approved and which he would sometimes see as offering the ideal exemplars for the future of German opera: Wagnerian opera out of the melodic spirit of Bellini!

Wagner attacked the tendency of modern opera composers to reduce opera to a 'colourless and nothing-saying mask for aria-singers'. He objected to singers, usually tenors, who could not act and sang as 'mechanized instruments' interested merely in exhibiting their 'throat dexterity'. Once musical speech is cut off from any object worth expressing, once it speaks without content and according to 'the bare caprice of operatic aria', it does little more than 'chirp and chatter'.[39] Opera's loss of expression echoed the same loss he perceived in instrumental music: Berlioz had reduced the orchestra to mechanism and music's effect to the 'unnatural'.

He once summed up his objections to opera in terms that literally applied to opera, although their sense again derived from his attacks on instrumental music. 'The error in the art-genre of Opera, consists herein,' he announced: *'that a Means of expression (Music) has been made the end, while the End of Expression (the Drama) has been made a means'*.[40] Obviously Wagner meant to reverse the terms, yet for this he paradoxically used Beethoven's Ninth. If you think that what is peculiar about the Ninth is that it is a purely instrumental work until its last movement, and that the presence of words at its end explains its end in drama, then you are thinking along the right lines, but you have missed the crucial point. Wagner argued that it was not the presence of words in the 'Ode to Joy' that

---

[37] 'Opera and Drama', ii. 94. I am grateful to Tom Grey for reminding me of the connection between this string of abuse and Beckmesser's 'garbled nonsense'.

[38] Quoted by Rose in his *Wagner: Race and Revolution*, 47.

[39] 'Opera and Drama', ii. 67.   [40] Ibid. ii. 17.

gave this symphony its end in drama. It was, rather, the reintroduction of the human voice, which, in singing, fulfilled the expressive promise of the preceding instrumental movements.

[I]t is not the meaning of the words that really takes us with this entry of the human voice, but the human character of that voice. Neither is it the thought expressed in Schiller's verses that occupies our minds thereafter, but the familiar sound of the choral chant in which we feel bidden to join and thus take part in an ideal Divine Service. . . . In fact . . . Schiller's words have been built . . . with no great skill, for this melody first unrolled its breadth before us as an entity *per se*, entrusted to the instruments alone, and there had thrilled us with the nameless joy of a paradise regained.[41]

Wagner had found an argument literally voiced in Beethoven's last symphony for the end of the dominance of instrumentalized music and the return to music of voiced expression.

But where did the drama enter in this account? Wagner answered—in the way the use of the voice, with its connection through expression to passion, made Beethoven's last symphony stand for the 'universal drama of humanity'. This drama—this artwork for the future—towered above the bounds of the poetry, and was the basis of expression. It brought 'light to chaos'. How? It depended upon people singing out those words as the ancient orators sung out their laws, laws that were as much political as musical. Original musicians, he explained, had all 'the gifts of godlike vision'; their musical expression illustrated that vision. Beethoven was an original musician: his Ninth moved us beyond the 'frontiers' of absolute music's 'dominion'. It reached a 'wide humanity' and raised music to an 'eternal, purely human type'. However, it achieved its full drama, not just because it was composed by a complete musician, but also because it was composed for complete performers.

By locating drama in the composing and performing voices of 'whole, entire, and warm-breathed human beings',[42] Wagner was not making music's content irrelevant to its meaning. It was just that the content would depend for its fullness of meaning on its connection to the expressive voice. The composer, as the performer, he decreed, 'must fill expression with content which will justify it', to reach music's 'highest poetic aim'.[43] More precisely,

[41] 'Beethoven', v. 102. [42] 'Judaism in Music', iii. 95.
[43] 'Opera and Drama', ii. 341.

because music's origin in expression is inexpressible, it must be expressed through content, so content matters. Wagner was anticipating the critical role that would later be given musical form, for critical formalism is committed precisely to showing how different musical forms historically reveal the different ways expression has been mediated through content, a mediation we also call technique.

Wagner further supported this doubleness of content and expression through an appeal to limits. In a fragment (partially quoted in Chapter 2), he noted: '"history of music = Christian expression": "where the word can no farther, there music begins" = *Beethoven*, 9th Symphony, proves on the contrary: "where music can no farther, there comes the word" (the word stands higher than the tone)'.[44] Influenced by Goethe, Wagner liked to use the formulation of limits and of ends and beginnings.[45] He used them to demarcate different domains as a response to modern separatism, and to show how metaphorical interchange could take place between these domains none the less. 'Tone speech [music]', he once wrote, 'is the beginning and end of word-speech, as feeling is the beginning and end of understanding, as myth is the beginning and end of history, as lyric is the beginning and end of poetry.'[46] In a similar vein, he also wrote that '[t]he secret and profound aspiration of poetry is to resolve itself finally into music', and that poetry does this when it arrives at the 'limit of its art-branch'.[47] Wagner was not suggesting that poetry literally becomes music, only that poetry becomes metaphorically musical at the point of its 'consummation', or when it 'becomes' or 'culminates in' pure expression. The idea that there is an aesthetic reaching[48] from literal to metaphorical meaning, or from content to expression, suggested in the formulation of one thing ending and another beginning, affirmed nineteenth-century aspirations towards transcendence. In aesthetic reaching, Wagner argued, poetry becomes music or it becomes

---

[44] 'Sketches and Fragments', viii. 362.

[45] Other formulations include 'where the speech of man stops short there Music's reign begins' ('A Happy Evening', vii. 73); and for a reference to Goethe in this context, 'Beethoven's Choral Symphony', vii. 247.

[46] 'Opera and Drama', ii. 224.

[47] 'Zukunftsmusik', iii. 312.

[48] This is my phrase, not Wagner's. Cf. Lacoue-Labarthe's discussion of the 'passage to the limit' (*Musica Ficta*, 12), also Jürgen Kühnel's discussion of a 'progression towards the acquisition of maximum human capacity' in 'The Prose Writings', in Müller and Wapnewski (eds.), *Wagner Handbook*, 594.

philosophy. At the source of both was the vocal call of a purely human expression or, in my terms, an inexpressible expression of the extramusical. Beethoven's Ninth had united the call.

Wagner's use of the Ninth as exemplar dictated his reading of music's history. Whereas he happily sang the praises of Bach, Mozart, and Gluck—because any mistake they made belonged to a pre-emancipated framework—he criticized most works composed around and after Beethoven's Ninth (including Beethoven's first eight symphonies and even his opera *Fidelio*). His reading was suggestively Schillerian: Mozart was naive, he was reflective. Meyerbeer was neither, because he worked with an understanding inappropriate for his times. Although sometimes harsh on 'early' music, his purpose here was to show that between Beethoven and himself no composer had fully comprehended Beethoven's legacy with 'open eyes'. He largely blamed formalism: 'To what a degree the narrow view of Music's mission still errs to this day, particularly under the terrifying impression of the misunderstood last works of Beethoven . . . [and] from the flat assertions of modern aesthetes when setting up their theories of the Beautiful in Music.'[49]

To set history's path aright, Wagner moved the concern with musical content back to a concern with expression. He used Schopenhauer's argument that content is related to expression as expression is to the inexpressible, as representation is to Will, as 'the outer' is to 'the inner'. From these equations, his cultural prescription followed. The prescription recalled Rousseau: the 'ear of hearing' that directs itself to the passions should guide the 'eye of hearing' that directs itself to the outer sound-patterns, because it is the 'inward facing side of consciousness' that leads us to the true character of things.[50] In more general terms, that the aesthetic should have this 'moral' recourse means that artists cannot remain mere eyewitnesses to the world; they must also be its earwitnesses.[51]

---

[49] 'A Music-School for Munich', iv. 217.

[50] 'Beethoven', v. 67.

[51] Recall the quotation (in Ch. 2) that 'we must take the era by the ears'. Cf. also Thomas Mann's worries about the distinction between ear- and eye-men: 'Goethe too says that music is something inborn and native, requiring no great nourishment from outside and no experience drawn from life. But after all there is the inner vision, the perception, which is something different and comprehends more than mere seeing. And more than that, it is profoundly contradictory that a man should have, as Leverkühn did, some feeling for the human eye, which after all speaks only

Wagner departed from Schopenhauer in the choice of a paradigm for expressive music. Wagner equated Schopenhauer with the Beethoven of the Fifth and regarded them as having jointly symbolized only the first step in music's emancipation. Both had released music from its former 'servitude' to word and occasion; both had demonstrated the primacy of the symphony by recognizing within it the proper place for expression and song. Yet neither had returned to music the full breadth of its outer form. Beethoven's Ninth had shown the way forward. Schopenhauer had usefully warned against the temptation in vocal music and opera to be distracted by their outer content, by what the words said and what the scenes showed. Even in opera, he had determined, one should listen to the 'unseen' expressive content of words, scenes, actions that was given by their melodic accompaniment. Music might be an accompaniment, but it was certainly not servile.

Wagner likewise advocated that the temptation to be distracted in the wrong way be surpassed by the temptation to be distracted in the right way. Towards this end the composer-poet must give to the inner image its most appropriate outer form. Restoring the outer form fully, in a way that neither Schopenhauer had urged nor Beethoven had done, would be Wagner's contribution to reconnecting music's 'lyrical voicing' of the inexpressible to its original dramatic deed.

'Only in what is human, does a person feel interest,'[52] he now stated to counter the thought that musicians are only interested in a 'narrowly meaningful' music. Then he explained what he meant by 'human'. It referred to the impulse towards uniting disparate elements in the form of a totalizing artwork—totalizing in impulse first, and in content second. He wrote of man's twofold nature and of the need to reunite ear and eye, the inner and the outer, feeling and intellect, tone and speech.[53] He wrote of harvesting 'the full *knowledge* of [the] true "mus[e]-ic art" of "*music*" in its broadest meaning . . . wherein poetry and tone-art are knit as one and indivisible'.[54] 'Tone's most living flesh is the *human voice*,' he ex-

to the eye, and yet refuse to perceive the outer world through that organ' (*Doctor Faustus*, tr. H. T. Lowe-Porter (Harmondsworth, 1947), 172).

[52] 'Pasticcio', viii. 66. The authorship of this essay is presently in question. However, the words are consistent with Wagner's view.

[53] 'The Art-Work of the Future', i. 91.

[54] 'On Musical Criticism', iii. 71.

plained, 'and the *word* is . . . the bone and muscle rhythm of this human voice.'[55] 'The poet has become musician, and the musician poet: now they are *both* entirely artistic man,'[56] but to become 'entire artists' they must also move towards *'gymnastics'*.[57] In giving back to music its full drama, it suffices not merely to sing songs, but to sing them in full, embodied presence, with the full outerness of bodily gesture. The drama, Wagner wrote, moves in full presence 'before our very eyes'; it is music's 'visible counterpart'. To find this drama we must look less in the actual *work* that Beethoven produced, Wagner concluded, than in its 'unparalleled artistic *deed* (*unerhörte künstlerische Tat*)'.[58]

Wagner pursued the point past composer, past performer, to audience. In reconciling 'absolute, self-sufficing melody' with 'unflinchingly true dramatic expression', the audience would be given the potential for a total synaesthetic experience. The experience would incorporate not only the total sensory input, but also the total emotion associated therewith. In Beethoven's Ninth Wagner had found the promise of this total emotion. In joy and in love, he explained, man is reunited with woman, as poetry with music, as composer and performer are with audience. With love and 'expressional significance', society could be restored to its wholeness; again he blamed a separatist 'understanding' (or, following *Tristan*, the 'daylight of reason') for decomposing it.

Opera as dramatic deed synthesized Beethoven and Shakespeare: it fulfilled both the literal and metaphorical demand that music be fully dramatic as well as purely (musically) expressive. It synthesized the audible and visual arts: a certain eye, 'when it faces inwards . . . becomes an ear when directed outwards'.[59] Wagner had redirected Schopenhauer's view to show how music exists 'on the boundary between dance and speech, feeling, and thought'. As such, it reconciles all outer forms. Think back to the ancient lyric, 'where the song, the sung word, gave fire at once and measure to the dance. Dance and song; rhythm and melody; so she stands both binding and dependent on the two uttermost faculties of man, of physical sensation and of spiritual thought. The ocean severs and unites—so music!'[60]

In all this talk of restoration Wagner was not urging the return of

---

[55] 'The Art-Work of the Future', i. 103.   [56] 'Opera and Drama', ii. 300.
[57] 'On Musical Criticism', iii. 71.   [58] 'Beethoven', v. 112.
[59] Ibid. v. 79.   [60] 'Sketches and Fragments', viii. 354.

music to an earlier or primitive state. Even when he spoke of
restoring to it its naturalness, his idea was always to consider music
at the most modern point of its development, in its most emancipated state. Consistent with contemporary thinking, he gave priority to art and humanity over nature. Humanity's expression
revealed its historical and revolutionary moment. Grasping passion
through the immediacy of tone was the modern aesthetic route by
which people were put in touch with their emotion. It had once
been the route ancient orators had used in public, political
speech.

Similarly, when Wagner spoke of restoring to music its origin in
folk-song, it was less the outer, formed content of the song that was
to be restored, than the fully embodied passion of the metaphysical
Volk. In this context, Wagner would also warn of the dangers
of defining 'Germanness' by external criteria.[61] National identity
derives from expression, not external content. Anyone, even foreigners, he said, can duplicate outer content. Antithetical to the
ominous tone, his appeal to origin was metaphysical. It was the sort
of origin Sachs had sought in Walther's 'Prize Song', an origin
that, in one formulation, expressed an aspiration towards a subjective freedom sufficiently unconstrained by society's formalist
routine.

Wagner went on to provide a theory of performance in which
one would not be taken in merely by the outer, external, or visible
content of performance. Yet the expansion he had already urged
sufficed to shift the emphasis away from the absolutist's conception
of the purely musical to a broader conception of the purely human.
This shift had given him his conception of the freedom of expression. Elucidating this concept in music's modern domain would be
his aesthetic contribution to society's 'life-of-the-future'. In his
view, it contradicted the contribution of the emancipated metaphy-
sicians who were concerning themselves with music's perfectibility
only for the most narrow of sakes.

5. All Instrumental Playing Aspires to the Condition of Singing

I shall return to Wagner's view of performance in the next chapter.
Here I want to focus only on the part of it that helps illuminate the

[61] 'Beethoven', v. 61–3.

philosophical content of a familiar figure of speech, that when we say of a musical instrument that it is played musically we say of it that it sings. Illuminating this saying will broaden the scope of the present argument both within and beyond Wagner's own view. Within this broader scope, a tenet emerges that it is incorrect to call a violin, a piano, or a flute an instrument as opposed to a *musical* instrument. The correction then prescribes concealment: treat a violin not as the object or mechanical tool that it is, but as you would your voice or body—an extension of your soul. To recall a lesson from William James, we need not strictly posit the soul as an existent to comprehend its convenient invocation in descriptions of musical performance.[62]

There are two different claims at hand: first, that instrumental music should approximate to the condition of song; secondly, that instrumental playing should approximate to the condition of singing. The first concerns the condition of music, the second its performance. In both claims, the sense of the prescription varies, depending on whether 'song' and 'singing' are understood literally or metaphorically. Wagner took the prescription both ways in both cases. His understanding generally countered the predominant (German) tendency of his time to treat work and performance in separation.

Wagner understood instrumental music's emancipation to have occurred primarily within the context of German music. When he spoke of restoring song to music, or singing to its performance, he was often thinking about German traditions in particular. But sometimes he meant by extension to restore the metaphorical spirit of singing to German society and then to society in general. 'Song, Song, and a third time Song, ye Germans!', he once proclaimed in the culturally specific case, but then his explanation turned more general. 'Song is the speech through which you should musically express yourself,' and if this language is not cultivated as other languages are cultivated, then 'nobody will understand you'.[63] All should cultivate their speech to 'the utmost of their ability'.[64] And every musician should take singing lessons, because

---

[62] From 'The Reality of the Unseen', in *The Varieties of Religious Experience* (New York, 1982), 53 ff.

[63] 'Bellini', viii. 68.

[64] 'A Music-School for Munich', iv. 187.

'[w]hoever does not know how to sing can neither write for the voice . . . nor imitate song on an instrument'.[65]

Wagner was not unique in his literal and metaphorical appeals to song. It was almost a commonplace in the nineteenth century (as it still is) to understand the seemingly local prescription that instrumental playing should approximate to the condition of singing as invoking the largest possible cultural plea. The plea was that to the modern, overly literalized world musicians should restore music's redemptive metaphor of song.

Part of the plea came in the form of a reminder, that a violin should be treated as more than a modern instrument; it should also always be treated as a *musical* instrument. The prescription that a violin should sing became a demand, in Wagner's terms, that dramatic expression should be the end towards which a player's use of her musical instrument strives, or, more generally, that style be the end of the violinist's technique which is his means. Combining the two claims, where the technique of *a violinist* ends, the style of *the musician* begins.

This prescription was thick with cultural content. First, theorists generally understood the condition of singing to be a condition to which instrumental players and singers equally had to aspire. Here, the condition of singing referred straightforwardly to qualities associated with being musical. Here, singing and instrumental playing were treated on a par. But theorists also liked to give to singing the priority: sometimes they claimed that it was 'more naturally' musical. 'The human voice is the practical basis of Music,' Wagner once explained, 'and however far the latter may journey on her primal path, the boldest combinations of the tone-setter, the most daring execution of the instrumental-virtuoso, will always have to hark back to the purely singable, to find the law for their achievements.'[66] Stendhal explained further that the voice can graduate 'sounds to a degree of perfection inconceivable in any mechanical device'.[67] It can achieve a degree of natural expressiveness that a mere violin never can, but to which nevertheless a violinist must always aspire.

Another version of the prescription appears in Willa Cather's *The Song of the Lark*, a novel clearly written in the Wagnerian spirit. One of its characters, Thomas, a violinist, has just completed

---

[65] 'A Music-School for Munich', iv. 187.   [66] Ibid.
[67] *The Life of Rossini*, 368.

a concert tour, and is recounting to his friend, the voice teacher Harsanyi, his sudden 'awakening' by Jenny Lind and Henrietta Sontag. 'They were the first great artists he had ever heard,' he recalls, 'and he never forgot his debt to them. . . . It was not the voice and execution alone. There was a greatness about them. They were great women, great artists. They opened a new world to me.' Cather continues:

Night after night he went to hear them, striving to reproduce the quality of their tone upon his violin. From that time his idea about strings was completely changed, and on his violin he tried always for the singing, vibrating tone, instead of the loud and somewhat harsh tone then prevalent among even the best German violinists. In later years he often advised violinists to study singing, and singers to study violin. He told Harsanyi that he got his first conception of tone quality from Jenny Lind. 'But, of course,' he added, 'the great thing I got from Lind and Sontag was the indefinite, not the definite thing . . . their inspiration was incalculable.'[68]

It was not just the singer's sound Thomas wanted to emulate, but that elusive 'something' he sensed behind the sound, a 'something' that was more than merely audible, and a 'something' that was definitely more than physical or mechanical. It was an indefinite 'something' extra of incalculable effect, an intimation apparently of the singer's 'greatness'.

Wagner likewise thought about singing in terms of the expressive origin of sounds. In his eulogy to Wilhelmine Schröder-Devrient he wrote that, listening to this marvellous singer, he did not think either of her voice or of her singing as such, but of her womanly soul 'streaming forth in wondrous sound'. He then accounted for the beauty of her singing in terms of her knowing how to use her breath. So even, to put the point extremely, if her vocal instrument did not matter, her breathing did.[69]

Singer and composer Reynaldo Hahn also focused on breathing, as voice teachers always naturally do, but he contributed to the discussion the distinction between the expressive breathing that should be heard from the physiological breathing that should not.[70] Expressive breathing, he wrote, animates or gives to singing its 'live

[68] *The Song of the Lark*, 205. Cf. Wagner's own mentions of Lind and Sontag (*My Life*, 516).
[69] 'Actors and Singers', v. 217–19.
[70] *On Singers and Singing: Lectures and an Essay*, tr. L. Simoneau (Portland, Oreg., 1990), 52.

spirit'; physiological breathing corresponds to 'dead technique'. He wrote further of how diction, accent, and articulation give to otherwise dead words their significance.[71] For Hahn, as for Wagner, as indeed for Rousseau, the singing out of words and the breathing out of spirit constituted an act of human expression that could not be reduced to 'deadening accounts' of the physiology of hearing or of the formal properties of sound. As 'the language of the heart', Wagner once wrote, music always proves herself 'victorious over formalism'.[72]

Whether theorists emphasized breathing (or bodily gesture more generally[73]) as the carrier of expression, they shared a resistance to accounting for the value of singing in terms either of the mechanics of the voice or of the sound produced. This had an important ramification. It allowed instrumentalists to appropriate the conditions for singing for their own conception of instrumental performance. This was the real point of Thomas's learning. By stressing the *musicality* of the instrument, rather than its 'instrumental' qualities, instrumentalists could claim to sing as singers sing.

Although the claim was made initially with respect to performance, it was soon extended to the music itself. If it could be shown that an instrumentalist could sing as a singer could sing, then instrumental music could sing, metaphorically speaking, as vocal music could sing. An even stronger claim soon beckoned, that instrumental music might meet the expressive condition of singing better than song itself, because, unlike song, it was unhampered by the cognitive interference of words. Instrumentalists were adapting an argument of abstraction that had been used to emancipate instrumental music itself. They borrowed a conception from a medium against which they wanted to assert their independence, and then claimed that that conception in fact suited their medium better. Wagner remained sceptical.

In their bid to prove their performance on a par with singing, instrumentalists began to speak of their instruments as humanized,

---

[71]   *On Singers and Singing*, 27 and 78.

[72]   'Opera and Drama', ii. 35.

[73]   Barthes gives a different emphasis to the human voice, to expand the voice into a vehicle of the body. 'The singing voice, that very specific space in which a tongue encounters a voice and permits those who know how to listen to it to hear what we can call its "grain"—the singing voice is not the breath but indeed the materiality of the body emerging from the throat, a site where the phonic metal hardens and takes shape.' For Barthes, to deny breath is not to deny the voice its expressive function ('Listening', in *The Responsibility of Forms*, 255).

as biological, as expressing the inner qualities of human souls. They spoke of their instruments as having energy, as breathing, and as having the immediacy and presence of a human body. Some said the body of their instrument moved emotionally through gestural expression. '[T]he piano is not a percussion instrument,' claimed piano theorist Frederick Horace Clark; it is a singing extension of one's hands. Our hands radiate 'outwards in gestures from the human centre which is, from the organic and corporeal point of view, the heart'.[74] Instruments were being thought of as immediate extensions of bodies; bodies extensions of souls. Of Liszt it was claimed that his ear acted on his fingers, and his soul on his ear.[75] Another observer wrote that Liszt's countenance expresses 'everything his fingers are singing'.[76] Clark wrote that if he raised his fingers too far from the piano, it caused 'a separation of the will, the body, and the mind.'[77] Another wrote more generally: 'If you do not awaken the eyes which are sleeping in your hands, you will never do anything of worth.'[78] Instrumentalists sometimes also spoke of feeling incomplete without their instruments. 'My piano is to me', Liszt wrote, 'what a frigate is to a sailor, what a war-horse is to an Arab,' and then he added, 'even more perhaps, because it is my speech, my life.'[79] All these statements pointed to the same thing: when Thomas was thinking of his violin as 'an organ of his soul', his interest shifted from the instrument as object to the instrument as his means of performing or expressing his self through the medium of music.

Performers seem to feel about their instruments as they do about their bodies and their voices, that they have both an inner and an outer aspect. Externally, they see their instruments as objects belonging to the world upon which they, as intentional beings, act; internally, they hear their instruments from the inside as imposing musical sound upon their world. When they play musically, when they use instruments in their musical performance, they make the instruments act as if they are 'indwelling' within their bodies.

---

[74] Bertrand Ott, *Lisztian Keyboard Energy/Liszt et la pédagogie du piano: An Essay on the Pianism of Franz Liszt*, tr. D. H. Windham (Lewiston, NY, 1992), 52. I am grateful to Estela Olevsky for alerting me to the many quotations in this book.

[75] Ibid. 15. Cf. the lines in a review signed as 'Guénier' (1834): Liszt 'has made his fingers into an admirable voice, submissive to the most delicate inflections of his soul' (ibid. 15).

[76] Ibid. 18 (Louise Gerson, 1844).   [77] Ibid. 51.

[78] Ibid., p. xix (Marie Jaëll).   [79] Ibid. 8 (1838).

When performers speak of pulling the energy or soul out of their instrument, what I think they really mean is that they are putting their energy into it. The way not to see a violin as an external, mechanical instrument is to see it as an extension of yourself, the violinist. What a musician does to an instrument is precisely how an instrument is made musical, how, according to many musicians, the instrument acquires a personality (whose personality is a difficult question).[80] To call an instrument a musical instrument is to distinguish it from any ordinary tool or instrument we use in our everyday lives. The more musically we play a violin, the more it loses its ordinary toolness. But it does not thereby lose its physicality; rather, at the moment of musical playing, its physicality, we could say, becomes inseparable from the pure expressiveness of our 'souls'.[81] At that moment, it effectively becomes concealed.

The paradox of artifice enters the account again. It appears in the claim that a musical performance consists in the overcoming of the instrumentality of the instrument to give way to the appearance of musicality in an artificial performance of art. Performers will even use the term 'naturalness' or naturalistic terms when describing this moment of musicality. 'The organism carries within itself a negation of art,' Liszt student Marie Jaëll once wrote.[82] Heine provided the explanation: 'It is enough that the musician have a perfect control of his instrument, that the material means shall be entirely lost sight of, and only the soul of music be felt.'[83] Schumann likewise wrote to Clara: 'The instrument burns, sparks fly beneath the fingers of the master [Liszt]. It is no longer a piano, but rather the expression of an artist with an impetuous nature in whose hands destiny placed the power of Art which dominates and conquers.'[84] Another wrote that Liszt's 'touch extracted the soul of the instrument and his playing was removed from any terrestrial or material

[80] Candidates include the personality of the player, the composer, the instrument itself, the music performed, or a combination of some or all of those. Perhaps one should not seek a specific determination of character at all.

[81] I have been helped in my thinking here by Maurice Natanson, 'Man as an Actor', in E. W. Straus and R. M. Griffiths (eds.), *Phenomenology of Will and Action* (Pittsburgh, 1967), 201–32; also by Merleau-Ponty's phenomenology, which connects intentionality to bodily expression and gesture.

[82] Ott, *Lisztian Keyboard Energy*, 38.

[83] 'The French Stage', in *The Works of Heinrich Heine*, tr. C. G. Leland (New York, 1920), vii. 277. All further Heine references are to this edition.

[84] Ott, *Lisztian Keyboard Energy*, 16 (1840).

element'.[85] Kodaly provides us our final statement of negation: 'There must be a strenuous attempt to replace music that comes from the fingers and the mechanical playing of instruments with music from the soul and based on singing.'[86]

Once more, the critical point about the paradox of artifice is not that artifice should be got rid of; it is indispensable. It just has to be put to the right use, as a means, not as an end. This is how performers think about technique: playing on the difference between eyes and ears, they wonder how they should use technique so that it may be *seen but not heard*. This, in the terms of my argument, is a question that begs for answers invoking doubleness or the paradoxical play between two elements. Liszt apparently agrees: 'All technique starts from and returns to touch,' he writes; 'great technique comes not so much from the fingers as from the deepest reaches of the spirit, and it is the spirit that gives technique all its strength.' 'Virtuosity exists only to permit the artist to reproduce everything that is expressible in art. It is indispensable and is never developed enough.' Fingers should not be obstacles: 'to express everything one feels, one must not be hindered by anything'.[87] The idea here is that at the moment that performers perfect their techniques, the technique is overcome or transfigured, as it were, into its opposing element—musicality. At this moment, the literally musical becomes extra- or metaphorically musical. For this transfiguration, for this aesthetic reaching, the two elements are at every moment required.

The seemingly simple prescription that instrumental playing should approximate to the condition of singing is not, we have now seen, simply a demand that the violin *sound like* a human voice. It is a demand that a violinist should sing as a singer sings, where the analogy between the violinist and singer depends upon an elusive metaphor of musicality usually expressed with all its Romantic and metaphysical grandeur.

The reverse prescription that a singer should not sound like an instrumentalist presupposes the same general understanding. We often describe a singer as failing to sing because she treats her voice like an instrument. Sometimes we articulate the criticism to leave it ambiguous whether we are criticizing the singer for sounding, say,

[85] Ibid. 21 (Eugen d'Albert, 1881).
[86] Preface to *Fifty-Five Two-Part Exercises*, ed. P. M. Young (London, 1955).
[87] Ott, *Lisztian Keyboard Energy*, 143, 250, 7, and 26.

as an oboe sounds, or criticizing the singer for sounding as any instrument might sound, as merely an instrument. Generally I think we mind far less, if we mind at all, when a baritone sounds like a cello, a mezzo like an oboe, a soprano like a flute, than when the baritone sounds like any machine sounds, if by this we mean to say that he captures only the instrumental or technical quality of the instrument and not its musical quality. Playing with metaphors, a soprano should sound like a flute if the flautist sings as a singer sings.

Finally, for the singer and instrumentalist alike, a performance is not merely 'for myself', but 'for our selves'. Performance is a social act of engagement. The musicality of my performance resides less in the instrument that I play than in the expression I convey from my self to others (perhaps to myself *qua* listener). In Wagner's terms, I must maintain the expression of the melody when I 'fiddle', 'blow', or 'hammer-out' my sounds on an instrument, if my melody is to be 'a real melody for the public'.[88] Performers accordingly speak of their souls speaking to each other through music. Heine once wrote of Chopin that he 'is not satisfied that his (dexterous) hands . . . shall be clapped by other hands; he strives for higher laurels; his fingers are but the servants of his soul, and that is applauded by people who hear not only with their ears, but also with their own souls.'[89] Sometimes performers have spoken of communicating with each other in silence, through the inner ear of expression. In so singing, they have said, their outer ears and eyes are blinded as their inner sense is brought to life. Connecting these statements is the belief that singing is a metaphor of social communication that captures the way in which musical performers express the inexpressible.

When Wagner adamantly stated that singers should never 'degrade themselves' by emulating instruments, he was thinking less about the musical condition of instrumental performance than the more general cultural tendency towards instrumentality. Wagner was here following, as he so often did, Heine's complaint. The complaint always moved from the specific to the general. The piano symbolized the modern victory of machinery. Virtuoso performers were largely to blame, because, with their 'technical facility', in Heine's words, they aspired towards 'the precision of an automaton'. They were finding their selves in their stringed wood, not their stringed wood in their selves. Humanity was being turned into 'a tuned instrument of sound'.[90] Heine could have been quoting Rousseau. He could also have been quoting any one of many nineteenth-century theorists who were complaining that technology had the ability to 'stop' human or expressive mediation.

To see the human voice stopped by the victory of technology is one way to see the modern condition of alienation. Another is to see the human voice as lost in processes of formalism and abstraction. Yet another is to see the voice, or, better now, certain expressions of voice, as repressed by voices that are heard or as excluded within certain forms of social and typically 'bourgeois' arrangement. Richard Leppert has recently explored metaphors of inexpressibility, silence, and expression in their historical (though mostly nineteenth-century) roles as antidotes to the increase in visual domination and the associated repression of the woman's voice within male-dominated social forms. He has written of women living in conditions of domesticity that were gendered as Woman, as Other. Men did not play music; they listened to it under the condition of silent, abstracted, and intellectual contemplation. Their silence was quite different from the secret 'delight and gratification' that women experienced making music. Man's silence signified men's control and domination of the world; woman's silence evidenced women's exclusion or repression, but also their unannounced private joy. Women were empowered: engendered as Woman, they sung out their subjectivity; engendered as Man, men listened to music, but not its song. Women's singing became a secret weapon—the enemy or negation of reason. Music, Leppert concludes, 'bears relation to the shadow: it is the not of that which is'. Music's refusal, its moment of non-identity, announces that 'this is not so'.[91]

Leppert finds in this argument a claim that seems to be about music's content, but is really about its metaphysical origin in expression. Music's power lies in its sonority rather than in its words. 'All that music adds to words is in effect taken from words.' Yet music 'betrays the very paucity of the words it sets, or rather it

[90] 'The French Stage', vii. 375–6. Cf. Max Weber, 'The History of the Piano', in *Selections in Translation*, ed. W. G. Runciman, tr. E. Matthews (New York, 1978), 378–82.
[91] *The Sight of Sound*, ch. 4; also 22 and 223.

makes emphatic the severe limitations of a reason that valorizes a rationality divorced from embodiment'.[92] That a whole sonorous world of song lies concealed or latent in the modern world gives Leppert, as it gave Wagner, a 'critical' theme. This theme is the main subject of my conclusion.

6. Resituating Musical Autonomy

Leppert acknowledges that certain nineteenth-century theorists (he names Schopenhauer and Pater) recognized that the 'condition' of emancipated music was less an aspiration of art in itself, than a desire for an embodied happiness which did not exist in material life. However, the ahistorical, formalist aesthetic of autonomy denied this desire. It concealed it by not naming it. Consequently, the aspiration had to break in by the back door. In my terms, in breaking in, the aesthetic of autonomy had its character changed. The break-in resituated music's freedom.

Theorists who have recently sought in music its political or social dimension have looked mostly at the revealed or concealed political nature of music's content. Sometimes they have described the various ways in which different combinations of sounds, modes, styles, and forms have been associated with certain, usually oppressive, social forms. Dialectically they have connected the internal, purely musical content of works with the framework of external social relations in terms of the latter's being mediated in or by the former. The arts, Leppert writes typically, 'discursively "transliterate" the political process into an aesthetic chronicle'.[93] The advantage of seeing the relation as one of mediation has been that it has allowed theorists to render music (or the arts more broadly) as non-reductively social. The non-reductive relation has then allowed theorists to find a space for music's free expression. However, in these accounts and despite appearances to the contrary, it has really been the music's antagonistic *relation* to society, not its form or content *per se*, that has sustained music's claim to autonomy. In other words, autonomy has been conceived paradoxically: though shown in the aesthetic appearance of purely musical formed content, music's autonomy has revealed an aspiration

---

[92] *The Sight of Sound*, 87.
[93] Ibid. 11. Cf. my 'Political Music and the Politics of Music', in which I list the many synonyms for 'mediation' employed in the recent literature.

much broader than that of a fidelity to the 'merely musical'. That finding is the distinguishing feature of critical formalism.

The argument of this chapter retains this paradoxical quality, but it further shifts the emphasis, of the antagonistic relation. It less stresses the relation in which a musical work stands to society than the relation in which people so stand. This relation has historically been exemplified by our acting through music's medium. To make sense of this claim, the argument has forced us to broaden our scope regarding the concept of the musical. For that concept must accommodate the idea that people who voice their freedom often sing in and through song. That singing is both a musical and a political act.

One advantage in changing the emphasis in our argument is that it does not immediately privilege the type of music produced, though it does privilege tokens of a type; it starts where nowadays most ethnomusicologists like to start, with the performance and production of music understood within the scope of particular communities. The argument also urges us to reverse the more usual course of our considerations. Rather than beginning with music's content and products, with works, and perfunctorily saying something about performance, it begins with a basic idea about human performance and voiced expression. It shifts our thinking away from the nature of the work to the freedom of expression exhibited in the act of performing that work. Once more, it does not make the consideration of content irrelevant; it just does not give it first or exclusive priority in the enquiry into autonomy. In doubling terms, it sees content as historically mediating expression. In cultural terms, it offers a prescription, that to speak or sing autonomously, in a way 'conducive to liberty' (Rousseau's phrase), we should first be 'true to our voice', as a precondition for our 'being true' to our works or texts, since our voices and performances are the fundamental carriers of expression. In this argument, the traditional *Werktreue* ideal is expanded beyond its usual formalist scope. (Of this, more next chapter.)

Someone may object that it is incorrect to think about autonomy as dependent upon a distinction between content and performance. In legal theory we usually think about autonomy as a right to say what we want when we want (albeit under certain constraints). This is a right that dictates a freedom of both performance *and* content. But I employed the distinction to draw attention to a particular history in the arts, and especially in music, in which autonomy has been attributed to the content of music, or, otherwise put, to the language of music in abstraction from its expression or performance. This abstraction restricted the scope in which we could locate freedom and the political in the musical world. It is an undesirable restriction.

The advantage of linking music back to expressive acts is that it allows us to claim that, in the broadest sense of 'political', musical practice is already political whether or not one finds in any given arrangement of notes an explicit ideological message. Music is political already in virtue of the fact that music is a practice of human expression or performance working itself out in the world, in particular communities, through the medium of melody. It might be thought an undesirable conclusion if we were to conclude that if music *is* political in this very broad sense, then every practice is broadly political. But this conclusion would only be undesirable if politics were always and automatically reduced to specific ideological forms of which one did not approve. It does not have to be.

The contemporary theoretical burden to 'prove' music political reflects our contemporary attempt to move beyond the dominance of a formalism that increasingly tended towards separating the significance of music's content from its origin in expression. But, as I have tried to show, the resistance to formalism was present in musical practice since formalism's inception. I actually think it had to be, for, without it, formalism would not have survived as the dominant paradigm it became. As I shall argue in the next chapter, formalism required this opposition precisely to preserve in musical practice all that it put aside as 'extramusical'. The general point is that a dominant world-view (or ideology), despite its claims to completeness, is always partial, but what it leaves out lies dormant or concealed in the practice it dominates.

The argument of this chapter newly connects music's claims for its emancipation and its autonomy. Putting Wagner's particular demands aside (i.e. what kind of music he believed suited his ideals of freedom, human expression, and drama most fully), we can interpret him as having described the kinds of conditions under which the music can lose its freedom both of musical and of political expression. Wagner might have said to those with whom he identified the negative impulses of modernism: not every kind of freedom is a freedom we want; some freedom produces a dull and lifeless music that no one *should* listen to. (I did not say 'wants to' because this is not a matter of merely suiting people's taste.) Not every music that claims to be emancipated is in fact so. We want effective 'freedom within', not ineffective complete 'freedom from'. So the point is not to defend music's emancipation in terms merely of what its proper content should be, but to defend its freedom to express itself musically or our freedom to express ourselves in the world through music's medium. Without compromising his formalism, Hanslick could have endorsed this principle, despite his disagreement with Wagner's use of it to support a particular type of music. Here is the cultural core of a commonality that cuts across the formalist–transcendentalist academic divide.

In formulating this argument I have not hesitated to use terms that are strikingly 'old-fashioned'. Yet I have recalled all those appeals 'to heart and soul' to demonstrate deliberately the noticeable lack of terminology for the residue that cannot be captured in empirical terms. That there is this lack reveals the 'negative' character of the domain of the 'inexpressible'. To be sure, many theorists have given positive and substantive content to these terms in ways that have rendered the aesthetic of expression sometimes conservative, sometimes naturalist, sometimes regressive. But this aesthetic can also be rendered otherwise. Giving the terms a negative character is, I am suggesting, one way to do this.

A significant feature of Wagner's commitment to the expressive origin of political community is that he was able to hold onto this commitment despite the variety of ideological stands he assumed through his lifetime, from anarchism to republicanism. The feature is significant because it motivates one to draw a distinction between his metaphysical and ideological positions. That such positions are mixed up in Wagner's own writings is obvious, as is the more general inseparability in practice of formal matters of principle and substantive commitments. Yet, from a theoretical standpoint, we can maintain the relevant distinction. Thus, to speak of the origins of community commits one only to a formal political demand which, until it is mediated ideologically by content suitable to musical or any other practice, is no more conservative than it is liberal, proto-fascist, or communist.

I previously described the distinction implied here in terms of a gap. This gap can help us meet two objections that are likely immediately to arise: first, that the potentially regressive dimension of the argument rests on positing the purely human as the expressive origin of a musical music; secondly, that, unless we can specify in what the purely human consists, to give guidance on what being musical means, the appeal ends up a vacuous theoretical posit. From a theoretical standpoint, the ideal of the purely human is deliberately empty of specific or 'prejudicial' content so that it can be filled out, mediated, or met in different ways in different practices. In being empty, this regulative ideal perhaps remains essential, but it is not regressively essentialist. It is also essential only as a formal demand or as a critical or transcendental requirement, and not because it has an a priori or naturalistic content. Until historically mediated it has no positive or constitutive content at all.[94] This position allows us to say of Wagner's view, at moments when it is relevant to do so, that it went profoundly wrong whenever he filled in the ideal of the purely human with, say, substantively anti-Jewish content. But it also allows us to say that the same formal view could have been filled in differently. A philosophical theory must accommodate the possibility that the historical realization or mediation of the formal ideals it articulates may turn out progressive, regressive, or both. This possibility creates a space for genuine debate about our ideological or substantive commitments. One might identify this last thought with some recent formulations of political liberalism.

References to ideals of the purely human function much as references to birdsong (to recall the previous chapter). They capture human aspirations, not natural states achieved. They are essentially negative inasmuch as they have no content until they are realized in our conventional states. It is the concrete realizations of our ideals that are subject to our judgements; we argue for our ideals at the level of theory. To maintain a gap between judgement and argu-

---

[94] In his *Innocence and Experience* (Cambridge, Mass., 1989), 73, Stuart Hampshire argues that 'a bare minimum concept of justice, underlying all the distinct, specific, and substantial conceptions, is indispensable, if there is to be a peaceful and coherent society. Evidently the difficulty is to specify what this minimum concept . . . ought to be, given that it must be independent of specific, and therefore, divisive, conceptions of the good.' My description of this 'underlying concept' as 'empty' also tries to avoid the assumption that it has (too much) 'content' independently of any, some, or all of the conceptions it underlies. The description I prefer is of a formal principle or regulative ideal that cannot function or materially be conceived independently of its being filled out or mediated historically by different contents. I use the term 'empty' to try to capture the necessity for historical mediation. Otherwise Hampshire's 'bare minimum' would do.

ment has two advantages. First, practices can remain open, critical, and historical. Secondly, we can release ourselves from the pressure to establish a substantive content once and for all for the ideal, say, of being musical. Our practice can function without such a determination. To leave our formal ideals underdetermined suits a view of open practices in which participants are required constantly and independently to reflect upon, and to judge, whether the actions undertaken and the products produced meet these ideals. Each and every example is subject to such a judgement. This view commits us to maintaining at the formal level of our philosophical theory a substantive emptiness precisely to give to our historical practices a substantive primacy. It commits us to a view of practices as regulated by metaphysical ideals and filled in by historical contingent acts. We cannot do without either.

Finally, this view matches my earlier description of the exemplary status of works. The important feature of treating a work as exemplary is that, in coming to understand it, we treat it as having a doubled character. We treat it first as a radically contingent particular and secondly as an embodiment, expression, or mediation of the general, formal ideals that regulate the practice within which those works are produced. (In Chapter 2, we thought about these ideals as revisable rules.) A philosophical theory has to recognize in a work this double aspect. However, it does so only when it acknowledges that a work *qua* exemplary particular exemplifies the general at the same time that it sets a new standard for what the general should be. The lesson holds true also for musical performance.

4

Conflicting Ideals of Performance Perfection in an Imperfect Practice

> Perhaps, said Kretschmar, it was music's deepest wish not to be heard at all, nor even seen, nor yet felt: but only—if that were possible—in some Beyond, the other side of sense and sentiment, to be perceived and contemplated as pure mind, pure spirit.
>
> (Thomas Mann[1])

> It's always seemed to me that when first people sat glued or wired to their crystal sets, what they really were recognizing was the phenomenon of another human voice. It wasn't the facts of the news reportage; it wasn't the vital weather information; it was the sheer mystery and challenge of another human voice.
>
> (Glenn Gould[2])

1. Introduction

In 1965 Glenn Gould predicted that 'the public concert as we know it today would no longer exist a century hence [because] its functions would have been entirely taken over by electronic media'.[3] As is well known, Gould stopped giving public concerts himself—in part to underwrite his prediction—and moved his musical life almost exclusively into the recording studio. His prediction startled the establishment, and this reaction startled him:

It had not occurred to me that [it] represented a particularly radical announcement. Indeed, I regarded it almost as self-evident truth and, in my case, as defining only one of the peripheral effects occasioned by develop-

---

[1] *Doctor Faustus*, 63.
[2] Quoted in G. Payzant, *Glenn Gould: Music and Mind* (Toronto, 1992), 71.
[3] 'The Prospects of Recording', in *The Glenn Gould Reader*, ed. Tim Page (New York, 1984), 331.

ments in the electronic age. But never has a statement of mine been so widely quoted—or so hotly disputed.[4]

Gould was right; his prediction was not as radical as all that. Certainly its gadfly sting dizzied the establishment, but its aesthetic and moral substance was familiar. Corresponding to a traditional conception of music's mission, the prediction just took it in a new direction. Gould had found that the technological conditions associated with recordings maintain more honesty in musical production and reception than the comparable conditions associated with live performances and the concert hall. In other words, the 'ministrations of radio and phonograph' had proved more successful in their 'moral' mission to convey divine works to contemplating listeners via interpretations performers tried to make as perfect as possible.

To what then did Gould's critics so strongly react—surely neither to his aim to produce perfect, exemplary, or ideal interpretations nor to his mere use of recording technology? What really troubled them, it seems, was the mode of performance they thought would dominate practice if his prediction proved true. He was asking them to conceive of performances as experienced by listeners in recorded form without the detrimental distractions of the performer's live presence. Performers would effectively become invisible; their actions, gestures, and technique would never again be seen. His critics were insisting, by contrast, that performances could still be successful even if visually present performers did figure in the listener's experiences. Indeed, they wondered whether their visual presence might not actually be necessary, if the traditional purpose of communicating expression between musicians and their public was properly to be fulfilled.

It might seem unusual to characterize Gould's quarrel with his critics in terms of two performance conceptions differing according to the presence or absence of visibly acting performers, or, more abstractly, to the degree of humanness involved. Yet the history of performance reveals just such a strange divergence, and though the divergence long precedes the quarrel about recording and live performance, it is made explicit by it. 'There are those ... who

[4] Ibid. Gould gives details of his critics' reactions in several of his essays; often he serves as his own harshest critic. See his 'Let's Ban Applause', 'Rubinstein', 'Music and Technology', and 'Glenn Gould Interviews Glenn Gould about Glenn Gould', in *The Glenn Gould Reader*.

counsel that only in the theatre, only with the direct communication of artist to listener, can we experience the high drama of
human communication,' Gould observes, but 'art on its loftiest
mission is scarcely human at all'.[5]

In this chapter I shall torment this last pronouncement, but not
by focusing on Gould. Rather, I shall focus on the more general
practice of performance, which since 1800 has accommodated a
conflict between two dominant performance conceptions. I shall
refer to them respectively as *the perfect performance of music*
and *the perfect musical performance*. The former stresses the vehicular and structured Apollonian ideal of a performance *qua*
performance-of-a-work; the latter the open, social, and spontaneous Dionysian ideal of musicianship involved in the performance
event. The former has generated more explicit theorizing than the
latter, partly because it has regulated a more elite space in the
practice and partly because of formalism's dominance. But the
latter conception has held its own, partly because it has claimed a
more popular appeal and partly because it has been sustained by an
anti-formalist aesthetic. The 'partly's are important, because,
though the conceptions have genuinely conflicted under the modern condition of musical practice, their successful functioning has
not been, because it could not be, contingent upon the conceptions
being mutually excluding. Further, it has been more their connection than their separation that has given sense to Gould-like proclamations on the humanness of art or desired lack thereof.

One purpose I have in distinguishing these two performance
conceptions is to highlight the tendency in the formalist aesthetic to
neglect the role of human action, a neglect stemming from an age-
old preference in Western thought for knowing over doing. As
Boethius long ago summed up the thought: 'How much more admirable . . . is the science of music in apprehending by reason than in
accomplishing by work and deed!'[6] To be sure, many theorists have
asserted that music has no meaningful existence other than through
its sounding out in performance, yet the role of performance, and

---

[5] 'Let's Ban Applause', 247. Cf. Harold Schonberg's remark: 'In a future, fully
automated age, it may be that . . . all performing musicians will be obsolete. But
until that unfortunate day is here, let us be thankful that there still remain interpre-
tive musicians to synthesize the product of the composer' (*The Great Conductors*
(New York, 1967), 23–4).

[6] O. Strunk (ed.), *Source Readings in Music History: From Classical Antiquity
through the Romantic Era* (New York, 1950), 85.

even more so that of the performer, remains surprisingly undertheorized.[7] I take this recent lack of attention to result from three characteristics of formalism: the denial of 'the social' implied by its content-orientated understanding of autonomy; its favouring of the work category over that of performance; and its propensity to see instrumental music as the only music that can be purely musical.

My major purpose is motivated by my interest in methodology and especially by a desire to present classical music as what I shall somewhat rhetorically call *an imperfect practice*. 'Imperfection' symbolizes now not only the negative motivation behind aspirations towards human betterment. It also symbolizes the positive quality of critical conflict within a practice that sustains the kind of humanness that depends precisely on a lack of perfection. Playing with both meanings, I shall argue that it has been the imperfect character of the practice of classical music that has allowed the practice to sustain at least these two genuinely conflicting conceptions of performance perfection. Motivating this argument is the thought that practices (musical, philosophical, or political) are desirably open when they are imperfect, and imperfect when they are critical, critical in the sense that practices survive their self-deceptive but necessary assertions of perfection by allowing strategies of conflict, criticism, and resistance constantly to keep them in check. The critical dimension arises, in other words, from the presence in a practice of competing conceptions that halt the absolutist pretensions of any single one.

To sustain the argument I shall highlight once again the transcendental strain that has consistently accompanied the formalist aesthetic. My general point is that the formalist aesthetic could never

[7] Cf. Hilde Hein, 'Performance as an Aesthetic Category', *Journal of Aesthetics and Art Criticism*, 28 (1970), 381–6, Paul Thom, *For an Audience: A Philosophy of the Performing Arts* (Philadelphia, 1993), and Henry Kingsbury, *Music, Talent, and Performance: A Conservatory Cultural System* (Philadelphia, 1988). Recent literature on the public concert is plentiful, as is that on performance art, but little from those literatures has been employed in philosophical ruminations about the performers' contribution to music. Thom's and Kingsbury's books partially remedy this situation, as does the recent special issue edited by Patrick Maynard, *Perspectives on the Arts and Technology, Journal of Aesthetics and Art Criticism*, 55/2 (1987). Of broader scope in recent musicology is Leppert, *The Sight of Sound*, which attends explicitly to how the intellectualization of music has removed music's meaning away from the practice of performance, R. Taruskin, *Text and Act: Essays on Music and Performance* (Oxford, 1995), and Jonathan Dunsby, *Performing Music: Shared Concerns* (Oxford, 1995).

have survived without its transcendental counter-strain, for much the same reasons that the literal concept of the purely musical could not have survived in genuine severance from the residue of the extramusical it tried to throw away, or for the same reasons that our interest in music's content was sustained by an interest in expression, or, finally, for the same reasons that the freedom of the purely musical was continually forced back into the domain of the human.

Thus far, in relation to each doubleness, I have described the element being returned as metaphysically concealed, transcendent, inexpressible, or unknowable. I have done this to support a philosophical technique that helps protect those elements from the academic and cultural dangers of either over-determination or reduction to their rejecting counterparts. Further, to counter the thought that transcendental concealment leaves what matters shrouded in mystery, I have deliberately stressed in this technique its ability to account for a practice in a way that honours the primacy of that practice. To honour that primacy is to allow the practice to maintain its freedom, in the best sense of allowing musicians to shape theory with their exemplary and expressive acts of composition, performance, and criticism. The technique is designed to hinder both philosophers and musicians from seeking the false security of a philosophical theory that fails to respect its own limits. This is a theory that closes the practice through over-determination.

2. Towards Two Modes of Evaluation

'Temporibus nostris super omnes homines fatui sunt cantores—in our time the silliest of all men are the singers.' So observed Guido d'Arrezzo in the eleventh century and so began Paul Hindemith in his chapter entitled 'Performers' 900 years later.[8] Hindemith's purpose, though it was not Guido's,[9] was to remind his readers of the unending history of derision and abuse to which performers, be they singers or instrumentalists, have been subject. Who has

---

[8] *A Composer's World: Horizons and Limitations* (Cambridge, Mass., 1969), 149.

[9] Guido explains his judgement from his *Prologus antiphonarii sui* (c.1025): 'For in any art those things which we know of ourselves are much more numerous than those which we learn from a master' (Strunk (ed.), *Source Readings in Music History*, 117). Guido developed a musical notation in part to allow singers to reduce their dependency on their masters.

criticized performers so strongly? Everyone: composers and listeners, theorists and teachers, concert impresarios and opera producers.

Hindemith identifies several historical criticisms: performers lack skill, but are overly confident none the less; they are often ignorant, manifest unappealing personality traits, and tend to maintain dubious social connections. Sometimes the criticisms are charitably explained, other times not. Compare the sober observation that performers are so devoted to the means of performance that they are 'unable to participate in any profound knowledge of music',[10] with the exasperated criticism that '[t]here are singers who have neither talent nor knowledge, but only vanity. This makes them audacious . . . singing more loudly and more brutally than the jackass, producing the most terrible cacophonies, and with their false phrasing they turn music into barbarism.'[11]

Of course Hindemith recognizes that accompanying this history of degradation has also been a history of praise extolling performers to the highest degree. Quoting Coclico, he refers his readers to those sixteenth-century singers who surpassed their contemporaries because they 'know the rules of art, which they learned from composers'. He continues: 'We may even count them among the composers, in that they improvise free counterpoints over given chorale melodies. The knowledge of all musical means of expression and possibilities of effects enable them to delight and enrapture men with their well-sounding, sweet, and solemn execution.'[12]

Hindemith draws the obvious conclusion. There are two extremes: 'For some critics [the performer] is nothing but the low grade medium of transmitting music, a contrivance to produce tones. . . . For others he is the almost superhuman being who, with the wings of his divine talent, carries us into heavenly regions.'[13] He employs this history to highlight what he calls the 'essential tragedy in the performer's existence'.[14] Yet his attempt to redeem their standing is reluctant: '[o]nce we accept the performer

---

[10] *A Composer's World*, 150. Hindemith is summarizing Boethius' view here that performers 'are separated from the intellect of musical science, since they are servants . . . nor do they bear anything of reason, being wholly destitute of speculation' (ibid. 86).
[11] *A Composer's World*. Hindemith is quoting Arnulf of San Gilleno of the 14th century.
[12] *A Composer's World*, 152.
[13] *A Composer's World*.   [14] *A Composer's World*, 168.

as an inevitable necessity in spite of his basic dubiousness, we may as well try to determine what properties make him estimable.'[15] My purpose is not to investigate Hindemith's surprisingly reluctant attitude towards performers (he was a devoted performer himself). It is only to provide more nuances to what he correctly identifies as a double-sided assessment of performers and their art.

As he recognizes, performer assessment has always reflected the changes taking place in the rankings and functions of musicians. However, no change was more decisive than that which occurred at the end of the eighteenth century. There were many transformations that took place in our understanding of music at that time,[16] transformations that affected every dimension of the musical world. Out of those transformations emerged new modes of performance assessment appropriate to a new conception of performance. This conception assumed its modern form as a result of a reconfiguring of conceptual borders. The pre-modern, fluid and continuous relation between compositional and performance activities was conceptually transformed into a more rigid distinction between them.

Traditionally, one of the principal modes of evaluation concentrated on the knowing–doing distinction: were performers mere practitioners, or composers and theorists in addition? Did they have merely skill, or understanding as well? Evaluation took place in a practice where performers either merely 'embellished' over a pre-given figured bass or, through 'improvisation', also composed as they performed. Mere embellishers tended to be lowly regarded as doers who understand not what they do; genuine improvisers were regarded more highly as both knowers and doers. Especially striking was the concern that performers endeavour to be 'musicians' in the fullest and most traditional sense: knowledgeable first in 'high' matters philosophical and second in 'mundane' matters technical. Such a concern fitted a practice that permitted continuity rather than rigid separation between its theoretical and practical, and its creative and reproductive, roles—hence, the common use of the term 'musician' to cover persons who theorized, composed, and/or performed. Recall the early craft conception of the mastersingers' art.

[15] *A Composer's world*, 154.
[16] See my *The Imaginary Museum of Musical Works* for a description of many of these transformations.

Continuity between roles was possible in part because early performance practice was conditioned by the expectation that musicians would bring to fruition a fully shaped composition through performance. Walter Wiora calls this practice *Ausführungspraxis* to distinguish it from the modern category of *Aufführungspraxis*.

Die Ausführungen do not correspond to the composition itself the way copies of a picture correspond to its original. The difference is particularly telling when—as was done in earlier times—one not only followed the prescription of the score but also followed another meaning of the term 'ausführen' by trying to give shape to the composition. This included the realization of the *basso continuo* and the embellishment of unadorned melodies.[17]

Aufführungspraxis, by contrast, is conditioned by the expectation that compositions be fully composed prior to performance, an expectation that releases performers from the obligation—indeed it forbids them—either to embellish or improvise, i.e. creatively to compose the music in performance. In this *Werktreue* practice performers are obligated to comply as perfectly as they can with the composers' fully notated scores and to interpret faithfully the works they perform.

Like performer function, performer evaluation shifted from being contingent upon composer–performer continuity to being contingent upon their separation. Of course, there would continue to be performers who composed and composers who performed, but, evaluatively as conceptually, composers would be held responsible for creating music, performers for its sounding out. Liszt is widely canonized, despite his also being a composer, as the first *modern* performer.

With their responsibilities so defined, composers and performers were each conceptually released also from the responsibilities of pure or mere theorists—philosophers, analysts, and critics. Future references to musicianship, and the knowledge associated therewith, would be constrained by a new degree of awareness of tasks appropriate to each musician type. Judgements sensitive to the new categories naturally helped legitimize them. But nothing prevented judgements of a comparative sort from also being made by and against those who now just 'did', now just 'created', or who now just 'thought' and 'criticized'.

---

[17] *Das Musikalische Kunstwerk* (Tützing, 1983), 40; my translation.

How have performers fared in this new arena of evaluation? Since about 1800 performer evaluation has been organized around two different modes. In one, performers are judged either as necessary evils or as the great interpreters of musical masterpieces. In the other, they are judged either as 'circus performers' or the 'devil's servants' or as inspired enchanters magically and mythically expressing the passions of the human soul through the transcendental musical language. In neither mode, though for different reasons, has the one judgement automatically precluded the other. What rationale lies behind these two familiar modes? To answer this question I shall now describe the two conceptions or ideals of perfection that together have sustained the performance of works as an emancipated category of modern musical conduct. One purpose in juxtaposing these two conceptions is to show, as I showed in the previous chapter, that behind the modern theorizing of our categories of music, work, and performance lurks the shadow of their pre-modern fluidity and fullness.

3. The Perfect Performance of Music

The performance conception referred to by the phrase 'the perfect performance of music' is most closely bound up with the solemn, sacred, serious, and sublime aesthetic[18] of the concert hall and with the *Werktreue* ideal central to the development of music as a fine art. It functions most clearly within the elite and autonomous aesthetic governing the symphonic tradition inaugurated by Beethoven, and idealized thereafter by 'the Beethoven cult'. It functions in its purest form within concerts of purely instrumental music. Its content is predominantly formalist, but the formalism is enhanced by a strong commitment to principles of transcendence.

The first step in comprehending the perfect performance of music is to regard music as a purely sonorous art. 'The sonorous element in music', wrote formalist Robert Zimmermann in 1865, '[is] the ultimate consideration.' Unlike poetry, in which the sonorous element 'has only a validity subordinate to thought', in

---

[18] This alliterative description is adapted from the 1910 *Technical Manifesto of Futurist Painting*, quoted in R. Goldberg, 'Performance: A Hidden History', in G. Battcock and R. Nickas (eds.), *The Art of Performance: A Critical Anthology* (New York, 1984), 29.

music the same element claims 'independent validity'.[19] Musical concerts are correspondingly conceived in their essence as purely sonorous events, 'pure' not in the sense that all essential qualities have literally to be sounded out, but in the sense that all such qualities have either to constitute or to derive from the sonorous material.

The perfect performance of music takes the *of* seriously. The perfect performance of music is the perfect performance of a work. Under a neutral, ontological description, works and performances are co-dependent. Works are made accessible to audiences via mediating performances; performances are necessarily performances of works. Under aesthetic evaluation, this neutrality is overwhelmed. At one extreme, performances are deemed subservient in purpose to the work, subordinate in value to the work, and derivative in nature of the work. At the other extreme, performers are judged the great interpreters of works that are created just to give them the opportunity to show their interpretative skills. Historically, however, the tilting towards each extreme has been neither equal nor balanced. First, the tilt has mostly favoured works; secondly, when the tilt has favoured performances or performers, the result has not been simply to favour performances over works, but to try to meet both extremes simultaneously. I shall describe each situation in turn.

3.1. *In Favour of Works*

One prominent thesis determines that most, if not all, value should be placed in the permanently existing works and not in their transitory and fleeting performances. 'The secret of perfection', Stravinsky once wrote, 'lies above all in [the interpreter's] consciousness of the law imposed upon him by the work he is performing.'[20] That value is placed more in what lasts than in ephemeral phenomena is not an unfamiliar claim in music's history, but in the nineteenth century it assumes an unreservedly (ontological) Platonic profile.

Accordingly, performances *qua* copies of works are regarded as necessarily imperfect. For performances to be perfect they would have to reach the condition of the work itself. But this is

---

[19] *Allgemeine Aesthetik als Formwissenschaft*, excerpted in Bujić (ed.), *Music in European Thought*, 46.
[20] *The Poetics of Music in the Form of Six Lessons* (Cambridge, Mass., 1942), 127.

ontologically impossible: works last, performances do not, and even if they did—say, in recordings—they would still only ever be perspectival representations of the perfect work. Thus, speaking about the perfect performance of music is oxymoronic unless one intends to capture an ideal of the practice that performers strive, but of necessity fail, to meet.

This necessary failure captures what Hindemith called the performer's 'essential tragedy', and what Stravinsky referred to as 'the great principle of submission'.[21] For from the recognition of a performance's necessary imperfection emerges a demand—for Stravinsky it was a 'moral responsibility'—that the best performance be one that most successfully negates its own presence. The demand here is for performance *transparency*: performances should be like windows through which audiences directly perceive works. Sometimes the demand is also for performer *invisibility*. 'The visual effect of the performance', wrote Zimmermann, 'does not belong to the work's essence. . . . It is for this reason that orchestral musicians rightly appear in the simplest clothes; it would be best if they were not visible at all.'[22]

Zimmerman's desire finds an interesting precedent in Goethe. Recall Goethe's observation attributed to Natalie's Uncle in *Wilhelm Meister's Apprenticeship*, his words being recalled by Natalie as she walks with Wilhelm around the 'Hall of the Past':

We have been spoilt too much by theaters, where music only serves the eye, accompanying movements, not feelings. In oratorios and concerts the physical presence of the singer is disturbing. . . . A lovely voice is the most universal thing . . . and if the limited individual producing it is visible, this disturbs the effect of universality. . . . [W]hen someone is singing he should be invisible, his appearance should not prejudice me.

Natalie continues on her Uncle's behalf: '[My uncle] also wanted players in an orchestra concealed as much as possible, because one

---

[21] Cf. Robert Hill's comments on 'the bliss of denial' in his 'Overcoming Romanticism: On the Modernization of Twentieth Century Performance Practice', in Bryan Gilliam (ed.), *Music and Performance during the Weimar Republic* (Cambridge, 1994), 44. Hill contrasts Romantic and Modernist performance practices in a way similar to my own. He identifies what I am calling the perfect performance of music with a Modernist, fidelity conception and the perfect musical performance with a Romantic, virtuoso conception. But whereas he sees his contrast as chronologically sequenced, I see mine as contemporaneous.

[22] Bujić (ed.), *Music in European Thought*, 49.

is only distracted and disturbed by the laborings and necessary strange gestures of musicians.'[23]

The ideal of invisibility embodies two demands, the second more severe than the first. The first asks that, given music's purely sonorous nature, the visual dimensions of a performance be disregarded by the audience as inessential or as necessary evils. Performers and audiences should separate from the total performance event the essential 'aural image' of the work. What is musical about a performance consists entirely in what is heard. Nietzsche once described this abstraction in terms of the gradual release of dependency of the ear from the eye:

As soon as men understood each other in gesture, a *symbolism* of gesture could evolve. I mean, one could agree on a language of tonal signs, in such a way that at first both tone and gesture (which were joined by tone symbolically) were produced, and later only the tone. It seems that in earlier times, something must often have occurred much like what is now going on before our ears and eyes in the development of music; namely of dramatic music: while music without explanatory dance and miming (language of gesture) is at first empty noise, long habituation to that juxtaposition of music and gesture teaches the ear an immediate understanding of the tonal figures. Finally, the ear reaches a level of rapid understanding such that it no longer requires visible movement, and *understands* the composer without it. Then we are talking about absolute music, that is, music in which everything can be understood symbolically, without further aids.[24]

The second demand for invisibility is related to the first. It reminds us that what is actually heard in the concrete soundings out of the works is far less valuable than the transcendent meaning of the works the soundings are supposed to convey. Performers should attempt, therefore, to create the illusion that the work is being conveyed immediately to the audience by undermining their own presence as necessarily flawed mediators.[25]

[23] *Wilhelm Meister's Apprenticeship*, ed. and tr. E. A. Blackall (New York, 1989), 332–3.

[24] *Human, all too Human: A Book for Free Spirits*, tr. M. Faber and S. Lehmann (Lincoln, Nebr., 1986), sect. 216. Supporting the abstractive process, Hanslick once drew a distinction between instrumentalists performing in a musical, as opposed to a declamatory, manner. He clearly approved more of the former than the latter.

[25] Cf. Hein: 'It would follow from this [*Werktreue*] view that the ideal performer should be a transparent medium. He imparts information while conveying a minimum of noise; yet, where necessary he alters the original content just sufficiently to

The aesthetic of sonorous transcendence offers the following rhetorical prescriptions: Divine composers should be neither seen nor heard, to underscore the mystery both of absence and of genius. Performers and their instruments should be heard but not seen, but 'heard' only as imperfect pointers towards the transcendent. And audiences, to complete the triad, should be seen but not heard, but 'seen' only in the sense of each listener being present to grasp the work in the privacy of his or her own contemplative experience. A traditional impetus lies behind these familiar aesthetic strictures: the more civilized the event, the 'higher' or 'finer' the condition, the less the appearance should be of ordinary, everyday behaviour and ordinary, everyday tools.

These strictures are fully evident in the history of performance. Recall E. T. A. Hoffmann's often quoted decree that performers should 'not make their personalities count in any way',[26] or Busoni's observation that since musical performance 'derives from those free heights from which music itself descended', then whenever the music is 'threatened by earthliness, the performance must elevate it and re-endow it with its original *ethereal* quality'.[27] Consider also Hindemith's recommendation that performers should never try to express their own feelings, as well as his instruction (inspired by the possibilities of technology) in his *Kammermusik*, no. 1, opus 24/1, 'die Vortragenden dem Publikum unsichtbar zu placieren'.[28] Or consider composers who have used computers or other compositional techniques to eliminate as far as possible the mediation of performers altogether. 'It is now possible for composers to make music directly,' announced John Cage in

make it comprehensible to its audience without deviating from its essential character. He is the bridge between artist and public or, better, a system of locks, designed to transmit the vessel of art from one level to another' ('Performance as an Aesthetic Category', 383).

[26] 'Beethovens Instrumentalmusik', in *Musikalische Novellen und Aufsätze*, i, ed. E. Istel (Regensburg, 1919), 69.

[27] 'Der Vortrag in der Musik stammt aus jenen freien Höhen, aus welchen die Tonkunst selbst herabstieg. Wo ihr droht, irdisch zu werden, hat er sie zu heben und ihr zu ihrem ursprünglichen *schwebenden* Zustand zu verhelfen' (*Entwurf einer neuen Ästhetik der Tonkunst* (Frankfurt, 1974), 26). My translation is partially taken from C. Debussy, F. Busoni, and C. Ives, *Three Classics in the Aesthetic of Music* (New York, 1962), 84.

[28] I am grateful to Stephen Hinton for providing me with this example and for telling me also of the provocative nature of Hindemith's instruction designed 'épater le bourgeois'.

1937, 'without the assistance of intermediary performers.'[29] One wonders, however, whether in any of these attempts to subvert the presence of performers, the intention has ever really been to disconnect 'the musical' from 'the human'.

3.2. In Favour of Performances

Performers would be unlikely to survive as an enthusiastic group of participants in the musical world if they completely concurred with the demand for transparency, invisibility, or personality negation. However accepting of their mediating role between composer and audience, performers usually aspire to be regarded as more than means. Rose Rosengard Subotnik correctly observes that the post-Kantian politics of individualism clashed with the attempt to embody the ideal of *Werktreue* by turning performers into automatons.[30] But how have performers tried to reconcile their desire to be treated as both means and ends?

One way has been for performers constantly to remind composers and critics that their activity of interpreting music indispensably mediates the activities of composition and reception. Composers and critics have always agreed. 'Interpretation', wrote Schoenberg, 'is necessary, to bridge the gap between the author's idea and the contemporary ear.'[31] A piece of music is 'strictly speaking, nothing but a recipe', wrote Paul Valéry; 'the cook who executes it plays an essential role'.[32] Extending the analogy, we might say that each performance does something different with the fixed recipe that is the work, and that it is the unique difference or execution in each performance that makes all the aesthetic difference. However, attending to the importance of performing has not resulted in granting to performers a complete freedom; it has only underscored instead the complexity of their interpretative activity within the strict confines of the *Werktreue* ideal. The resulting position for performers has been strained as they have tried to reconcile their belief that the perfect performance of music is the product both of

---

[29] 'The Future of Music: Credo', in *Silence: Lectures and Writings* (Middletown, Conn., 1939), 4.

[30] 'Individualism in Western Art Music and its Cultural Costs', in *Developing Variations: Style and Ideology in Western Music* (Minneapolis, 1991), 256.

[31] 'Mechanical Musical Instruments', in *Style and Idea*, 328.

[32] 'A Discourse on the Declamation of Verse', in *Selected Writings of Paul Valéry*, tr. M. Cowley (New York, 1950), 155.

a *free* interpretation and of an *unfree* rendition in full compliance with the composer's commands. Stravinsky recognized the problem:

The idea of interpretation implies the limitations imposed upon the performer or those which the performer imposes upon himself in his proper function which is to transmit music to the listener.

The idea of execution implies the strict putting into effect of an explicit will that contains nothing beyond what it specifically commands.

It is the conflict of these two principles—execution and interpretation—that is at the root of all the errors, all the sins, all the misunderstandings that interpose themselves between the musical work and the listener.[33]

In his book *Form and Performance*, Schoenberg's student Erwin Stein shows how close the interaction between rendition and interpretation must be if the performer is faithfully to perform the work. Stein believes that expression and interpretation, like rendition, flow directly out of an understanding of a work's form or structure. 'Many performers would have the necessary musicality and skill if they understood the implications of musical structure.'[34] Stein takes seriously the etymology of the term 'perlformlance': a performance is the stylistic completion or accomplishment of the work in due form.

Stein's understanding of performance is widely shared. Musicality in performance emerges from a thorough understanding of the work. Where, perhaps, performers tend to depart from Stein is in the greater emphasis they want to give to their conviction that their performance requires something more. Certainly, correct rendition and faithful interpretation depend upon knowledge of the work, but performance is more than a demonstration of this knowledge; it is also an *act* of musicianship. As one singer says: 'The moment of truth is the doing.' In the actual doing, the intellectual work comes to an end and the instinct takes over. 'Fidelity . . . is elemental,' comments Daniel Barenboim, 'but you cannot stop there.'[35] Stein concedes the point: 'When all has been said and done,' he writes, 'the truth remains that musical performance is less a matter of historical faithfulness, than of artistic sincerity.'[36] In these appeals

---

[33] *The Poetics of Music in the Form of Six Lessons*, 122.

[34] (New York, 1962), 20.

[35] From Robert Jacobson, *Reverberations: Interviews with the World's Leading Musicians* (New York, 1974), 17.

[36] *Form and Performance*, 11.

to musical instinct, to artistic sincerity, performers begin to find their satisfaction within the confines of the *Werktreue* ideal.

These appeals are found most often in discussions of 'technique and style'. Constrained as both are by a composer's commands, their understanding is closely linked to matters of interpretation and rendition. In this regard, they tell us something about the relationship of performance to work. They also tell us something about performance itself.

Technique and style are related not simply by conjunction, but, as we saw in the last chapter, more closely, as two sides of a coin. Performers generally say that there is no adequate employment of style without a mastery of technique and no adequate use of technique without a feeling for style. But where does technique end and style begin? How does one confine the other or help secure its satisfactory expression? Barenboim offers a typical answer:

You cannot divide technique and making music. It doesn't work like that because you should know where one ends and another begins. If I play a passage loudly or softly, it is both a technical *and* a musical problem. When you have musical demands made in the music, then your technique comes into use to carry it out. For most people, a great technique means fast fingers—but a good technique means doing what you must do musically in terms of dynamics, touch and so on—musicianship, in a word.[37]

But what is musicianship? Philosopher Francis Sparshott thinks the question cannot be fully answered:

The question has scarcely been asked, although few terms play more important roles in our critical chitchat. . . . The ancient contrast between learned and practical music is one thing that has distracted attention from the concept. One can at least say that a performer shows musicianship by displaying a grasp of musical meanings, both structural and affective, rather than just following the score from point to point. . . . [But can one] specify further? Presumably not [because] one is speaking rather of the *level* of understanding shown than of any specifiable matter to be understood.[38]

Sparshott's awareness of our having reached the limits of description has a strong precedent. Whereas technique has traditionally been described in the language of rules and form, style has not received so systematic a description. Nor could it, because, as

---

[37] *Reverberations*, 17.
[38] 'Aesthetics of Music: Limits and Grounds', in P. Alperson (ed.), *What is Music? An Introduction to the Philosophy of Music* (New York, 1987), 84.

Berlioz put it so explicitly on one occasion, style captures that part of music that is 'sentiment' not 'science'.[39] Other musicians have expressed the same point differently: learning rules or teaching technique is straightforward, but learning how to be an intelligent musician or teaching a performer to play with style requires something more. Again, what is this elusive *more*? To be sure, it requires instinct and inspiration, but, with more specificity, it also requires an understanding of how technique and style together fill what we might usefully call the 'performance space' that remains once the work has been left behind. This was the 'extra' space Beckmesser so obviously failed to fill.

One way performers have captured the elusive 'more' of their musicianship is by appeal to the illusion that they are actually creating the music. 'The greatest thing for [performers]', comments Janet Baker, 'is to make a phrase sound like you never heard it before.'[40] '[W]hen you are onstage playing,' remarks pianist Gary Graffman, 'you should sound as if you are composing the music.' Of course the illusion of creativity has to be just that, an illusion, because *Werktreue* performers do not strictly speaking create. 'So it is crucial', Graffman adds, that performers 'begin with the music first'.[41]

But performers have then moved on to describe their performance space as an occasion for the theatrical expression of spontaneity, immediacy, and freedom, of feeling and breathing, of conviction and commitment. It is the space in which they bring the works out of the abstract and dead museum and infuse them with dramatic vitality. It is a space in which the sameness of the work and the difference of the particular performance compete in an exciting tension. It is a space in which tradition and culture inform the act of performance, and a space, finally, in which a unique acoustical environment is created. With assertions like these, performers have then felt confident about drawing this conclusion also, that their full visible presence, in all its dramatic intensity and glory, is required. 'It [is] not enough to hear music,' once declared Stravinsky 'it must also be seen.'[42]

[39] Cf. *À travers chants* (Paris, 1862); excerpted in P. Weiss and R. Taruskin (eds.), *Music in the Western World: A History in Documents* (New York, 1984), 349. Recall, also Oscar Wilde's comment (p. 41 above).

[40] *Reverberations*, 11.
[41] Ibid. 76–7.   [42] *The Poetics of Music*, 128.

However, despite the plethora of assertions of this sort, the performer's space has been more suggested than systematically investigated within the aesthetic dominated by the *Werktreue* ideal. But the suggestiveness has not been employed arbitrarily, because lurking in the background has been another conception of performance altogether.

4. The Perfect Musical Performance

The conception of a perfect musical performance is broader than that of the perfect performance of music. It attends to the general, although elusive, dimension of musicianship inherent in a performance *whether or not* the performance is a performance of a work. It restores to the more literal or formal concept of music as the art of tone its extramusical significance. It does this by modifying the tendency merely to engage, as T. E. Hulme once put it, in metaphors of flight that transport music into the spheres of 'circumambient gas', with the demand that musical performance be treated as a profoundly social activity. Rejecting Humboldt's widely shared dictum that the arts move us from the world of reality to the world of ideas, the perfect musical performance celebrates the so-called 'lower' actions of the human, the ephemeral, and the active as *the route by which* musicians express the 'higher' aspirations of 'the purely human spirit'. The emphasis on the aspiring human resists the temptation to see transcendence as separated from the world; it sees it, rather, as a dimension immanent within it. It also resists the temptation to think of performers mechanistically as 'automatons' or 'transformer stations'. The principal idea in this conception is that it is 'all-too-human' performing beings who aspire to achieve the sublime heights of musical perfection. Their performing acts are exemplary of their aspirations.

Despite the human emphasis in the conception, the perfect musical performance does not bring the meaning and function of performance completely down to earth, where 'down to earth' suggests a reduction to the mundane. Rather, it strives to make the mundane unmundane, or the 'human' more 'Human'. So, as with the perfect performance of music, the perfect musical performance uses operations of transformation, transfiguration, abstraction, and transcendence. In both cases, the operations derive from the same ground. It is a ground constituted by an aesthetic theory that emerged out of early secular and sacred traditions of theatre, drama, ritual, and spectacle, adapted to music's modern emancipated concerns. However, despite the common ground, the operations still sustain conflicting conceptions of performance.

The perfect musical performance suitably adapts an age-old purpose of secular and sacred drama, to transform and transport the audience through transfiguration, or, in other alliterative terms, to elevate and educate through entertainment. It adapts from these traditions the idea of theatrical transfiguration in which meanings are stripped of their habitual or 'taken-for-granted' associations and invested by performers with traits of the symbolic, metaphorical, mythical, and *extra*ordinary.[43] It also carries over from these traditions both their more and less elite, social and participatory aims.

Coleridge once defined theatre as an 'amusement thro' the ear or eye in which men assemble in order to be amused by some entertainment presented to all at the same time'.[44] The 'all at the same time' principle is perhaps subverted when the aesthetic principle dictates a silent and lonely contemplation in a darkened concert hall of an ideally purely audible event. But it is not subverted when the aesthetic regards the total event of performance as a 'socialized activity', to use Leppert's recent phrase,[45] or as 'a musical occasion' that, as Edward Said has recently written, is 'always located in a uniquely endowed site, and what occurs then and there is part of the cultural life of modern society'.[46] The stress given here to the social and cultural dimensions of performance accentuates the extent to which communicative 'circuits'[47] are generated between composers, performers, and listeners in their active and collective engagement with the music.

---

[43] For more on this transfigurative process, see R. Schechner and W. Appel (eds.), *By Means of Performance: Intercultural Studies of Theatre and Ritual* (Cambridge, 1990).

[44] Quoted by Keir Elan in 'Much Ado about Doing Things with Words (and Other Means): Some Problems in the Pragmatics of Theatre and Drama', in M. Issacharoff and R. F. Jones (eds.), *Performing Texts* (Philadelphia, 1988), 55.

[45] 'When people hear a musical performance, they see it as an embodied activity. . . . the musical event is perceived as a socialized activity' (*The Sight of Sound*, p. xxii).

[46] *Musical Elaborations* (London, 1991), p. xv.

[47] The term 'circuit' is employed by J. L. Styan in his 'The Mystery of the Play Experience: Quince's Questions', in Issacharoff and Jones (eds.), *Performing Texts*, 25.

The perfect musical performance places its emphasis more upon the actions involved in the total context of the performance than upon the mediating language conceived in isolation from this context. Transfiguration or revelation is rooted in the participatory act of interpreting the message or 'the work itself' in one's capacity of either performer or listener. Transferring a notion from the great teacher of the theatre Stanislavsky, the condition to be achieved by both performer and listener is a 'creative state of mind', a condition that is achieved through the training of mental attitude and, in the performer's case, of bodily gesture and gait, breathing and muscular movement. In the perfect musical performance, value resides in the creative acts of individuals who give meaning to music in each moment of their act of performing or engagement with music.

But the 'creative state' implicit within the perfect musical performance does not necessarily involve acting as one would take on a role in a play (though soon we shall see circumstances in which it does). The uncoupling of performing and acting is as much historical as conceptual. It enabled the perfect musical performance to serve as a specifically musical conception for the performance of instrumental music, despite its broader roots in theatre. The uncoupling, as I suggested earlier, occurred through a process of abstraction and negation. Just as instrumental musical language shed itself of its occasional and representational content, the act of performance underwent a process of abstraction and developed into something like an empty play—a play without content. Performers played out movements on the stage recalling those of traditional theatre, but the meaning of those movements became purely formal, gestural, or specifically musical. Stravinsky captured a significant part of the idea when he described the instrumentalist as 'an orator who speaks an unarticulated language'.[48] But it is not only the performer who speaks an unarticulated language; it is the performance, too, that becomes an unarticulated or dematerialized act, an act that generates the appearance of the musician's inexpressible musicality.

To describe the perfect musical performance in this way is intended to give stress to its specifically musical character, but it is not intended thereby to exclude the emphasis that this conception

---

[48] *Poetics of Music*, 128.

also gives to dramatic or visual spectacle. Nor could it, because during the nineteenth century the perfect musical performance became identified as much with popular forms of performance as with more elite ones. So widely identified, it resisted the dominating *Werktreue* ideal and catered to the broader demands of different kinds of audience in different kinds of social setting.[49]

The two traditions exemplifying the conception of the perfect musical performance are those of the virtuoso or instrumental soloist and of opera. I shall treat each briefly in turn, although they share much in common. Henry Raynor once described the commonality when he wrote that '[t]he virtuoso introduced a new element into instrumental performance. He won a new audience through his mastery of showmanship, transferring to the concert hall from the opera house the element of danger and physical excitement.'[50] However, the commonality runs deeper than this.

4.1. Virtuoso Performance and Visual Spectacle

Within the virtuoso tradition, performers such as Liszt, Chopin, and Paganini were regarded as incarnations of either God or the Devil, as inspired performers or as circus actors. Debussy once straddled the contrast:

The attraction of the virtuoso for the public is very like that of the circus for the crowd. There is always a hope that something dangerous may happen: Mr. X may play the violin with Mr. Y on his shoulders; or Mr. Z may conclude his piece by lifting the piano with his teeth. [But when] X plays Bach's violin concerto ... he has that freedom of expression, that unaffected beauty of tone, which are essential for its interpretation.[51]

Two questions typically shaped the assessment of the virtuoso: did the open display of Romantic inspiration through physical pyrotechnics enamour or horrify the audience, and did the virtuosi's overly physical and visual spectacle on the stage undermine their

---

[49] Cf. Eric Gans's observation that '[t]he high/low cultural distinction ... is not founded on the sociological opposition between mass and elite, but on that between individuality and participation' ('Art and Entertainment', in John Rahn (ed.), *Perspectives on Musical Aesthetics* (New York, 1994), 51–2).

[50] *Music and Society since 1815*, 66.

[51] *Three Classics in the Aesthetic of Music*, 22.

integrity as musicians? All the expected positive and negative answers were given.

Mulling over these dubious questions at least gave the critics the opportunity to recognize the virtuosi's dependence upon *live* performance. Accentuated first in live performance is the one-off, non-repeatable unfolding of time. It is a condition that sustains in the performance the qualities of immediacy, spontaneity, and uniqueness, and in the attending audience the qualities of fear, expectation, and excitement. Adorno once employed Beckett's notion of 'je vais continuer' to capture the sense in which music is 'as irreversible as time itself' and bound to the 'fact of succession'. 'By starting', the musical performance 'commits itself to carrying on, to becoming something new, to developing'.[52]

Developing through musical time, in its transitory and fleeting expression, music aspires towards its transcendence and freedom. Romantic theorists comparably understood temporality to sustain the possibility of music's creative and free spontaneity and its transcendental immediacy. Much more so than the formalist *Werktreue* ideal, the virtuoso ideal stressed improvisatory ideals of instrumental music-making, ideals conceived in terms of the 'endless melody pointing towards the infinite'. Liszt once wrote:

As instrumental music progresses, develops, and frees itself from its original bonds, it tends to become stamped more and more with that identity which marks perfection in the plastic arts, to become not just a simple combination of sounds but a poetic language more apt than poetry itself perhaps to express everything inside us that passes beyond the usual horizons, everything that defies analysis, everything that is connected to inaccessible depths of imperishable desires and infinite presentiments.[53]

The emphasis on progression (or aesthetic reaching, as I earlier called it) gave value to the idea that it is the fleeting performance itself rather than the work that carries musical meaning. The

---

[52] 'Stravinsky', in *Quasi una fantasia: Essays on Modern Music*, tr. R. Livingstone (London, 1992), 150–1. Said writes similarly: 'To know a piece of music . . . is always to acknowledge the ineluctable temporal modality, or one-timeness, of the audible; you cannot experience it, as you can, say, when you pause before or walk around a painting or a sculpture, without also submitting to the tyranny of its forward logic or impulse' (*Musical Elaborations*, 76).

[53] From Liszt's foreword to his *Années de Pèlerinage*, quoted in Ott, *Lisztian Keyboard Energy*, 9.

temporal performance embodies the transcendental musical drama: it sets into play the ritual of transformation through which performers communicate their message to a public. 'The demon began to flex his muscles,' Schumann wrote of Liszt in 1840:

> He first played along with [the members of the audience], as if to feel them out, and then gave them a taste of something more substantial until, with his magic, he had ensnared each and every one and could move them this way or that as he chose. It is unlikely that any artist, excepting only Paganini, has the power to lift, carry and deposit an audience in such high degree.[54]

The virtuosi's drama would not have made sense to its audience if temporality alone had constituted its essence, if the emphasis on temporality had led to the performers' visibility or presence being denied. Liszt's performance 'simply has to be heard—and seen', continued Schumann. 'If Liszt were to play behind the scenes, a considerable portion of poetry would be lost.'[55] The intriguing idea that Liszt might do so was obviously for many a worrying thought. 'We have now heard [Liszt],' wrote another critic, 'the strange wonder, whom the superstition of past ages, possessed by the delusion that such things could never be done without the help of the Evil One, would undoubtedly have condemned without mercy to the stake—we have heard him, and seen him too, which, of course, makes a part of the affair'.[56] Another critic, reviewing a Paganini concert for the London *Tatler*, chose to record his momentary dismay when a 'packed audience' threatened to hide Paganini from view, leaving the critic merely to 'hear' him. Fortunately, '[a] lucky interval between a gentleman's head and a lady's bonnet' favoured his endeavour to see 'the long, pale face of the musical marvel'.[57] It must have been the prevalence of these sorts of comments that led Paganini himself once to complain that 'no one ever asks if you have heard Paganini, but if you have seen him'.

When pressed to explain visibility's part in the musical affair, critics tended to move first to discussions of the metaphorical inner eye. As 'much as I love Liszt', Heine wrote,

---

[54] *Schumann on Music: A Selection from his Writings*, tr. and ed. H. Pleasants (New York, 1965), 157.
[55] Ibid. 158.
[56] Weiss and Taruskin (eds.), *Music in the Western World*, 363.
[57] Ibid. 343.

his music does not produce on my soul pleasant impressions, the more so because I am also a Sunday child, and see ghosts which others only hear; and, as you know, that at every chord which the hand strikes from the piano, the corresponding figure of sound (*Klangfigur*) leaps up in my spirit—in short, the music becomes visible to my inner sight.[58]

Another French reviewer of Liszt, one Saint-Rieul Dupouy, now provided Heine's inner vision with its corresponding, external image:

[Liszt's] soul leads his hands, and indeed he plays more with his heart, his intelligence, his whole being than with his fingers. At times he leans backwards and seems to be reading, in the air, music that is dreamed, or to be translating something that is sung up there in the region of harmonies. Then he leans his head over the keyboard as if to bring it to life; he grasps it bodily, struggles with it, tames it, embraces it, magnetizes it with his powerful hands. Then it is no longer a piano that you hear; it is an orchestra of a thousand voices.[59]

Decades later, Stravinsky elaborated the argument for visibility: 'Those who maintain that they only enjoy music to the full with their eyes shut do not hear better than when they have them open.' Closing one's eyes is just an excuse to attend to one's feelings while giving the appearance that one is listening to the music. Stravinsky also had a less cynical reason: the details an audience sees actually shape its understanding of performance. 'The sight of the gestures and movements of the various parts of the bodies producing the music is fundamentally necessary if [the music] is to be grasped in all its fullness. All music created . . . demands some exteriorization for the perception of the listener.'[60] In his *Poetics of Music*, he offered more detail:

What shall we say of the ill-breeding of those grimacers who too often take it upon themselves to deliver the 'inner meaning' of music by disfiguring it with their affected airs? For, I repeat, one sees music. An experienced eye follows and judges, sometimes unconsciously, the performer's least gesture. From this point of view one might conceive the process of performance as the creation of new values that call for the solution of problems similar to those which arise in the realm of choreography. In both cases we give special attention to the control of gestures.

[58] 'Letters on the French Stage', vii. 273.
[59] Quoted by Ott, *Lisztian Keyboard Energy*, 18.
[60] *An Autobiography* (New York, 1936), 72–3.

Because 'music does not move in the abstract', he concluded, '[i]ts translation into plastic terms requires exactitude and beauty'.[61]

4.1. Operatic Performance as Dramatic Deed of Music Made Visible[62]

No one would have encouraged this translation more than Wagner. What he would have recognized in it would have been his own description of the synaesthetic experience of ear and eye, as well as the synthesis that could be achieved between musical expression and dramatic deed. These were the connections he had sought in modelling his own particular conception of German opera, as he saw it, on the more broadly and ideally conceived Italian and French forms as opposed to the more narrowly 'formalist' or 'modern' forms of his immediate 'German' predecessors.

Using my terms, Wagner worked out his conception of the perfect musical performance within his vision of Bayreuth. He worked it out in antagonistic contradistinction to that of the perfect performance of music. He suggested that if the ideal of *Werktreue* is to avoid formalistic emptiness and serve its combined political and aesthetic function, it would have to function in tandem with an older and more fluid conception of the relationship between work and performance. He wondered, in other words, whether one could not give a perfect musical performance at the same time that one was giving a perfect performance of a work.

Wagner offered a complex list of instructions for Bayreuth, some of which seemingly had more theoretical plausibility than they did practical. Despite the dominant conception of work as end and performance as means, he instructed that a performance also be conceived as an end, i.e. as the completion of the work's deed. At the completion of the performance event, the dramatic space could be destroyed. Bayreuth, Wagner once announced, should be erected only as a temporary 'festival' structure. But what did he mean by 'temporary'? Reading as much meaning as we can into this term, more perhaps than Wagner put there, we come to see something more than a grand or 'insane' gesture.[63] We come,

---

[61] *Poetics of Music*, 128.

[62] Adapted from Wagner's definition of opera as 'deeds of music brought to sight (*ersichtlich gewordene Thaten der Musik*)', from a letter on 'The name "Musikdrama"', v. 303.

[63] For discussion of the 'insanity' of Wagner's instruction, see Manfred Eger, 'The Bayreuth Festival and the Wagner Family', in Müller and Wapnewski (eds.), *Wagner Handbook*, 487.

rather, to see something intriguing in the claim that the dramatic deed of a performance accounts for both its expression and its completion. The explanation is somewhat circuitous.

Wagner intended to transform the traditional prosaic theatre into a sacred and monumental dramatic site for the musical expression of 'the purely human'.[64] He sought the appropriate conditions of presence, absence, visibility, and invisibility that would allow the outer, plastic, and expressive face of a performance in each of its three—audible, visual, and verbal—dimensions to show its inner, natural, and inexpressible face. What he called the dual nature of the artistic or dramatic deed depended on aesthetic illusion and transcendental suggestion. It depended upon musicians and actor-singers creating a 'mystic gulf' between an 'imaginary stage world' and the 'ordinary' world.

He gave visual sense to this gulf by describing a space in which an almost hallowed world of hazy and dreamlike effects would be created. Within that carefully circumscribed visual world actors would act and sing in a 'wholly human' way so as to reveal their naturalness as human beings. '[B]efore all else' his dramatic characters were human beings. They were human beings before they were singers or actors, and before they assumed their superhuman or mythical forms.[65]

Wagner again invoked the paradox of artifice: every detailed instruction he gave to the actors was to be followed carefully so as to reveal *in and through* the artifice of artful performance a purely human expressiveness, naturalness, spontaneity, and transcendental ephemerality. To be true to the artifice or outer form of the performance was the means by which it could be concealed or seen through. It was not a matter of performers showing their true selves, but, through their individual selves, the potential self

---

[64] Geoffrey Skelton describes the three fundamental tenets of the Bayreuth vision as demonstrating how sacredness is invested in dramatic performance, how it elevates and ennobles the human spirit, and how it symbolizes Romantic, revolutionary ideals ('The Idea of Bayreuth', in P. Burbidge and R. Sutton (eds.), *The Wagner Companion* (London, 1979), 389–411). Skelton expands this account in his *Wagner in Thought and Practice* (Portland, Oreg., 1991). He stays very close to Wagner's own account given in 'Bayreuth' (v. 307–40).

[65] Wagner concluded, after some earlier statements to the contrary, that though an artist acts through self-denial of his personality, still, the best acting emanates from the artist's good soul. '[I]t has been proved that a high-souled art . . . cannot possibly be borne upon a petty heart, the source of badness of character, for truthfulness is the indispensable condition of all artistic being, and no less of all worthiness of character' ('Actors and Singers', v. 226).

of any human being. Performers should therefore ask of their audience that they look at them not as themselves, but as what they are capable of being. In other words, dramatic characters had to be exemplary human beings. Here the aesthetic ideal of *Werktreue* was expanded through its reconnection to the political. To be true to the work was to be true to the purpose of its performance. To act and sing correctly—under the composers' strict control—involved a technique of self-denial, which was required if the mythic or aesthetic space of the work was to be transformed into an ideal, socialized space. In the latter space a performer's inexpressible expression, achieved through aesthetic illusion, could serve its noble, normative, cathartic, and exemplary ends. Performer transparency had clearly come to mean something much more enigmatic and paradoxical than merely vehicular invisibility.

As Wagner sought illusory qualities for the visual world, he sought them for the audible world. '[I]n the perfect drama,' he wrote in a note:

the full shapes of a dream-vision or the other world are projected before us in a lifelike way as if by a magic lantern. It is a ghostly seeing in which all the figures of all times and places become distinct before our eyes. Music is the lamp of this lantern. . . . It is often said that in opera one needs to see something because its music does not fill us. With this attitude, the ear is depotenced—we no longer take in the music intensively. However, [in my opinion] music should be able to inspire the sight so that we see the music in shapes.[66]

To give music its visual shape (or to give the expression of the inexpressible its proper function within the dramatic deed), he instructed that his orchestra be made invisible. It was literally to be placed in a sunken pit in front of the stage and covered by a tin roof. 'To explain the plan of the festival theatre now in course of erection,' he wrote, '. . . I cannot do better than begin with the need I felt first, that of rendering invisible the mechanical source of its music, to wit the orchestra; for this one requirement led step by step to a total transformation of the auditorium of our neo-European theatre.'[67]

Though cognizant of partially concealed and lowered orchestra

---

[66] 'Sketches and Fragments', viii. 373. I have modified the translation here.
[67] 'Bayreuth', v. 333.

pits in other auditoriums (in Riga, for example),[68] and recalling
Goethe's description in *Wilhelm Meister*, Wagner believed that the
idea of rendering the orchestral players completely invisible first
became clear to him in 1840 after arriving late at a rehearsal in
Paris for a Beethoven symphony. As Geoffrey Skelton reports
the story: '[Wagner] was put in a room divided from the main
concert hall by a partition stopping short of the ceiling. As he
recalled . . . the sound of the orchestra reaching over the partition
amazed him: the music, freed of all mechanical side-effects, "came
to the ear in a compact and ethereal sort of unity".'[69] Only by
concealing the orchestra could one create the illusion that the
music was mysteriously emerging out of the silence from nowhere
and thus from everywhere.[70]

But could not Wagner have made the demand for an invisible

[68] Cf. Daniel J. Koury's summary of precedents:

> [Hans] Haas quoted Gassner as claiming [in 1842] that an invisible orchestra in
> church would be very 'edifying' and in the theater would 'undoubtedly contribute
> to the elevation of expression.' Haas also stated that Karl Friedrich Schinkel
> desired a sunken orchestra for Berlin as early as 1817, even providing a sketch for
> it. Haas also claimed that Verdi showed himself in favor of a lowered orchestra in
> a letter on *Aida* to Ricordi in 1871, and that even before Schinkel a certain L.
> Catel recommended such in 1802 for improving the Schausspielhaus in Berlin.
> Also, de Marette had suggested lowering the orchestra in a memoir in Paris in
> 1775! And according to Schinkel, Count C. di Benvello in Turin had put forth a
> plan for lowering the orchestra entirely under the stage floor in 1841. ('Orchestral
> Performance Practices in the Nineteenth Century: Size, Proportions, and Seat-
> ing', Ph.D. thesis, University of Michigan, 1986, 270)

[69] 'The Idea of Bayreuth', 390–1. Cf. Kierkegaard's description after attending a
performance of *Don Giovanni*:

> We know from experience that it is not pleasant to strain two senses at the same
> time, and it is often very confusing if we have to use our eyes hard when our ears
> are already occupied. Therefore we have a tendency to close our eyes when
> hearing music. This is true of all music more or less, and of *Don Juan* in *sensu
> eminentiori*. As soon as the eyes are engaged, the impression becomes confused;
> for the dramatic unity which presents itself to the eye is always subordinate and
> imperfect in comparison with the musical unity which is heard at the same time.
> This, at least, has been my own experience. I have sat close up, I have sat farther
> and farther back, I have tried a corner in the theater where I could completely
> lose myself in the music. The better I understood it . . . the farther I was away
> from it, not from coldness, but from love, for it is better understood at a
> distance. . . . Now . . . I stand outside in the corridor; I lean up against the parti-
> tion which divides me from the auditorium, and then the impression is most
> powerful; it is a world by itself, separated from me; I can see nothing, but I am
> near enough to hear, and yet so infinitely far away. (*Either/Or*, tr. D. F. and L. M.
> Swenson (New York, 1959), i. 119.)

[70] Frederic Spotts makes this point in his *Bayreuth: A History of the Wagner
Festival* (New Haven, 1984), 8.

orchestra more metaphorical than literal, more experiential than architectural? He once thought this possible: 'In my article on Beethoven, I explained how fine performances of ideal works of music may make this evil [i.e. the mechanical apparatus of production] imperceptible at last, through our eyesight being neutralised, as it were, by the rapt subversion of the whole sensorium.' Perhaps rapt subversion would suffice for purely instrumental concerts, but not, he realized, in opera. 'With a dramatic representation, it is a matter of focusing the eye itself upon the stage-picture (*Bild*); and that can be done only by leading it away from any sight of bodies lying in-between.'[71]

An invisible orchestra would not only hide the mechanics of the sound production. It would also help the audience maintain without distraction direct visual contact with the stage. This was its final purpose.[72] It would help meet Wagner's demand that the audience experience the performance in total darkness but in aesthetic light. With no light emanating from the orchestra pit, with the auditorium lights put out, with no distracting 'cheap adornments' on the ceiling or walls, and with no diverting social stratification of seating, the audience would do what they had rarely ever done before—focus exclusively through a totalizing experience on the spectacle at hand. No allowance would even be made for reading programme notes: the audience, Wagner hoped, would already know the libretto. 'One sees the proceedings on the stage without obstruction—and nothing else,' remarked one observant audience member—Hanslick.[73]

---

[71] 'Bayreuth', v. 333.

[72] Contrary to some commentators, I do not think Wagner gave his instruction merely so as to hide the mundane and mechanical origins of performance (though that was central), nor merely to release the absolute expression of music from any 'extramusical' element. He issued this instruction as part of his larger project, to show the proper place of the musical expression of the inexpressible in a transfigurative dramatic deed. This reading is important if we are to differentiate Wagner's conception of invisibility from the one I described earlier pertaining to the perfect performance of music. In the first printed version of this essay, I thought they were identical. I was misled by the parallel Dahlhaus drew (too quickly I now believe) between the Small Auditorium of the Copenhagen Concert Palais of 1904 that has a screen built on stage and Bayreuth's fully concealed orchestra. 'The prevailing doctrine of nineteenth-century music aesthetics,' Dahlhaus wrote, 'the idea of "absolute" music, divorced from purposes and cares . . . gave rise again and again . . . to the demand for an "invisible orchestra" concealing the mundane origins of transcendental music' (*Nineteenth-Century Music*, 394). Dahlhaus rather misleadingly suggests here that Wagner was motivated by the formalist idea of 'absolute' music.

[73] 'Richard Wagner's Stage Festival in Bayreuth', in *Music Criticisms*, 138.

Wagner further expected the audience to sit in silence: no inter-rupting applause as occurs in other (popular) theatres. He intended also that his theatre be built sufficiently far from the urban city to help his audiences release themselves from their daily cares. All these negating conditions would accentuate the required psycho-logical and aesthetic distance Wagner was demanding for his audience.

But to what end was this aesthetic distancing intended? In an-swering, Wagner finally gave sense to his conception of a perform-ance as the end of the work's deed. What lay behind his conception of the completion of the dramatic deed—and what therefore made the instruction to destroy Bayreuth plausible—was his political (Schillerian) idea that art's completion is not the completion of the aesthetic event *per se*, but the transfiguration of a public commu-nity that ideally follows upon that event. The completion of the dramatic deed contained within a work of the magnitude of the *Ring* was the fulfilment of the deed's political purpose, a purpose reminiscent of the ancient Greek festival.[74] The perfection of a perfect musical performance was the perfection of the public (the third element in the communicative circuit) and not the aesthetic event itself conceived merely as an aesthetic event. The public, ideally, would be perfected if it took its transfiguring experiences away from Bayreuth and back into its ordinary life. In so doing, presumably its ordinary life would cease to be mundane and sBayreuth (like the Church) would no longer—at least for a time—be necessary. That had clearly been one of the 'temporary' restora-tive intents of *Die Meistersinger*'s *Volk* festival.

In polemical terms belonging to his cultural critique, Wagner also saw in the end of drama the end of the activity he disliked most: music criticism and the production of academic journals. 'When we have reached our goal' in the work of art, we will have been redeemed. 'Our criticism will be at an end', and we will have turned ourselves 'into artists and people enjoying art'.[75] But to be artists and people enjoying art demanded this strong metaphysico-political change. Art's transfigurative experience entailed much more than the mere presence of art, but the total transfiguration of

[74] For more on the 'political' connotation of Wagner's use of the term 'deed', see e.g. David B. Dennis, *Beethoven in German Politics, 1870–1989* (New Haven, 1996), 40 ff.

[75] 'On Music Criticism', iii. 73. Cf. also Susan Bernstein's account in 'In Formel: Wagner and Liszt', Levin (ed.), *Richard Wagner*, 85–97.

German community through drama's exemplary performance. It was this transfiguration that would put the community, as Wagner put it, into the 'secret' and 'solidly lasting' condition of the 'genuine essence of the German spirit', or into the spirit, metaphorically speaking, of music. It was the transfiguration of 'the artwork-of-the-future', in other Wagnerian terms, into a community's 'life-of the-future'.[76] Whether, however, Wagner was expressing here so affirmative a picture, whether he really believed that transfiguration was possible in 'real' political terms and not just in the aspirational terms of the aesthetic spectacle, depends again on the metaphysical weight that, following Schopenhauer, he accorded his secrecy.

Needless to say, apart from the period when Bayreuth and Wagner's operas were ideologically appropriated, say, by the National Socialists, most people present at Bayreuth's performances responded far more as a concert 'audience' than as a (German) 'public'. And from the musicians in the audience, it was the invisible orchestra that received the most comment. For many, the invisible orchestra simply convinced them that, despite Wagner's protestations to the contrary, he had in fact perfected, rather than expanded or side-tracked, the conditions for the perfect performance of absolute music. The orchestra has been given 'an unprecedented role' in Wagner's operas: '[t]he orchestra is all', declared composer Edward Grieg after attending a performance of the *Ring*. And for critics like George Bernard Shaw, who liked to listen and not look, concealing the orchestra was a bonus. Concealing the stage as well would have been even better! Wagner had already given the idea some thought.[77] Hanslick approached the matter more pragmatically.

Most noteworthy of all is the invisible orchestra. . . . The orchestra is set so deep that one is reminded of the engine room of a steamship. It is, moreover, almost entirely hidden by a kind of tin roof. The musicians haven't the slightest view of the stage or of the public. . . . Wagner's inspired idea

---

[76] 'Bayreuth', v. 316.

[77] I have borrowed these examples from Spotts, *Bayreuth*, 71–3. Cf. Shaw's 'Bayreuth', in *Shaw on Music: A Selection of the Music Criticism of Bernard Shaw*, ed. E. Bentley (New York, 1955), 116–27. Wagner famously spoke himself of an 'invisible theatre', but, by this, he meant only to hide the mechanics of stage production. The idea was interpreted minimalistically by Wieland Wagner and later directors, who not only hid the mechanics but also reduced the visual image to bare essentials. Cf. Skelton, 'The Idea of Bayreuth', 409, and Spotts, *Bayreuth*, 78 and 216.

of sparing us the disturbing spectacle of the musicians' fiddling and puffing . . . is something to which I gave my blessing long ago and for which . . . I have even campaigned. The lowering of the orchestra is one of the most reasonable and enduring of Wagner's reforms; it has already taken hold in the legitimate theatres. . . . And yet, it seems to me that Wagner has gone too far, or . . . too deep; for in . . . *Das Rheingold* I missed, if not the precision, at least the brilliance of the orchestra. . . . This is . . . a boon for the singers, but at some cost to the role of the instruments, to which, especially in this work, is assigned much of the most significant and the most beautiful.[78]

Hanslick was partly articulating the unhappiness of the Bayreuth orchestral players, who, as one put it, had begun to feel more like machines than musicians, despite Wagner's intentions to the contrary.[79] But Hanslick was also pointing to practical disadvantages, because the manner in which Wagner had concealed the orchestra had made the musicians more than invisible. In Hanslick's judgement, they had also been made unhearable. As Hanslick noticed, the singers of course were pleased: for once, they could be heard over the orchestra. Of course, in concealing the orchestra Wagner had not had the singers' vocal volume first and foremost in mind. He had been much more concerned with their contribution as singer-actors to the total human drama.

Practical problems aside, Hanslick and Wagner shared an ideal common to both the perfect performance of music and the perfect musical performance, that of making the mechanical and mundane means of production invisible—literally or metaphorically—in the name of transfigurative experience. There was no quarrel between them there. But there was a quarrel over whether performers should *therefore* be conceived as merely mechanical and/or as merely mundane means. Certainly for the 'democratic' Wagner of Bayreuth (and following Kant's ethics), no one engaged in artistic performance should ever be treated merely as a means. Why, we might ask in retrospect, did he seem to think that his formalist critics already needed to be reminded of that fact?

As time passed, performers turned increasingly to recording and the apparatus associated therewith, but rarely because they favoured technology or mechanism *per se* (although some of course did). Rather, they saw in technology a way to serve their

---

[78] *Music Criticisms*, 138–9.   [79] Cf. Spotts, *Bayreuth*, 12.

aspirations towards the sort of musical perfection and purity that favoured concealing a single fact, that performers are 'imperfect', 'huffing and puffing' human beings. Was it the concealing of these 'lowly' human qualities that would direct musical perfection regressively towards an overly mechanized rationality? Only, objectors seemed to say, if the 'higher' moral qualities of the 'Human' were thereby also concealed.

With this fear in mind, performers invoked their expanded conception of performance whenever they could. They stressed that performance was something more than the abstracted sonorous event and something more than a means merely to opening up access to the work. Even if the sonorous event associated with the work remained central, the perfect musical performance, unlike the perfect performance of music, took that event as inseparable from the actual performers who produced the sounds, from the formal, visual choreography of their musical movements, and from the real spaces or environments, acoustic, social, and cultural, which shaped it. Yet this expansion had to be nuanced. For the design of the perfect musical performance was not intended necessarily to extend the borders of the category of music itself: music could remain, if musicians so chose, essentially the audible art of sound. In the end, the point was not really about music's *content*. It was about leaving open a space for musical performance to acknowledge, as the conception of the perfect performance of music was increasingly denying, that the humanization of the performance directed towards social ends was not necessarily to a performance's failing (though it could be), but to its genuine aesthetic merit. Therefore, whereas a perfect performance of music ideally achieved its transcendent meaning by negating itself to better illuminate the work it performed, a perfect musical performance ideally communicated its sublime message by asserting its uniqueness as a transfiguring, ephemeral event that was fully socially, audibly, and visibly situated.[80]

What happens now to a practice which moves in different directions at the same time? What is the nature of the conflict

---

[80] To recall the concerns of Chapter 1, 19th-century censorship policy-makers assumed that live, acted-out performances were more dangerous than (private) 'readings' of works, and that singing texts was more dangerous than reading them silently to oneself. (Cf. Goldstein, *Political Censorship of the Arts and the Press in Nineteenth-Century Europe*, 162.)

that emerges when two competing conceptions or ideals of perfection vie with one another for the dominant role in the practice? The interesting quality of the conflict, I shall argue, derives less from what differentiates the two conceptions *per se*, than from what differentiates them *given all that they obviously share*.

5. Towards a Philosophical Conclusion

When Glenn Gould wrote that 'for better or worse, recording will forever alter our notions about what is appropriate to the performance of music',[81] he offered an argument comparable to that regarding photography's impact on painting. In both cases, the technology of recording or reproduction would make possible a new degree of fidelity, representational or interpretative, formerly unrealizable. Unless the paintbrush could approximate to the condition of the camera, or the concert hall to that of the recording studio, painting and live performance would both have to re-evaluate their traditional aesthetic, social, and moral possibilities.

Concert halls have long tried to accommodate technological advancement as they have striven for acoustic perfection. Gould acknowledged this fact, though he was critical of it. Regardless, he had overriding arguments. In a recording studio, musicians could produce their most truthful interpretation of a work in solitude—a prerequisite for genuine creativity, he said. They would be released from the pressure of playing the work in one sitting; they would have the 'take-two' opportunity and, then, the opportunity to edit and splice. Musicians could avoid engaging in the 'wooing' showmanship demanded by live audiences; one would find interpretations being judged more than 'performers'. '[O]ne should not voyeuristically watch one's fellow human beings', Gould wrote, 'in testing situations that do not pragmatically need to be tested.'[82] Musicians could avoid anti-democratically imposing upon their listeners their particular interpretations. Gould was thinking here about the critical distance granted to listeners who, in the privacy of home, could listen to recordings in their own time and as

---

[81] 'The Prospects of Recording', 337.
[82] 'Glenn Gould in Conversation with Tim Page', in *The Glenn Gould Reader*, 452.

individuals without their judgement or experience of the works being influenced by the authoritatively dressed performer or by 'the herd' judgement of status-conscious audiences. (Of course, as he well recognized, lurking now would be the danger that listeners would not listen at all, but adopt a 'casual attitude' by turning music into comfortable, wallpaper muzak.)[83] He had more arguments, but it suffices to repeat their shared conclusion: the technology offered by the recording studio could bring musical performance closer to meeting the aspirations of the conception of the perfect performance of music than concert halls had ever yet done or ever could do.

Gould's democratic demands did not convince his critics. They mostly retaliated by reminding him of all that would be lost in musical performance if the conception of what I have called the perfect musical performance—with its emphasis on human presence, visibility, drama, and the immediacy of communication—were to be rejected altogether in favour of recordings. But they did not then argue in favour of one performance conception over another; weakly, they seemed content to allow the continuing functioning of both.[84]

However, they could have looked back to Wagner to strengthen their position. Gould shared with Wagner the worry that the conditions of modern concert halls were hardly ever suitable for an appropriately transfigurative aesthetic experience to take place. Both were highly critical (and often in comparable satirical tone) of the extraneous noises and events—all signs of a general lack of respect for music—occurring in what was desired to be an aestheticized space designed for the purest expression and experience. Both were critical of the potential alienation incurred by the anti-democratic composer–performer–audience triad. Both preferred to listen to music, as Gould once put it, 'in the wings'.[85] But whereas Gould opted for the recording studio, Wagner attempted to build a perfect temple to the *Gesamtkunstwerk* of music. Where, in principle, they might have shared common ground is in the

---

[83] I have collected these objections together from numerous essays by Gould.

[84] Cf. Gould's conversation with Arthur Rubinstein, in *The Glenn Gould Reader*, 283–90.

[85] Gould was stating a preference here for avoiding the distractions etc. that come with sitting in and with an audience (Payzant, *Glenn Gould*, 22). Recall Kierkegaard's reservations described above (n. 69).

principle that one should listen to recordings *as if* one were attending live performances under ideal circumstances.[86]

But would Gould have thought that listeners should fill in the
visible presence of performers, as it were, in their interpretations of
works? It is unlikely. He seemed to endorse a narrow conception of
the scope of the musical, as the purely audible art of tone, a conception that suggests that all listeners really have to do is listen to the
expressive content of the work. He was not even really concerned
with the performance of the work. He was not so much arguing for
recording as a better model of *performance*, but for recording as
a quite different means by which people could access works. He
seemed to be getting rid of the 'authoritarian' and 'oratorial' performance altogether. Given the tendency for performers to substitute a pure, private, and 'inner-directed' expression for public and
'showy' artifice, his real aim in recordings seems to have been to
bring about the end of the artifice of art as it exhibited itself in its
performing manifestation.

Gould was offering a rather old-fashioned purist thesis on the
'end' of art, in this case, a thesis which proclaimed that for music
truly to serve its spiritual mission, a technology should be introduced, as he himself put it, that would 'transcend the idea of art
itself'. To bring about the end of the artifice of art was to open the
way for music's pure or 'extra-human' expression. Like an instrument played, so a recording should not be treated as a technological instrument, but as a mechanism made to function solely in the
service of music's mission.[87] It was the commitment to music's pure
expression that ultimately lay behind his description of music or art
as 'scarcely human at all'.

Wagner had offered a similar thesis, but had stressed much
more explicitly than Gould the paradoxical relation between
means and ends. He had articulated his solution to the woes
of performance not by rejecting live performance but by seeking within it the paradoxical condition of its perfection. He
had stressed the role of artifice within live performance as the

---

[86] Cf. Payzant's description of Gould's view that 'The New New Listener, instead
of participating actively, will allow himself to be transported in imagination to the
Concertgebouw, or the Royal Festival Hall, or to whatever concert hall in which at
that moment he would like to hear the music' (ibid. 32).

[87] Cf. ibid. 120–1 for a comparable interpretation.

indispensable means to revealing the 'higher' end. Historically, he was not in a position to be able to abandon the transfigurative means supported by the conception of the perfect musical performance in favour of an entirely new means. Furthermore, he had supported a broad conception of the musical in which the inner ear functions as the channel to the soul, and to which both the outer ear and the eye must direct themselves. So the kind of developments in technology he would have supported—already apparent in Bayreuth—are those we now associate with film. But how, Wagner might have wondered had he been transported into this century, could the mechanical apparatus of film ever be sufficiently concealed, to create the illusion for the public that a performance is taking place 'here and now' for the social or political benefit of this particular public?

Despite the differences of articulation, Gould and Wagner started out with surprisingly similar complaints, and, in matters of motivation, both seem to have been inspired by comparable aesthetic and even political ideals which led them to announce the end of an art that was overly artificed. But whereas Gould announced the end of the concert hall in favour of recording technology, Wagner announced the end of the misuse of the concert hall in favour of its proper use. In retrospect, it is unclear which solution was the more radical. Is it so obvious (as Benjamin and Adorno would ask at a historical juncture midway between Wagner and Gould) whether embracing or resisting recording technology over the traditional technology of the concert hall is the more radical solution to the problems of art's artifice?

It is to this kind of unclarity, and to the openness or space for possibilities in musical practice it sustains, that I now want to appeal, in order to motivate my philosophical conclusion. It is a conclusion couched in meta-practical terms. Hence, it does not advise musicians how to perform music (that answer would be inconsistent with my claims). It only says something about how we might think about our 'all-too-human' practices that contain competing conceptions within them.

6. A Philosophical Conclusion

My first suggestion is this: when we strive to embody one conception of perfection sustained by a performance tradition we should not demand that that tradition be homogeneous or singular in such a conception; different conceptions of perfection can, and sometimes have to, coexist within a single tradition. This suggestion acknowledges only the mere phenomenon of coexistence; it does not yet address in any detail the situation in which conceptions coexist but conflict.

There are different ways to understand the conflicts that emerge within traditions or practices, or, more specifically, between the conceptions, ideals, or values they support. It suffices to describe only the kind of conflict that arises when a shared ground—perhaps a world-view, a theory, or a basic set of values—finds itself expressed by, or realized in, genuinely conflicting conceptions or ideals. Expressions of a shared ground may differ from one another if the shared ground is essentially limited, incomplete, or underdetermined, and, in this sense, imperfect. Expressions are attempts to make determinate or to perfect an imperfect ground. The relation between the shared ground and its expressions is akin to the relation that holds at a local level between a prescriptive theory and its correlative determinate actions, a stage direction and its enactments by actors, or an architectural drawing and the particular buildings which are its realizations. That which is prescribed is made precise in each action or realization, but the latter may permissibly assume different forms. Returning to the general level, genuine conflict between expressions of a shared ground arises when these expressions (conceptions, ideals, or values) are incommensurable, incommensurable because they cannot be ranked so as to give one priority over the other, or when no clear trade-off or easy synthesis between them is forthcoming.

One may respond to genuine conflict in more or less radical ways. Adopting a radical attitude one might regard it most expedient to endorse one expression or conception anyway, and in so doing reject any rival conception out of hand. Often this endorsement will be accompanied by a claim that the conflict no longer exists because it has been resolved. Perhaps one will employ previously unforeseen criteria to show how the rival conceptions can now be ranked. The non-radical attitude, by contrast, suggests tolerance: if one acknowledges that alternative expressions of a shared ground are possible, one may well allow the alternatives to coexist. One may well see that being tolerant has clear advantages regardless of the continuation of conflict.

Recall the two conceptions of performance. Both realize or track a shared ground of aesthetic theory, and against one another they pit themselves in a position of genuine conflict. How should one characterize the historical expressions and responses to this conflict and the consequences that emerge therefrom?

The conflict came to be expressed partly through a marking-off of a modern practice of performance from its pre-modern counterpart. It was also expressed through an attempted division of elite and popular forms of classical music practice. It also came to be expressed, somewhat paradoxically, through a division between (*a*) the orchestral or community-based symphonic tradition that stressed the individualistic nature of performance and aesthetic experience, and (*b*) the individualistic virtuoso tradition that stressed the social nature and purpose of performing. But we also know that this last division never became so sharp as to allow either conception ever to become wholly or exclusively identified with either tradition. Both conceptions were more or less obviously present in both traditions even though the balance of power between them varied. So despite my deliberately polarized description, we must recognize the historical interaction and overlap that has existed between the performance traditions, conceptions, and thus also the modes of evaluation that together, and not in separation, have constituted the modern practice of classical music.

But this interaction and overlap neither emerged out of, nor resulted in, relations merely of uncritical tolerance or consolidation, but rather out of and in critical antagonisms. This is demonstrated best by the isolated moments and historical tendencies when and in which the conflict received various combinations of radical and non-radical articulations and similar combinations of responses.

Recall how the Gould conflict presented a moment of threatened radical conflict. For Gould, the outcome was unsatisfactory, the concert hall still exists. But out of the conflict perhaps performers learned something more and something both new and old about what it means to perform. They became conscious of their striving to be both ends and means, to be both heard and heard through, and, when seen, both seen and seen through. From Gould's case we learn at least that when a challenge is posed in the extreme it is *not* required, for the challenge to be constructive, that it be met with an equally ardent response, although it may be.

Consider next the broader tendency towards radical conflict that arose when the perfect performance of music emerged as the conception most closely identified with the high-bourgeois culture of the German symphonic tradition and the formalism increasingly associated with it. In the name of purity and fineness, it found itself increasingly articulated independently of its rival conception, as if it could do all the work in the practice on its own: this is how genuine conflict arises, with the move towards the radical denial of a rival. However, this move proved self-deceptive in practice. For the perfect performance of music never succeeded in regulating even the *Werktreue* tradition on its own. This conception always required, to function successfully and to sustain its very assertion of transcendence, the conceptual, aesthetic, as well as the commercial co-presence or shadow of its counter-conception. Wagner's project, we might say, was precisely to show the emerging formalists that deep dependency. We might appropriately explain this relation of dependency by saying that the self-deceptive claim on behalf of the conception of the perfect performance of music was sustained by, as in turn it forced, a critical position of antagonistic tolerance.

Recall those performers who upheld the virtuoso tradition and brought to the public's attention the merits of the perfect musical performance. Did they respond radically to the extreme demands of the ideal of the perfect performance of music? I do not think so. They carved out a position in which they accepted the principle of the *Werktreue* ideal but resisted the most stringent demands of the performance conception to which that ideal had become most closely associated. Many performers—and Liszt was exemplary—thus aimed to be both great virtuoso and great *Werktreue* performers at the same time, and they did this by aspiring to produce a perfect performance of music as they aspired also to produce a perfect musical performance. Their resulting position demonstrated not only that *the performing of a performance* is a complex event in so far as the performers may simultaneously strive to meet historically conflicting ideals. It also demonstrated that the less elite conception of virtuoso performance striving towards the ideal of the perfect musical performance had a legitimate, although antagonistic, role to play in a practice increasingly seeing itself in elite terms. Once again, the less elite conception served to sustain the existence of the more elite conception, and by constantly asserting itself as different, it kept its opposition in check.

What conclusion should a meta-theorist draw when confronted with a practice that has historically been regulated by conflicting conceptions? Consider one viable position extrapolated from certain dialectical strains of Critical Theory. On finding that the conceptions regulating a practice are self-deceptive, incomplete, or dependent, we might recommend that those conceptions and the associated practice be clarified. This critical procedure would take what is truthful from any given conception with the purpose of transforming the practice into one that no longer depended upon, or was maintained by, any self-deceptive or antagonistic elements or conflicts. The procedure would not hope to leave everything as it is, but would intend for its outcome to have a transformative effect on the practice. In other words, the philosophical outcome of that procedure would play a revisory role within the practice itself.

I certainly favour philosophical clarification not leaving everything as it is, but I think its revisory role is undermined when it strives to do away with conflict and seeks instead a reconciliatory synthesis for the practice based on conflict-free ideals. For, by seeking such a synthesis, it ignores the potentially transformative or creative consequences that may emerge from the presence in a practice of more than one conception, any one of which might have some element of self-deception, and any one of which might conflict with another. I believe that creative performance—new problems and solutions, new activities, and greater learning—may emerge precisely from the constructive recognition by a practice's participants of the precise points of difference between its conflicting conceptions. I prefer, therefore, to allow the modern practice of classical music to remain imperfect or essentially limited both in its ground and in its expressions of that ground, precisely because this space or gap for antagonistic imperfection serves as an indispensable condition for its critical functioning.

However, whether the presence of this critical or doubling function is all one needs to produce creative products remains the crucial, but as yet unanswered, question. I pose this question in my final chapter. My conclusion for this one is that the practice of music should remain imperfect in its ground precisely because that imperfection leaves open a space for those in the practice who act. To give practice this primacy is to give its participants the spontaneous freedom to be musical in the performance of their music.

5

Music and Musicians in Exile: The Romantic Legacy of a Double Life

A linguistic work translated into another language is like
someone going across the border without his skin and donning
the local garb on the other side.

(Karl Kraus[1])

1. Preamble

The day I received the invitation to give the Bloch Lectures at the
University of California, I happened to be writing about Ernst
Bloch. I thought it quite fortuitous until I realized I was thinking
about the wrong Bloch—the philosopher not the composer. But
since I was writing about issues of double identity anyway, I decided to keep working on the one Bloch even as I was honouring
the other. My decision subsequently turned out not to be too
serious, because my lectures and then this book ended up focused
on neither Bloch, but on Wagner, the composer to whom both
Blochs were deeply devoted.

I had learnt of Bloch the composer's devotion to Wagner from
his 90-year-old daughter, Suzanne. Feeling a little guilty that I was
writing about Wagner, not her father, I asked her about her father's
attitude towards him. She answered that her father was convinced
that to understand music one has to understand Wagner, and that
he had taken a score of Wagner to bed with him every night.
Knowing that Bloch was also devoted to Jewish subjects, I then
asked her what he had thought about Wagner's anti-Judaism. She
sidestepped the question enough to tell me that her father believed

[1] *Half-Truths and One-and-a-Half Truths: Selected Aphorisms*, tr. H. Zohn
(Chicago, 1990), 66.

that even composers who are so-called 'Jewish composers' should aim to write music that speaks to all people. Music should speak universally, *whatever* its thematic or cultural identity. Suzanne continued to talk, but I could not get her 'whatever' out of my mind. I recalled Wagner's own reflection on the matter:

> Difficult as it must always appear to the thinker to satisfactorily define the true relation of a great artist to his nation, that difficulty is enormously increased when the subject is neither a poet nor a painter (*Bildner*), but a musician.... [For] neither through language, nor through any form wherein his country or his people greets the eye, does the musician reveal his origin. It has generally been assumed, therefore, that tone-speech belongs to the whole human race alike, that melody is an absolute tongue, in power whereof the musician speaks to every heart. However, upon closer examination ... we recognise that it is very possible to talk of a German ... music.[2]

I knew Wagner had also forwarded a thesis on the universality of German music from which he had chosen nevertheless to exclude Jews. Yet, even according to his paradoxical thesis, I had never been convinced that their exclusion was warranted. *He could have concluded differently.* To show this, we must consider once more the progressive and regressive tendencies of Wagner's aesthetic theory, viewed now in this chapter from a retrospective position.

2. Close to Home

During the Second World War my grandfather somewhat inadvertently assumed a double identity: he even went by two names. Under the safe, English-sounding name George Walter he composed film music, light music, and music for the allied war effort, specifically for the BBC's propaganda newsreels. Under his German birth name, Walter Goehr, he continued the career he had pursued in Berlin predominantly as symphonic conductor but also as composer. He regarded not only his birth name as the more self-authenticating of the two, but also the musical activity it symbolized. 'I have worked very hard for many years,' he wrote in wartime correspondence to his former teacher Schoenberg (now in America), 'and lately I am happy to say I find more time for

---

[2] 'Beethoven', v. 61.

composing. . . . This is the only thing in life I feel is worth while. . . . Whenever I try to compose . . . old times appear clearly before me.'[3]

For my grandfather, as for others in my family who have lived in countries different from those of their birth, their musical activity has been one of their strongest connections to home. Unreflectively, 'home' names a place and a life once lived; reflectively, it names a continually transforming set of bonds organized by activities, conversations, and relationships that trace memories of the past, establish patterns of present significance, and suggest desires for the future. 'Home' is largely synonymous with 'family': when a family finds itself in no place in particular, the bonds (musical or otherwise) between its members carry the significance of home.

The constant questioning about 'the soil of a family's significance'[4] is no different for those who emigrate in freedom than for those who emigrate because of political exile, even if the urgency of the questioning is. In contrast to the relative comfort of the freely moving immigrant, the often indescribable suffering of political exile links the questioning to extreme emotions: melancholy mixed with relief in leaving, happiness mixed with guilt for surviving, excitement mixed with trepidation about the new life to be lived. The principal reason my grandfather had written to Schoenberg was to thank him for all he had done for his brother Rudolf. 'I hope he will be able to get to the USA. At the moment it seems very difficult to accomplish.'

My great-uncle did eventually reach the United States, but the journey was agonizing. Exiled from Germany and interned in France, Rudi was himself writing to Schoenberg with a desperate request: could his former teacher help him obtain a visa or work permit for entry to America? His writing travelled across the languages of German, French, and English as he described the camps of his internment, his places of hiding and refuge. 'I hope you

---

[3] Letter of 17 July 1941. All quotations from the correspondence between Schoenberg and the Goehr family originate in documents collected at the Schoenberg Archive. I have corrected spelling, grammar, etc. in these letters for the sake of readability.

[4] I have borrowed this Sartrean phrase from Eva Hoffman's autobiographical *Lost in Translation: A Life in a New Language* (New York, 1989): 'Pattern is the soil of significance; and it is surely one of the hazards of emigration, and exile, and extreme mobility, that one is uprooted from that soil' (278).

received my postcards,' he wrote shortly after the occupation of France. 'Unfortunately, I am in a camp now, but I hope to be free soon and to see my wife.'

It was really a miracle, the German army stopped its advance just 5 miles before the village. So I escaped them. But now, know all is very sad. There will not be any chance for me to work again in France and I don't know what to do. Could you help me? I am very sorry to disturb you, but my situation is very serious. I know, after a week in America, all could be so easy—I mean, I could perhaps try my chance.[5]

Rudi did try his chance, but he did not find America so easy. 'Life is very hard in New York,' he wrote after his arrival:

Weather and thinking, thinking and weather. It's a terrible conflict, but I always have the impression that somehow it will work out. These days I make music with Rudi Kolish. We are playing the Bartók Violin Concerto, and it's great fun. . . . But besides this, one only hears here Shostakovich, Shostakovich, and more Shostakovich.

Rudi joined the army. 'Three months in the Army and already an American citizen,' he told Schoenberg on 4 February 1944,

I am writing to you again. The infantry never did much like musicians, so I have to wait and see what is going to happen. . . . But I got wonderful news from my brother, always conducting concerts with very interesting programmes. . . . [By the way, did you know that] I was—before I came here—arranger and musical director of the Eastman Kodak Show on NBC?

The purpose of having music on the Eastman Show was unapologetically commercial: it was used to encourage new Kodak customers to take snapshots with their cameras on picnic outings.[6] 'The musical direction of programming is not very interesting,' Rudi wrote while commuting between Rochester and New York. 'Beethoven is not nearly so loved as Sousa!' Apparently, some of Rudi's early musical activities in America were not so different in style from those of his brother known in Britain as George.

It is clear from Schoenberg's replies to Walter and Rudi that he wanted to help his former students, and sometimes succeeded in doing so, but was not confident at any point that he *could* do so. Schoenberg had surmised early on that his position in America

[5] Letter dated 7 July.
[6] I am grateful to an Eastman House archivist for giving me this information.

would not be exactly what it had been in Europe: 'I'd like to know too if I can do anything for you in America,' he wrote in 1933, responding to a plea for help from Alban Berg (and before his own departure)—but he added, 'always supposing that I should have the power. . . . For there's no knowing how disregarded, slighted, and without influence I may be there.'[7] Had his students not been facing quite desperate circumstances, they too would have recognized that, in exile, as every other kind of family is transformed, so also is a family of musicians.

This chapter investigates the transformations that occur to a musical family in exile, specifically the mass move of European composers to America prompted by Germany's National Socialism. It investigates the tensions that arose in musical practice when a powerful and widely accepted nineteenth-century metaphysical thesis about music and musicians was converted into the most extreme of ideological terms, when, more particularly, purportedly universal ideals were converted into racially bounded ones. However, the ultimate concern of this chapter is again less historical than philosophical. By 'a musical family' I will not just mean a family of persons who were musicians, or the relations holding between composition teachers and their pupils who in turn became composers and teachers. I will also include a family of philosophical views about music.

The kinds of view I will include are those specifically invoking doubleness. Bonding the family will be the view that composers, who because of exile were propelled into foreignness, began to live what the philosopher Ernst Bloch called in 1939 the double, rather than divided, life of frontiersmen. I shall show, first through a detailed description of composers' responses to exile, and later through conceptual clarification, that the doubleness involved in this frontier life has had numerous expressions of a musical, historical, aesthetic, and metaphysical sort. Recall that doubleness exists in practices of thought and activity that invoke two-sided, mediating, or conflicting ideals, productions, or conditions. It has been expressed in, for example, mergers between the languages and idioms of music and those of text, strategies of adaptation and resistance, articulations of insider and outsider positions, and in

---

[7] *Arnold Schoenberg Letters*, ed. E. Stein, tr. E. Wilkins and E. Kaiser (London, 1964), 184.

Romantic–Modernist theories invoking limits. These diverse expressions of doubleness do not together form a neatly unified picture of musical practice in the broadest sense, nor do they always mesh exactly with one another, though they are often employed as if they do. Nor do they together refer to a single way of conceiving of doubleness. Rather they stand to one another at best, and now quite appropriately, as family resemblant.

Doubleness pervades this century's thinking about the exile of musicians as part of its thinking about the exile of artists and intellectuals more generally. Highly Modernist thinking tends to take the two notions of language and creativity as constitutive in artistic and intellectual practices and the socio-political notions of expression and freedom as regulative. Its theorists then ask whether living on foreign soil affects a person's freedom of expression or whether being forced to speak a foreign language renders an artist more or less creative.

In historical mode, theorists answer these two questions by determining whether or not artists and intellectuals were exiled to places that provided them with adequate living conditions so that they could continue to create and write in comfort and freedom. They also study the impact of exile on the quality and quantity of the exiles' artistic and intellectual creation. But they also investigate exile as an existential or psychological condition. 'Being an exile is not a matter of needing a passport,' Henry Pachter once wrote; 'it is a state of mind.'[8] An exile is any artist or intellectual who maintains a critical distance from what Adorno called the 'administered world'. Thus, even if artists are not living in political exile, they may live none the less in a state of psychological or inner exile. Some theorists even claim that this inner exile is required for creative work or authentic expression, because it marks the free human subject. Political or outer exile may be just the thing to shock the artist out of a comfortable complacency, but, by itself, it is neither necessary nor sufficient for creative work.

This highly positive view of the state of exile is countered by an

---

[8] 'On being an Exile', in R. Boyers (ed.), *The Legacy of the German Refugee Intellectuals* (New York, 1972), 16. Cf. Louis Wirth's comment that 'intellectuals are always nomads in the universe of the mind and should feel at home anywhere' (quoted by Claus Dieter Krohn in his *Intellectuals in Exile: Refugee Scholars and the New School for Social Research*, tr. R. and R. Kimber (Amherst, Mass., 1993), 179).

equally positive view of the state of rootedness in home. Some argue that exile, in either its inner or outer form, is deadening, not awakening. Exile from one's culture, losing the use of a native language, does not quicken the fancy but places it far out of reach. 'To be rooted', wrote Simone Weil, 'is perhaps the most important and least recognized need of the human soul.'[9] Creativity and the language of free artistic expression require more the sense of belonging, more a native or saturated cultural understanding, than the purportedly alienating and empty condition of political or social freedom. In this view, rootedness, not exile, is the true condition of the creative spirit.[10]

To complicate matters these two opposing views are not always presented as such. In paradoxical flourish some theorists play with the meaning of 'home'. The artist is truly at home when not at home. Home for an artist is a place that allows her to feel constructively alienated from home—for truth is better grasped at a distance. If paradox (irony and laughter) once fuelled Groucho Marx's rejection of belonging to a club, it has also fuelled the artist's position more generally.

Yet it is just this complication of paradox that allows us to see the duality of home and estrangement less in mutually excluding, than in doubling, terms. Estrangement (linked to freedom, reflectiveness, and openness) and home (linked to understanding, identity, and involvement) capture in their mutual mediation a constructive Modernist attitude people may take in relation to the society in which they live. The cosmopolitan wants to be both estranged from and at home in the Modern metropolis. Of course, in times of intense social and political upheaval, the terms are usually employed in excluding and not in mediating ways, so that the duality between home and estrangement prompts negative claims of opposition, rigidity, and purity. Such terms are encouraged by a society's different groups—by those 'at home' *and* by those 'estranged'—according to their respective advantage. In the history of mass and individual exile we should not be surprised to find, therefore, the home–estrangement duality being used in wiser (political) mo-

---

[9] Quoted by Said in his 'Reflections on Exile', in M. Robinson (ed.), *Altogether Elsewhere: Writers on Exile* (Boston, 1994), 146.

[10] Cf. Pachter: 'The myth that exile produces Dantes, Marxes, Bartóks, and Avicennas certainly is not justified in the mass. More often exile destroys talent, or it means the loss of the environment that nourished the talent morally, socially, and physically' (ibid. 17).

ments in its doubling or mediating form, and in extreme (ideological) moments in its most dividing and polarizing form.

However, the polarization that may regressively affect a practice may disrupt without permanently destroying the practice's ability to accommodate the progressive condition of doubleness. When investigating a given practice, it is necessary to view it from both descriptive and normative perspectives, to see how it *is* conditioned at any given time and how it could and should be conditioned, and to see how the practice *is being described* and how in fact *it is working*. This dual perspective allows us to see past a polarization that forces us to conclude either that creativity demands estrangement or that it demands home, and allows us to conclude that, if it really demands either, then it most likely demands both.

This dual perspective also suits a musical practice whose Romantic–Modernist character is captured precisely in a myriad of doubling views. One view we have already seen at work describes music's other-worldly or aesthetic status on the one hand, and its worldly or historical character on the other. Another describes the play between inner and outer exile, i.e. between the psychological exile musicians experienced 'at home' in Europe and the actual exile they experienced in their move to America. In this chapter, these doubling views are closely connected.

The philosophy of music has thrived on claims about the language of music as bound or not bound to a nation, as free, expressive, and creative. But exiled musicians challenged two basic claims of their Romantic heritage: that music is a language and that creativity is causally or otherwise connected to the condition either of exile or of home. However, their challenge consisted less in a rejection of these views than in showing their limits. Chiefly, their experiences revealed the limits of describing music monologically, as one might an ordinary conceptual or cognitive language, because the description failed to capture the full significance of music, notably its creative or aesthetic moment. The resemblant, Critical claim was made contemporaneously that music could not be reduced to its social conditioning or embodiment because that reduction failed to recognize music's resisting, 'musical' aspects. For the last time, the Romantic–Modernist legacy in the philosophy of music has been exemplary in showing the need for recognizing limits and doubleness, and thus the dangers of reductionism, in both our theories and our practices.

The double life of the exiled musician makes explicit the double-sided character of music that the sometimes more comfortable life of the musician at home leaves implicit. My cast of characters is chosen for the manifold ways each character lived both 'homed' and 'foreign' lives. The primary cast comprises composers.[11] All moved to a country with a different spoken language. Most were Jewish (by birth, or by force or choice of return) and already had some understanding of the condition of religious exile. Some had experienced exile or 'inner emigration'[12] at home for their political views. All had experienced historical or psychological exile *en masse* or as individual targets.[13] The philosophical chorus comprises thinkers closely connected to the aforementioned composers, to issues of musical composition and creativity, and who themselves experienced exile or emigration. The doubly destructive and inspirational spirit of Wagner will burst once more onto the stage to overshadow the entire proceedings.

3. Experiences of Exile

In 1950 Albert Goldberg of the *Los Angeles Times* asked several exiled composers to respond to a claim made by a composer of European birth who, despite being 'distinguished', remained nameless. The claim was that 'European composers had changed since they lost contact with their native countries and the music the majority of them had written [in the United States] did not

---

[11] Although performers and musicologists wrote also of their conflicting experiences of exile, my account records only those of composers. The account could easily be extended.

[12] Hans Werner Henze describes this state in his *Music and Politics: Collected Writings, 1953–81*, tr. P. Labanyi (London, 1982), 35 and 275.

[13] Many composers were outcast from Germany or left or escaped not because of what their music said as such (or was believed to say), but because they were Jews, Communists, etc. In this sense, they were more refugees than individual exiles. Moreover, contrary to statements that followed their 'exile', we must acknowledge that they did not all come to America with the impression that their music was the immediate cause of their banishment, despite the crude comparisons the Nazis helped promote between (*a*) racial characteristics of composers and the music they composed, and (*b*) racial characteristics of music and certain 'modern', 'degenerate' musical forms. According to Nazi ideology, non-Jews could compose 'Jewish' or 'degenerate' music, but Jewish composers always composed Jewish music whatever the form or content. Some composers may not have thought about their music as Jewish or non-Jewish *per se* until forced by ideological circumstance to do so.

equal that... previously composed.'[14] Of the many responses given, Schoenberg's statement that he was unconscious that his exile changed him has been the most frequently cited by theorists to characterize him as the composer who most resisted Americanization.[15] Taken in isolation, Schoenberg's statement fails to capture what was, as one would expect, a much more complex reaction.

Drawing on a range of documents, I shall show in the present section that composers' responses to exile were usually too varied for us crudely to characterize them as merely assimilating or merely resisting Americanization.[16] To be sure, some variation within and across individual cases was due to context of utterance: whether, say, the responses were politically strategic or guided by particular emotions. But some variation reflects the conflicting views composers often held regarding the need for their creativity and use of the musical language to be positioned sometimes at a distance from, and sometimes as rooted in, home. Following conventional discursive patterns, they responded to exile dichotomously. They distinguished between their *inner* and *outer* lives, and between the *transcendence* and *situatedness* of their music. They gave flesh to these distinctions by distinguishing between the productions of *high* and *low* art, between judgements regarding the *quality* and *quantity* of their work, and between their *resistance* and their *concessions* to market pressures.

Precisely because there is no perfect fit between these different distinctions, and because composers often wanted to endorse both

[14] The interviews are printed in sect. iv, 14, 21, and 28 May, under the heading 'The Sounding Board'. Many composers interviewed were employed as film composers in the Hollywood studios. On that connection, see Christopher Palmer, *The Composer in Hollywood* (London, 1990). Cf. also Barbara Zeisl Schoenberg, 'The Reception of Austrian Composers in Los Angeles: 1934–1950', *Modern Austrian Literature*, 20/3–4 (1987), 135–44.

[15] See Gunter Berghaus (ed.), *Theatre and Film in Exile: German Artists in Great Britain, 1933–45* (Oxford, 1989), 19; and Jarrell C. Jackman, 'German Émigrés in Southern California', in Jackman and C. M. Borden (eds.), *The Muses Flee Hitler: Cultural Transfer and Adaptation, 1930–1945* (Washington, 1983), 98; and Walter Rubsamen, 'Schoenberg in America', *Musical Quarterly*, 37/4 (Oct. 1951), 485–6.

[16] A comparable story would temper the long-standing assessment of Adorno as a one-sided resister. See his *Minima moralia: Reflections from Damaged Life*, tr. E. F. N. Jephcott (London, 1974) and his 'Scientific Experiences of a European Scholar in America', in D. Fleming and B. Bailyn (eds.), *The Intellectual Migration: Europe and America, 1930–1960* (Cambridge, Mass., 1969), 338–70; and Martin Jay, *Permanent Exiles: Essays on the Intellectual Migration from Germany to America* (New York, 1986).

sides, we find constructive conflicts in the overall picture of music as a language and of conditions of creativity. Or to put the point slightly differently, it was precisely in mixing the particular exigencies of their exile with the aesthetic views they inherited that composers' responses to exile became deeply conflicted. My overall claim, reiterated throughout this book, is that these conflicts are best interpreted in doubling terms and that these terms have potentially empowering ramifications for how we speak and philosophize about music.

Schoenberg attached his famed response to a question a Spanish musician once asked him about the effect a country's climate or character could have upon his compositional style. He replied rhetorically at first: should my style be cold in Alaska, but hot near the Equator? But then he replied more soberly: whereas the quantity of his compositional output might have been affected, the quality could not have been, because quality comes from within.[17] Schoenberg was not the only one to reply this way. Quoting the exile Albert Einstein, Mario Castelnuovo-Tedesco responded to Goldberg: 'The bitter and the sweet come from the outside, the hard from within, from one's own efforts. For the most part I do the thing which my own nature drives me to.' And of Bela Bartók, Yehudi Menuhin recalled that 'exile made of him [an] unaccommodated man, solitary, intense, requiring for material support only a bed, a table to write.' But, Menuhin speculates, perhaps these conditions were not entirely unconducive to Bartók, because they gave him what some would regard a 'luxury', the condition of 'absolute quiet, in which his inner concentration might bear fruit'.[18]

Many exiles believed that the reliance upon their 'inner natures' had grown in proportion to the decline they experienced in external support. Although some admitted that they were just too old to adapt to new conditions ('I was a finished product of the old world,' remarked Eric Zeisl), others blamed the conditions of American musical life. Something is 'missing in America's musical scene', complained Miklos Rózsa, 'the bubbling, fertile, and germinating artistic atmosphere of prewar Europe that gave inspiration to many masterpieces'. Composers are isolated in America, the protesters continued; concert audiences only want to hear the

---

[17] Unless otherwise noted, all views recorded in this section are taken from Goldberg's interviews in the *Los Angeles Times*.
[18] M. Gillies (ed.), *Bartók Remembered* (New York, 1990), 186.

old warhorses; there is a 'critical lack of demand for contemporary music' and a lack of performance opportunities; performers are vain, conductors are temperamental. Comparing himself to Schoenberg, Stravinsky commented with some irony: '[We shared a] common exile to the same alien culture, in which we wrote some of our best works (his Fourth Quartet, my *Abraham and Isaac*) and in which we are still played far less than in the Europe that exiled us.'[19]

The moderate conclusion drawn from these complaints was that relying on one's inner nature was a contingent consequence of one's exile: one may not be able to 'overlook' external conditions, Castelnuovo-Tedesco remarked, but one must try to 'overlive' them. Some composers drew a stronger conclusion: since exile reveals the true relation between creativity and the inner life, exile is a necessary condition. Zeisl explained that the artist

is always unhappy and maladjusted to his society and that it is this [condition] . . . which prompts him to dig so deeply into the hidden resources of his soul. . . . The more harassed he is, the stronger the medicines with which he will come up for his own benefit and the benefit of mankind. (See Beethoven, Mozart, Wagner, etc.) Longing, nostalgia, loneliness, and strife. I . . . know of no better nourishment for the artist's soul, and we have in proof the fact that the world's most beautiful works of art and music have frequently been created in exile and far from home. (Wagner, Chopin, Stravinsky, Hindemith, etc.)

Stravinsky agreed at least with the last sentiment. Despite his warning against generalities and dismissing Goldberg's subject as 'not worth a column of [his] pen', he still felt obliged to comment that the Soviets had tried to intimidate artists by warning them that their creativity would be impoverished by exile. However, the Soviet's claim, he said, had been 'brilliantly refuted' throughout history, by 'Handel, Gogol, Chopin, Picasso'. Strategically composers should never admit defeat; according to Stravinsky, fortunately they rarely, if ever, had had to.

Some composers were sceptical of the advantages of exile. Bitingly attributing his creativity in exile to the torment of boredom, Hanns Eisler dismissed the glorification of the masochistic suffering of exile.[20] (Virgil Thomson commented similarly when he wrote

---

[19] Stravinsky and R. Craft, *Dialogues and a Diary* (London, 1968), 108.
[20] *A Rebel in Music: Selected Writings*, ed. M. Grabs (New York, 1978), 14. Cf. Albrecht Betz, *Hanns Eisler, Political Musician*, 14 and 153.

that one does not have to be poor to be an artist[21]). If exile was inspiring, it was not because of the suffering involved, but because exile has the positive effect of making one see the world anew. Seeing distant lands, Eisler argued in 1935, tests our methods of reasoning. Exiles are never absolutists. Eisler was seeing a critical link others would see too, a link between thinking differently and being creative.[22]

Ernst Krenek expressed his scepticism regarding the link between exile and creativity more strongly than Eisler. He initially severed the connection between the condition of exile from that of a composer's inner life altogether.[23] Exile is an external condition; it is simply the condition of composing away from home. He then reasoned this way: some exiles' works followed in the tradition of 'the European output' and some 'were written for American opportunities'. But because we do not know how composers would have composed had they stayed in Europe, we cannot determine whether exile made them more or less creative. External conditions affect composition wherever you live, so the safest conclusion is not to consider them. 'It is amazing that the pattern of one's [creative] life does not change,' Krenek reflected autobiographically in 1941, 'in spite of the most comprehensive outward changes.'[24]

Many exiled composers enjoyed reminding each other that external conditions in their native lands had not always been so good. Modern (dissonant) music was already alienated in Europe; even European audiences preferred their warhorses.[25] That conditions before and after exile could be more similar than different was a point made by one composer, who just reminded his fellow exiles

[21] *Virgil Thomson* (London, 1967), 346, ending his chapter 'Europe in America'.
[22] 'A Musical Journey through America', in *A Rebel in Music*, 82. Cf. Adorno's observation that his outsider lack of involvement maintained a freshness of judgement in his writings on American themes ('Scientific Experiences of a European Scholar in America', 341); also Paul Tillich's influential exploration of the 'essential relationship between mind and migration': 'mind in its very nature is migratory and ... human mental creativity and man's migrating power belong together' ('Mind and Migration', *Social Research*, 4 (1937), 295).
[23] See his 'America's Influence on its Émigré Composers', tr. D. Harran, *Perspectives of New Music*, 'Colloquy and Review' (Spring–Summer 1970), 112.
[24] *Die Amerikanischen Tagebücher, 1937–1942. Dokumente aus dem Exil*, ed. C. M. Zenck (Vienna, 1992), 192.
[25] In his 'Weimar Culture: The Outsider as Insider', Peter Gay describes the extent to which exiles were already alienated before their emigration. He argues that Weimar culture was the creation of outsiders (in Fleming and Bailyn (eds.), *The Intellectual Migration*, 11–93).

that they were now ten or fifteen years older and, if their creativity were lessened, it might simply be because they had 'not discovered the pills which Wagner took to write his *Parzifal* and Verdi to write his *Falstaff*'.

Still, composers generally agreed that dismissing the impact of exile altogether was untenable. Krenek remarked that a total disregard would probably be motivated by defensiveness, although he retained his scepticism.[26] Describing his composition as always having been guided by two contradictory tendencies of the pure and the situated, or the purely musical and the socially influenced, he maintained that he had never been able to tell which tendency had made his work better.[27]

Some composers used the pure–situated dichotomy to draw precisely the same conclusions as the inner–outer one. Having already asserted that 'nothing comes out, [that wasn't already] in', Schoenberg unhesitatingly moved from 'inside' to 'beyond'. A musical idea or style, he said, is like a mathematical truth and 'two times two equals four in every climate'. He then used this claim to stake out a position of artistic integrity: 'Maybe I had four times harder to work for a living. But I made no concessions to the market.' And then he used the implied distinction between loyalty to a pure musical tradition and conceding to market pressures to support the traditional distinction between autonomous 'high' art and dependent 'low' art—although to the latter he refused to give the name art. 'No serious composer in this country is capable of living from his *art*,' he wrote in 1945: 'Only popular composers earn enough.' But then he proclaimed with rather too much confidence, they are not producing '*art*'.[28]

Exiled composers generally agreed that they could not live from 'serious composition' alone and were having to spend their energy on teaching or 'producing' film music. ('The only way to escape Hollywood is to live in it,' once snapped Stravinsky.[29]) If composers were living by composition alone, it must be because they were compromising. Rózsa warned of the dangers of writing down to the American public and of diluting one's art, and, like Schoenberg, concluded that real art is only produced with full conviction:

[26] 'America's Influence on its Émigré Composers', 112.
[27] 'Self-Analysis', *New Mexico Quarterly*, 23 (Spring 1953), 7.
[28] *Arnold Schoenberg Letters*, 233.
[29] Vera Stravinsky, *Stravinsky in Pictures and Documents* (New York, 1978), 347.

compromise is 'synonymous with the ruin of all artistic endeavor.' '"Adjustment"', Castelnuovo-Tedesco wrote similarly, 'shouldn't mean "opportunism" or obedience to transitory fashions. I believe that only by following sincerely and honestly my natural trend can I bring some contribution . . . to musical art.'

Expressing resistance to external pressures in terms of a retreat into one's private inner world enabled exiled composers to articulate the continuity they needed to feel across the radical disrupture they had experienced. What would have been the point of conceding that their lives' work, their creative inspiration, had been inhibited by exile? Most frighteningly, it would have been to admit the triumph of National Socialism. Composers had to believe that they could compose anywhere.

On the other hand, the sense of a composer's belonging to a place captures another side of exile experience. Sixteen years before Schoenberg spoke to the *Los Angeles Times* he wrote:

It is perhaps [to be] expected that now I am in a new world I should feel its amenities to be ample compensation for the loss I have sustained and which I had foreseen for more than a decade. Indeed, I parted from the old world not without feeling the wrench in my very bones, for I was not prepared for the fact that it would render me not only homeless but speechless, languageless.[30]

'Languageless?'—surely Schoenberg had not lost his music? To make sense of his statement, perhaps we have to assume that he was referring only to speech and language associated with nation and tongue. The idea that music (at least purely instrumental music) is not nation-bound, and the related idea that if music is a language then it is not an ordinary one, are familiar ideas in the history of music. They are familiar also in exile theory. Jarrell C. Jackman has written recently that '[t]he great advantage the émigré composers and musicians had over writers and actors was not being bound to language for economic survival'.[31] In this claim, music is not even classified as a language. Günter Berghaus writes that '[t]hose artists who relied in their profession on verbal language and linguistic skills had to overcome considerably greater difficulties than those who worked in [arts which were] more international

---

[30] *Arnold Schoenberg Letters*, 191–2. Cf. Hannah Arendt's observation: 'We lost our language . . . the naturalness of reactions, the simplicity of gestures, the unaffected expression of feelings' ('We Refugees', in Robinson (ed.), *Altogether Elsewhere*, 110).

[31] 'German Émigrés in Southern California', 101.

in their general outlook'.[32] At least Berghaus assumes that the difference between nation-bound and international arts is one of degree. Only the exiled musician Boris Schwarz tempers his account appropriately: 'On the surface the fate of a musician forced to emigrate seems less onerous than that of an actor, writer, or scientist. Music is an international language; a musician—with his instrument in hand—can play and be understood in Paris, New York, or Rio, without the need to communicate through spoken works.' However, composers are 'more difficult to transplant: there are subtle national differences in musical tastes and customs'.[33]

The appeal to music as abstract, unbounded, or international clearly provided composers a way to resist the impact of exile. But it could only be used so far because exiled composers also had a very strong sense of their carrying a national musical identity with them into their new and foreign lives. Thus, within their responses arose a conflict between two claims, that music was an abstract language on the one hand and that it was nation-bound on the other. (This conflict had already been embroiled in Krenek's distinction between pure and situated tendencies.)[34]

'As much as I have an accent in my language,' a painter exiled to Britain once remarked, 'I have an accent in my painting.'[35] Could not the same be said about music? Apparently Schoenberg sometimes thought so: 'Artistically speaking,' he had written as early as 1928, 'it is all the same whether someone paints, writes, or composes; his style is anchored in his time.'[36] Later, after his geographical exile, he might well have added: and his style is anchored in his place. Maybe he really did feel he had lost his musical language.

Certainly he used the conflict between music's abstraction and its being culture- or nation-bound strategically. It allowed him to

[32] *Theatre and Film in Exile*, p. xiv. Berghaus discusses this claim again on p. 18 in a different context. There, he acknowledges the language difficulties faced by all types of artist.
[33] 'The Music World in Migration', in Jackman and Borden (eds.), *The Muses Flee Hitler*, 137.
[34] This dichotomy is also related to Aron Gurwitsch's 1944 description of the contemporary refugee as coming 'in one sense out of the void, in another sense out of a 3000-year past' (Alfred Schutz and Aron Gurwitsch, *Philosophers in Exile: The Correspondence of Alfred Schutz and Aron Gurwitsch, 1939–1959*, ed. R. Grathoff, tr. J. Claude Evans (Bloomington, Ind., 1989), p. xvi).
[35] Quoted by Berghaus (*Theatre and Film in Exile*, 18).
[36] 'Does the World Lack a Peace-Hymn?', in *Style and Idea*, 500.

retreat from explicit involvement in war and politics. 'I did not come into this marvellous country to speak about terrors—but to forget them.'[37] He had long ago motivated this act of forgetting: 'There are . . . reasons', he had already written in 1928, 'why one cannot seriously believe that the arts influence political happenings. . . . [B]y what chord would one diagnose the Marxist confession in a piece of music, and by what colour the Fascist one in a picture?'[38] Schoenberg was not being naive. Music, he knew, could be a powerful language: 'Composers speak symbolically of philosophy, morals, etc.,' he wrote in 1943; it is just that music speaks without a defined vocabulary.[39] As a symbolic language, music could function without a vocabulary but convey values none the less. Schoenberg seemed to be adapting here the traditional Romantic strategy of claiming that music, unable to express meaning in ordinary referential or conceptual terms, resists its description as a language, yet in this negation succeeds in expressing, in its unique musical or extraordinary terms, philosophical, moral, and social value.[40]

Describing music this way gave composers the confidence to maintain both that in exile nothing had changed (because the musical language is abstract or universal), and that they had brought with them a language thoroughly permeated by value, and when it suited a national value. But to sustain their confidence they had to employ yet another distinction. To conserve a musical culture or tradition abroad required that the idea of music's being, for example, German be separated from the idea of its being situated in Germany. This separation was already a staple of exile discourse. Many German-speaking artists and intellectuals were proclaiming that it was they who defined German culture and not a country's geographical or social–political condition. 'German culture', Thomas Mann apparently once announced, 'is where I am.'[41] German culture was being maintained abroad because it no

[37] 'Two Speeches on the Jewish Situation', in *Style and Idea*, 502.

[38] 'Does the World Lack a Peace-Hymn?', 500.

[39] *Arnold Schoenberg Letters*, 217.

[40] In post-war works, e.g. in his *Ode to Napoleon*, he adopted a more explicit approach.

[41] Brecht ascribed these words to Mann, as James K. Lyon explains in his *Bertolt Brecht in America* (Princeton, 1980), 252. For more on Mann's conflicting attitudes towards exile, see Henry Hatfield, 'Thomas Mann and America', in Boyers (ed.), *The Legacy of the German Refugee Intellectuals*, 174–85.

longer existed in Nazi Germany. If one could found a 'university in exile'—a space for academic freedom—why not also a culture—a space for autonomous cultural expression?[42]

For many musicians, composition in exile was an act of not merely personal survival, but also cultural survival. As Berghaus describes them, the exiled composers were *Kulturvermittler* (cultural ambassadors), keepers of a tradition abroad, because the country in which this musical tradition originated had expelled its proponents.[43] Krenek spoke of the political necessity of continuing to use the twelve-tone technique, despite its often negative reception, just because the Nazis had banned it.[44] Darius Milhaud commented that even in exile the 'profound impulses of race endure'. '[Y]ou cannot make a mistake as to the nature of a creative artist (and he mentioned Verdi now). It is idle to pretend that any great composer fails to demonstrate the racial origins of his expression.'[45] Eugene Zador likewise denied 'the hypothesis that a composer must live in the country of his birth, even when his musical style is based on native folk-lore. Stravinsky's ballets, written in Paris, are Russian, just as Bartók's 'Concerto', written in America, is Hungarian.' Stravinsky agreed: 'A man has one birth place, one fatherland, one country—he *can* only have one country—and the place of his birth is the most important fact of his life.'[46] Castelnuovo-Tedesco, finally, spoke of his having never felt 'cut off' in exile from either his Jewish ancestry or Latin culture, because they were 'a wealth which I had acquired once and for all: which were in me forever'.

In these responses, exiled composers were now asserting continuity between their personal, cultural, and national selves, rather than severance. Looking back at this period, Elliott Carter explained that the maintenance of the European culture of serious music was one of the things that made composers 'who and what

---

[42] For more on the university in exile or the New School for Social Research, see Krohn, *Intellectuals in Exile*.

[43] *Theatre and Film in Exile*, pp. xvi and 33.

[44] 'Self-Analysis', 32.

[45] 21 July 1940, ix. 8. Recorded in David Josephson, 'Documentation of the Upheaval and Immigration in *The New York Times* and the *Grove Dictionaries*', (6 May 1994), 26.

[46] Quoted by John Warrack, 'Stravinsky', *Tempo*, 81 (1967), 9, to confirm his general point that theorists have underestimated the fact of Stravinsky's Russianness and have tried to denationalize him.

they are'.[47] Further sense to this identification was again given by Thomas Mann when he described his own work as requiring 'long roots in my life'; 'secret connections must lead from it to earliest childhood dreams if I am to consider myself entitled to it. . . . The arbitrary reaching for a subject to which one does not have traditional claims of sympathy and knowledge, seems senseless and amateurish to me.'[48]

If one could separate a tradition from its originating country, one could similarly separate a language. Bertolt Brecht distinguished the language spoken in Nazi Germany from the 'true' German language, and claimed to take the latter wherever he went.[49] Profoundly sceptical of the possibility that one could be creative in a foreign language, he asked in song: 'Wozu in einer fremden Grammatik blättern? | Die Nachricht, die dich heimruft | Ist in bekannter Sprache geschrieben.'[50]

If Brecht held passionately on to his familiar and native language, other exiles just as passionately gave it up. Bartók refused to speak or write German just because it was the language of the enemy, yet he did not feel obliged, according to György Sandor, to reject the 'German' tradition of music. Bartók, Sandor writes, was 'strongly anti-German in all his activities, except [in] his musical work'.[51] Bartók thus sought continuity in his musical language (Hungarian–German) but discontinuity in his spoken language. So, too, in the case of Brecht's former collaborator Kurt Weill—but with a twist.

Weill sometimes described himself as having given up speaking German,[52] as being 'the same composer as before', but denied that

[47] Allen Edwards, *Flawed Words and Stubborn Sounds: A Conversation with Elliott Carter* (New York, 1971), 13.

[48] Quoted by Jackman, 'German Émigrés in Southern California', 103.

[49] Cf. Lyon's description of Brecht's position as being directly influenced by the philosopher Bloch (*Bertolt Brecht in America*, 30 and 251–62).

[50] 'Thoughts Concerning the Duration of Exile', in *Selected Poems*, tr. H. R. Hays (New York, 1947), 166, set to music by Hanns Eisler. Cf. Benjamin's remarks in 'The Task of the Translator', in *Illuminations: Walter Benjamin. Essays and Reflections*, ed. H. Arendt, tr. H. Zohn (New York, 1968), 69–82.

[51] Gillies (ed.), *Bartók Remembered*, 201. Cf. the comparable recollection by Bartók's publisher Hans W. Heinsheimer; ibid. 177.

[52] He once described his resolve 'to speak nothing but English', and recalled asking his German friends how they ever could become Americans if they held onto the language and customs of a country that had 'become the most un-American country in the world' (quoted in Ronald Taylor, *Kurt Weill: Composer in a Divided World* (Boston, 1991), 227). Cf. Pachter's observation regarding the guilt and inbreeding on the part of those exiles who preserved German culture: unwilling to allow their daily language to develop with the times, they used a language that 'froze at the point of emigration' ('On being an exile', 18).

he was any longer a 'German composer'.[53] Of course, it was not clear that Weill had been a German composer for a long time. Stephen Hinton records Constant Lambert's prophetic, though incongruous, description of Weill as an American composer even before exile.[54] What seemed to motivate this description was the fact that the musical tradition Weill had been developing since the mid-1920s, and which he had transported from Germany to America, was, according to contemporary views, more 'American' than 'German' to begin with. It was a tradition, as Weill described it himself, that saw music not as composed for posterity but, unlike the tradition of 'serious' music, for contemporary lives and times. Its techniques and materials were, therefore, of a 'popular' sort.[55]

But contrary to the crude assessment of Weill as the great assimilator, or the 'popular' composer who 'sold out' to commercial pressures, a more subtle assessment recognizes that, though he composed in a 'popular' vein, he saw himself as doing what he had always done, and that what he had always done was as much resistant as it was adaptive to popular or social demands. 'My position in America has become so secure', he explained, 'that I am now able to contemplate making my earlier works better known here than they have been up to now. . . . I have now completely settled down and feel absolutely at home.' But, he continued, 'it is heavy going in America, especially for someone who speaks his own musical language, but in the theatre the situation is still better and more favourable here than anywhere else, and I am sure that I shall reach the point where I can carry forward here what I began in Europe'.[56]

Apparently, though he conceived of his music as thoroughly situated in the world, he did not believe that it thereby had to be dictated by the world. That music is immanent in society is different from its being merely instrumental (i.e. in service to it): immanent music still has the freedom to resist. In these matters of resistance and continuity Weill was no different from Schoenberg: they just did not agree on how and in what ways music should be anchored in time and place. For the exiles, that was precisely the matter in dispute.

[53] See Kim Kowalke, 'Formerly German: Kurt Weill in America', in K. Kowalke and H. Edler (eds.), *A Stranger here myself: Kurt Weill-Studien* (Hildesheim, 1993), 35–57.

[54] Hinton (ed.), *The Threepenny Opera* (Cambridge, 1990), 70.

[55] Recorded in Taylor, *Kurt Weill*, 251.

[56] Ibid. 233.

If Weill was not, crudely, an adapter, then Schoenberg was not, crudely, a resister. Consider this description Schoenberg once gave of his expatriation. Contrasting his experience to that of the snake who 'was driven out of paradise' and 'sentenced to go on its belly and to eat dust all the days of its life', he experienced, he said, a new freedom: 'I . . . came from one country into another, where neither dust nor better food is rationed and where I am allowed to go on my feet, where my head can be erect, where kindness and cheerfulness is dominating, and where to live is a joy and to be an expatriate of another country is the grace of God.' 'I', he concluded, 'was driven into paradise.'[57] Other composers also saw the promise of paradise—or at least freedom—at the end of their tunnel of complaints. Having detailed the utter physical and mental torment of exile, Castelnuovo-Tedesco closed his interview with Goldberg by saying: 'On the other hand, America gave me something I didn't have before or perhaps I hadn't fully developed: a greater sense of freedom and a better understanding of social conditions and of community life.'

Nowadays the 'on the one hand–on the other hand' style of argument is often dismissed as unappealing academese, but it serves none the less to capture conceptually the often conflicting aspects of human experience. We have seen this style employed constantly by exiled composers to convey a complex pattern of different distinctions. These distinctions demonstrated that, in the matter of musical creativity, composers saw both the advantages and disadvantages of exile doubly conceived as an inner and outer condition, even though in claiming the one given side they often spoke as if they were dismissing the other. To see constructive doubleness emerging from their distinctions, rather than polarized one-sidedness, one simply must be cognizant of the hand with which a composer speaks at any given time.

4. Wagner's Legacy

This section begins to fortify with conceptual clarification the historical construction of the double-sided discourse of music and

[57] 'Two Speeches on the Jewish Situation', 502. Boris Schwarz comments on Schoenberg's dual position this way: 'Although Schoenberg is known to have been rather uncompromising in his musical views, he did make some concessions so that his writing would be more accessible to the American public, particularly to young American musicians' ('The Music World in Migration', 141).

musicians in exile. Certain philosophical claims and distinctions need to be detached from their particular historical expression. The palatable claim that music and musicians are bounded to nation, tradition, or culture must be separated from the more difficult and disturbing historical fact that they were once so bounded according to a racial criterion.

Wagner psychologically exiled many composers from the tradition of German music long before Hitler geographically exiled them, and he did so with thoughts that pervaded exile discourse. In his sinister essay 'Judaism in Music',[58] he conflated his broad metaphysical concept of Judaism (which, to recall, he used synonymously with his negative concept of the rootless, wandering, modern cosmopolite) with a more local and racial criterion to demarcate a class of living persons—the Jews. He spoke of 'the effect the Jews produce on us through [their] speech; and [of] . . . the Jewish influence upon music'. 'The Jew', he wrote, 'speaks the language of the nation in whose midst he dwells from generation to generation, but he speaks it always as an alien.' He described this alienation first in terms of the early 'violent severance' of Jews from 'Christian Civilization', and then in terms relating to language use: 'the [modern] Jew talks the modern European languages merely as learned, and not as mother tongues'. This fact, he continued at some length,

must necessarily debar him from any capability of expressing himself idiomatically, independently, and conformably to his nature. A language, with its expression and its evolution, is not the work of scattered units, but of a historical community; only he who has unconsciously grown up within the bonds of this community can take any share of its creations. . . . [T]o make poetry in a foreign tongue has hitherto been impossible, even to geniuses of the highest rank. . . . [T]he Jew can only after-speak. . . . He cannot truly make a poem of his words, an artwork of his doings. . . . If the aforesaid qualities . . . make the Jew almost incapable of giving artistic enunciation to his feelings . . . through *talk*, they make his aptitude for enunciation through *song* . . . even smaller, because song is just talk aroused to the highest passion.

Wagner went on to describe what he saw to be the apparent success but real failure of Jews in the musical world. He attributed their apparent success to their ability to deceive, to present the

---

[58] Wagner wrote this essay initially in 1850 under the pseudonym K. Freigedank (iii. 75–122). He revised and reissued it in 1869.

appearance of being German; their real failure he had attributed to their lack of ability to express themselves as purely human. Combining the appearance and the reality, he wrote: 'If we hear a Jew speak, we are unconsciously offended by the entire lack of purely-human expression.'[59] From this he concluded that, despite external appearance to the contrary, Jews can only participate in the German musical tradition as second-hand thinkers.

Wagner's reading of Jewish second-handedness was reread many times along the path of its pervasive influence. In his remarks that might well have been gathered together for 'friends . . . scattered throughout the corners of the globe', Wittgenstein once described, with Wagner in mind, how Jews had been measured in Western civilization 'on scales which [did] not fit them', and of their having been either over- or underestimated but, the suggestion is, never judged aright.[60] Wittgenstein then reminded his readers that Jews believe that '"genius" is found only in the holy man', and thus that 'even the greatest of Jewish thinkers' takes himself to be 'no more than talented'. 'Myself for instance', he wrote, and added: 'There is some truth in my idea that I really only think reproductively.' In this context, being second-handed is not a negative quality: following Jewish law, to think reproductively is to think in truthfulness; it is to think (albeit imperfectly of course) in the image of G–d.

For Wittgenstein, truthfulness was linked to one's being 'at home' in a language. Prima facie, and certainly Nazi doctrine supposed this, 'being at home in Jewish tradition' was incompatible with 'being at home in German tradition'. But, upon reflection, this incompatibility is at most contingent. For it is false that belonging to one tradition automatically precludes one from belonging to another.[61]

Wittgenstein spoke of the need for an expression sometimes 'to be withdrawn from language and sent for cleaning'. My purpose in

[59] Quoted in Rose, *Wagner*, 70.

[60] The reference to 'friends around the globe' is from Wittgenstein's 'Sketch for a Foreword' (printed as a foreword to *Philosophical Remarks*, ed. Rush Rhees), and printed in *Culture and Value*, tr. P. Winch, ed. G. H. von Wright (Oxford, 1980). All quotations from Wittgenstein, unless specified otherwise, are from this book: remarks 16, 18, 35, 39, 49, and 50.

[61] Cf. Karl Löwith's interesting observations on the Nazi separation of the Germans from the Jews, and of his own retreat into internal emigration, in his *My Life in Germany before and after 1933*, tr. E. King (Urbana, Ill., 1994), 139–40; also George Steiner, 'A Kind of Survivor', in *Language and Silence* (New York, 1967), 119–35.

comparing Wagner's remarks with Wittgenstein's was to show how the latter withdrew Wagner's judgement on the alienation of the Jews and tried to clean it. Schoenberg once tried the same thing. In the second of his 'Two Speeches on the Jewish Situation' given in 1935,[62] he recalled young Austrian Jewish artists growing up in circumstances in which their 'self-esteem suffered very much'. It was a time (the late nineteenth century) when Wagner's 'victorious career' was beginning to have its impact. Wagner, according to Schoenberg, had challenged the Jews to try to become true Germans, but racism had interfered. Camp-followers had distorted Wagner's views by turning his 'mild' views into 'harsh and excessive' ones. (Wagner had not made the distortion so difficult.) According to Schoenberg, the impact on young artists was severe: how could one create if one was not convinced of one's creative capacity? He then described the resistance that Jewish artists and intellectuals had tried to muster against this destructive view, but commented sadly that Jewish audiences had been too compliant: Aryans, he wrote, were more appreciative of his music than Jews. But he concluded positively: we should not pity Jews for being second-handed, but celebrate the fact that they are G–d's chosen people. We might say 'he is only a Jew', but by this we should mean that 'he is a Jew and therefore is probably of great importance'. Schoenberg was obviously trying to turn the anti-Jewish propaganda on its head.

Both Schoenberg and Wittgenstein could have concluded their remarks by identifying a special quality not of a racial or religious group (though historically we can understand why they did the contrary), but of a particular condition, namely that of being second-handed: because this condition by itself may foster qualities in people which contradict outright the judgement that they are second-rate.

This possibility was given its first steps towards credibility in the philosopher Ernst Bloch's insightful speech of 1939 entitled 'Disrupted Language, Disrupted Culture',[63] in which he dismissed the exiles suffering from *divided* loyalties and embraced their celebrating their *double* loyalties. Bloch generated his doubleness thesis specifically as a response to the conflict that arises when exiles or

[62] *Style and Idea*, 501–5.
[63] *Exiled German Writers, Art, Fiction, Documentary Material*, Special Issue, *Direction* (Dec. 1939), 16–17 and 36.

refugees (and he was thinking here explicitly of writers) recognize that they are bound to the language of their home, but are forced to fulfil their cultural task in a foreign place. He described the difficulties of translation and of trying to create art in an alien or second language, and the role of language in the shaping and maintaining of 'the culture-world', a world resulting from the mediation between subject and object. Where the mediation is disrupted, where the 'I' meets the 'Other' in shock, he explained, where the language does not mediate through a feeling of belonging, so the cultural task is temporarily arrested. What, he asked, is the exile to do?

Bloch narrated the exile's temptation to drift towards the extreme either of resistance or of adaptation, but argued that either temptation conceived in isolation from the other is incorrect. The correct attitude is 'as far from insipid intrusion as it is from introverted foreignness'. Exiles 'bring their roots with them . . . to America' but 'remain faithful to them not by making museum-pieces of them, but by testing and quickening their powers of expression on the new stuff of life'. The point is not to produce 'travel-books about America', but to produce an American literature in the German language. Crying out to be translated, this literature will reach a multilingual audience, but in so far as it succeeds, it will remain a 'deeply original creation'. It will have been 'fostered by double but not divided loyalties—by memory and a vigorous faith in the future'. 'We are creating on the frontier of two epochs,' he concluded: 'We, German writers in America, are frontiersmen in a doubly legitimate sense—both temporally and spatially—and we are working at the one necessary task: the realization of the rights of man.'

Bloch showed how the transition from divided to double loyalties demanded a twofold account, of doubleness itself and of the creativity, expression, or originality of composition issuing therefrom. But what he left more implicit than explicit in this demand were the many forms of doubleness supporting the construction of exile discourse. Most of the rest of this chapter attends to making those forms explicit.

5. Patterns of Doubleness

Bloch's thesis derived from exiles using their native language in a new country. But the same thesis could be derived were they to

adopt the new language as well. Given the many elements involved—languages, genres, styles, customs, traditions, cultures,
and countries—and the fact that these elements are not related by
simple one-to-one correspondences, the ways of mixing the so-
called old with the new are countless. One may change country, but
retain the customs, change the style but retain the language, and so
on.

Essential to the exile's experience is the feeling of doubled kinship. Exiles always have two elements in mind—broadly referred to
as the old and the new—that share a common function. 'As for the
posited central kinship of languages,' Benjamin once wrote, 'it is
marked by a distinctive convergence. Languages are not strangers
to one another, but are, *a priori* and apart from all historical relationships, interrelated in what they want to express.'[64] Accordingly,
if exiles always experienced the old and the new as mutually exclusive, their choices would be straightforward. But because they
more often experience the old and the new as interpenetrating or
mediating one another, their tasks are complex. Mediation allows
symmetric and asymmetric processes of transfiguration to occur in
the relata, say, when the use of a secondary language in a new
country brings changes to the dominant primary language, and/or
vice versa, or when the mixing of two musical traditions or styles
brings changes to one or both. These processes are capable of
generating different creative outcomes. One outcome recognizes
new products arising from the doubleness; here the 'two-tone'
character is preserved. The other outcome rests upon the
doubleness's being overcome: when aspects of continuity overshadow aspects of discontinuity, a synthesis or a 'supervenient
unity'[65] may be formed (say, a new or third language) on the basis
of which new products may then be created.[66]

---

[64] 'The Task of the Translator', 72.
[65] This phrase is employed by Wolfgang Grassl and Barry Smith in 'A Theory of
Austria', in *From Bolzano to Wittgenstein: The Tradition of Austrian Philosophy*
(Vienna, 1986), 17. Their article considers different models of centre and periphery,
purity and diversity, to account for Austria's particularly creative *fin de siècle*
period.
[66] I have profited from Alasdair MacIntyre, 'Relativism, Power, and Philosophy',
in M. Krausz (ed.), *Relativism: Interpretation and Confrontation* (Notre Dame, Ind.,
1989), 182–203. MacIntyre discusses the bordering status of persons occupying two
rival linguistic communities, the problems of translatability, the primary and secondary (native and strange use of terms), the benefits of conflicts, and the possibilities
of forming a third language.

Recall Bloch's recommendation that exiled writers express their double rather than divided loyalties by producing an American .literature in the German language. This production might involve the use of American themes and content and a foreign literary form or genre, or the form or genre may be American too and only the language foreign. But the recommendation could be extended to allow authors to write of German concerns in the language(s) of America. Extending this recommendation also to the other arts, one soon sees that there are myriad ways in which exiled artists may match the old with the new and thereby demonstrate the many creative possibilities available to them.[67]

Against this background, consider some musical works composed in exile in America of which we might judge that 'they could only have been composed by foreigners'. Many composers set American or new-life lyrics or themes to what was still generally regarded a German or European (old-world) language of music: Eisler's exile *Lieder* (the *Hollywood Songbook*), Stravinsky's a cappella arrangement of the *Star-Spangled Banner*, Weill's *Down in the Valley* or *Four Walt Whitman Songs*, Schoenberg's mixed-language *A Survivor from Warsaw*, and finally Krenek's orchestral composition based on the Carolina song 'I wonder as I wander'.[68] (Perhaps we should also include the Britten–Auden opera *Paul Bunyan*.) What is shared by these and other examples (whether the compositions end up being purely instrumental or not) is the dialogical play between the words (or themes) and music where the presence of the foreign music transfigures the conventional significance of the text or theme, and/or vice versa.[69]

These transfigurative possibilities illustrate the creative possibilities of doubleness. They illustrate well the very general principle that changing the context may change the meaning. They also illustrate the principle that setting the familiar against the unfamiliar, the new against the old, the native against the foreign, may result in a changed understanding of the two sides. The musical

---

[67] Although the identification of nations is not a necessary feature of this mixed production, it is common, linked as the mixing often is with experiences of travel and exile. Note also that 'German' and 'American' stand for historical complexes and are neither related nor opposed as pure elements.

[68] Apparently the song turned out not to be authentic folk-song at all. See John L. Stewart's account of the piece and its context in his *Ernst Krenek: The Man and his Music* (Berkeley, Calif., 1991), 243.

[69] Cf. Hinton (ed.), *The Threepenny Opera*, 5, 102, and 118.

examples also attest to the possibility of there being different kinds of creative or expressive outcomes. Composers, for example, who imagined their 'old-world' language transformed into a future 'American' language were imagining, in relative terms, a synthetic 'third' language. Composers, by contrast, who still saw their compositions as embodying 'unlovely', parodistic, or Aesopian antagonisms generated through the mixing of languages would not have been so eager for eventual synthesis, or at least 'not yet'. Think of the Brecht–Eisler song 'Under the Green Pepper Trees'.[70]

So far I have extended Bloch's thesis of doubleness to accommodate, first, the production of different mixes of German–American literatures, and, then, comparable production in the other arts. I have also allowed the creative possibilities to be twofold, depending on the maintenance of doubleness, on the one hand, or following upon synthesis, on the other. But another extension is possible, because the doubleness pervasive in exile discourse also describes the position of artists as artists rather than as exiles.

The doubleness embroiled in the desire of exiles to hold onto the old as they negotiate the new is guided by the same ideal of creativity as the doubleness embroiled in the long-standing claim that artists, from their position of difference or distance—from their standing, as it were, at the limits of the world—undertake to transfigure the familiar. For artists the doubleness is conventionally expressed in the vertical distinction between the transcendent and the ordinary; for exiles it is expressed horizontally between the old and the new. But what artists and exiles share is their experience of being both insiders and outsiders. In doubling terms, by seeing outside, beyond, or above, they claim to see more truthfully the 'here and now' within. It is perhaps incongruous, in the context of this chapter, that the long-exiled Wagner played on the advantages of this shared double position as explicitly as any composer ever has.

This shared position can be seen as having already infused European artistic culture before the war. Recall the sense of newness, linked increasingly to their psychological exile, composers were cultivating as they experimented with compositions mixing familiar and unfamiliar themes. Looking back, it seems tragically prophetic

[70] For more on 'unlovely' antagonisms, see Hatfield, 'Thomas Mann and America', 175.

that they voiced their desired doubleness by contrasting the European 'old world' and an Amerikan 'new world'. But it was less the European-influenced establishment of America to which they looked, than the music of alienated 'black' America. There they found similarities with their experience of alienation at home. Fusing 'American' motifs of jazz, folk-song, and poetry with European idioms to suggest idealistic, utopian, or avant-gardist visions had already been tried by Puccini, Ravel, and Dvořák, and certainly by the composer Bloch in his 1916 composition *America*, but the practice was given increasing political urgency in the music of Milhaud, Chavez, Krenek, Hindemith, Zemlinsky, and Weill. (It was also being developed in America by Ives, Copland, and Gershwin.) Probably the most explicit doubling examples coming from Europe were the unofficially, but appropriately, named 'zonks'—German-sounding American-styled songs—of the Brecht–Weill collaboration.[71] Another telling example is found in Zemlinsky's *Symphonische Gesänge* of 1929 (especially the 'Afrikan Tanz'), in which he mixed tonal and atonal idioms with Dixieland and African idioms. This piece gave urgent expression to the message he had already conveyed in the opening of his *Lyrische Symphonie* of 1924, in which he used the words of the Bengali poet Tagore to cry: 'I am a stranger in a strange land' and 'am athirst for far-away things'.[72]

The visionary or revolutionary moment captured in the doubled compositional style of the doubly exiled artist prompts us to extend Bloch's thesis a step further. This moment has also been invoked in Modernist and more recent descriptions of the condition and progressive potential of migrating, marginal, and minority social groups. These descriptions have forced us to think with dynamic models and travelling terms. They have stressed the importance of difference and duality in opening up spaces for multiple and new voices, and have stressed mediation to overcome static dichotomies. They have spoken of borders and frontiers as sites for constructive displacings of the centre. James Clifford has thus recently written of Diaspora cultures as mediating 'in a lived tension, the experiences of separation and entanglement, of living here and remembering/desiring another place', and of Diaspora conscious-

---

[71] For more on 'zonks', see Taylor, *Kurt Weill*, 107.

[72] I am grateful to one commentator who pointed out that pieces containing visions of America would not have been composed in America in the same way.

ness as a product of 'cultures and histories in collision and dialogue'.[73]

The doubling thesis so extended allows us to see, as we have seen in each of the previous chapters, that *it is less the 'twoness' than the 'more-than-oneness'*[74] that sustains the progressive tendency. For, multiply situated, a person is taken beyond the limits of the familiar and sees that there is more than one way to view the world. The doubleness thesis is compatible, in other words, with a fundamental openness or a purposive ambivalence to the world ('let's see what the world is like'). When exiles spoke of their losing their absolutism (Eisler), of America's deprovincializing them, or of their learning not to take things for granted or to 'regard as natural the circumstances that had developed in Europe' (Adorno),[75] they were suggesting not that these new conditions were leading them all to think the same new thing, but that, in seeing the world anew, each had a genuine option about how he or she would shape his or her home in permanent exile or eventual return. Santayana made the point earlier and most poetically: 'migration like birth is heroic: the soul is signing away her safety for a blank cheque'.[76] Said made the point more recently, when he spoke about the painfulness, but also the benefits, of an exile's contrapuntal awareness.[77] (Neither in my thinking nor in Said's is the musical term 'contrapuntal' accidental.)

However, neither openness nor the condition of doubleness carries progressive value by itself. According to most exile theorists, they are valuable in connection to the integrity of the now non-integrated self. In this connection, the condition becomes linked also to a person's actions. In other words, whether exiles described themselves as feeling at home, or as estranged, or as oscillating

---

[73] 'Diasporas', *Cultural Anthropology*, 9/3 (1994), 311 and 319. Cf. Janet Wolff, *Resident Alien: Feminist Cultural Criticism* (New Haven, 1995), and Adi Wimmer, ' "Expelled and Banished:" The Exile Experience of Austrian "Anschluss" Victims in Personal Histories and Literary Documents', in W. Hölbling and R. Wagnleitner (eds.), *The European Emigrant Experience in the USA* (Tübingen, 1992), 67, in which he discusses Julia Kristeva's dual discourse of the language of desire.
[74] Put this way, my view is not only committed to doubleness but, and this might be more appropriate for contemporary society, also triplenesses etc. The 'more-than-oneness' is the crucial moment. I am grateful to Martin Jay for reminding me to emphasize this point.
[75] Adorno, 'Scientific Experiences of a European Scholar in America', 367.
[76] 'The Philosophy of Travel', in Robinson (ed.), *Altogether Elsewhere*, 44.
[77] 'Reflections on Exile', 148.

between the two, they believed, rightly I think, that they would and should be judged more on the outcome of their condition than on the condition itself—on their deeds. Victor Hugo once wrote that 'an exile is a decent man who persists in decency',[78] but, for exiled composers, the concern was also whether, as creative people, they had persisted in productive deeds. The two concerns were not necessarily unconnected, as the composer Bloch now makes explicit: 'When art becomes an expression of a philosophy of life, it is no longer a luxury ... It is a storm that carries one away, unites all [people] in a unit of solidarity, shakes them to the bottom of the soul, waking them to the greatest problems of their common destiny.'[79]

I have suggested that the philosopher Bloch's thesis of doubleness establishes with my extensions a link between the condition in which exiles and artists found themselves and their products and/or deeds. But it would be quite wrong to think that the link is a sufficient condition. Even were composers to be 'ideally' saturated in a culture *and* critically estranged from it, there would be no guarantee that their products would be creative or suitably expressive. So similarly must we apply this proviso to the claim about the doubleness of a work's content: that composers might have chosen to employ a double language never guaranteed that they would say or express anything new. But that the link is not one of a guarantee does not mean that there is not a link at all. Rather, the link is one of opening up a space—an autonomous or critical gap that allows us to make assessments of creativity or expression by looking not at the conditions or modes of production *per se*, but at the productions—the works—themselves. Merleau-Ponty captured this change of emphasis when he suggested that an exemplary work or an artist's life work calls for the conditions—rather, presumably he meant, than vice versa. 'Although it is certain that a man's life does not *explain* his work, it is equally certain that the two are connected. The truth is that *this work to be done called for this life*.'[80]

So describing the link forestalls reductionist arguments, asser-

[78] 'What Exile Is', in Robinson (ed.), *Altogether Elsewhere*, 79.
[79] David Ewen, *American Composers: A Biographical Dictionary* (New York, 1982), 78.
[80] 'Cézanne's Doubt', in *Sense and Non-Sense*, tr. H. L. and P. A. Dreyfus (Evanston, Ill., 1964), 20.

tions of causal links, or specifications of necessary and sufficient conditions, all of which close or reduce the gap between the conditions of musical practice and its creative productions. The attempt to preserve this gap is an attempt to account for music's aesthetic moment within philosophical theory or, as I have otherwise put it, its double quality of being purely musical and deeply worlded at the same time. The attempt to preserve the gap is a way to show within philosophical theory the presence and immanence, but also the non-reducibility, of the extraordinary in the most ordinary examples of our human deeds. The extraordinary symbolizes here our freedom to be musical.

Using doubleness as a technique of philosophical description impels us to extend Bloch's thesis one last time. This extension asks us to see the limits of conditions and of philosophical descriptions in a positive light. It asks us to follow Nietzsche in seeing philosophy and language as ideally approximating to the condition of music, and not vice versa. 'Compared with music, all communication by words is shameless; words dilute and brutalize; words depersonalize; words make the uncommon common.'[81]

To reiterate again a major thesis of German Romanticism, the true significance of music—its creative or aesthetic moment—is ineffable and inexpressible; it fails to be accounted for even in the most complete description not only of its conditions of production, but also of its own form and content. In this chapter we have seen this view invoked by exiled composers when they spoke of music as partially surpassing its concrete situation, and it was this characterization that led them to conclude that music was not wholly, even if it were in part, an ordinary nation- or culture-bound language. But suppose exiled composers had focused more than they did on these so-called ordinary or common languages, and had noticed the extent to which they too were capable of being taken, as it were, abroad and transfigured. What they might then have seen is that ordinary language is much more like the 'non-ordinary' language of music than the 'non-ordinary' language of music is like 'ordinary' language.

---

[81] *The Will to Power*, sect. 810, in *Complete Works*, tr. and ed. W. Kaufmann (New York, 1968), 15, 254. Also quoted (in a way that connects us back to Ch. 1) in Robert Morgan's relevantly titled article 'Secret Languages: The Roots of Musical Modernism', in M. Chefdor, R. Quinones, and A. Wachtel (eds.), *Modernism: Challenges and Perspectives* (Urbana, Ill., 1986), 33–53.

Recall Alfred Schutz's explanation of William James's 'fringes' in his 1944 discussion of 'the stranger':

Every word and every sentence is . . . surrounded by 'fringes' connecting them, on the one hand, with past and future elements of the universe of discourse to which they pertain and surrounding them, on the other hand, with a halo of emotional values and irrational implications which themselves remain ineffable. The fringes are the stuff poetry is made of; they are capable of being set to music but they are not translatable.[82]

In this picture, ordinary language has always the possibility of a double identity: it has ordinary, conceptual significance and extra-ordinary fringes. As such, it may be seen ideally to approximate now to the condition of suggestiveness or expressiveness we find in lyric poetry or music, or paradigmatically in song.

Following James and Schutz, and not accidentally the Wittgenstein of the *Tractatus*, one may likewise say of philosophical theory itself that its full meaning fails to be grasped in what it tries ordinarily, by means of reason and logic, to say. For its meaning is captured as well in what a theory suggests or shows 'between the lines', or even in what it fails to say in its spaces and silences. In other terms, meaning is captured in the doubling condition of a philosophical theory, in, that is to say, a theory that allows what it says to be weathered and/or defied by what it shows. Just as the doubling condition of the exiled composer opens up a gap without fully accounting for any creativity that might follow, so the apparent failure or limits of a philosophical theory to account for everything is precisely the positive condition in which it reveals its polysemous meaning(s). Autonomous music, to reiterate the conclusion of Chapter 1, cautions philosophy to see its limits as positive.

This chapter drew a philosophical picture out of an exemplary instance, this being the fact of my grandfather's having once adopted a double identity. Like an aphorism, the exemplar suggested a fractured world of significance. It was a world that revealed much more constructive conflict or contrapuntal doubleness than it did either simple logical opposition or harmonious theory. It was a world that challenged two claims prevalent in exile theory: the closed, 'Wagnerian' line that exile precludes creativity, and the

---

[82] 'The Stranger: An Essay in Social Psychology', *American Journal of Sociology*, 49/6 (1944), 504.

diminishing line, articulated (though not ultimately supported) by Said, that an exile 'exists in a median state, beset by half-involvements and half-detachments'. In contrast to both these positions, this chapter argued that exiled composers, as exiles and composers, alienated at home or living abroad, have the possibility to live constructively in a condition of doubleness, not division. Under this possibility, exile may prove a route for genuine political empowerment and emancipation. The philosophical accent, as it has been throughout this book, is focused on the 'may'. It is an accent, I have been arguing, that leaves the theoretical claim open enough to let us seek its proof in the pudding of the practice. It is an accent that has historically defined the quest for the autonomous musical voice.

Bibliography

ABBATE, C., *Unsung Voices: Opera and Musical Narrative in the Nineteenth Century* (Princeton, 1991).

——and PARKER, R. (eds.), *Analyzing Opera: Verdi and Wagner* (Berkeley, Calif. 1989).

ADORNO, T. W. A., *Philosophy of Modern Music*, tr. A. G. Mitchell and W. V. Blomster (New York, 1973).

——*Negative Dialectics*, tr. E. B. Ashton (London, 1973).

——*Minima moralia: Reflections from Damaged Life*, tr. E. F. N. Jephcott (London, 1974).

——*In Search of Wagner*, tr. R. Livingstone (London, 1981).

——*Prisms*, tr. S. and S. Weber (Cambridge, Mass., 1981).

——*Introduction to the Sociology of Music*, tr. E. B. Ashton (New York, 1988).

——*Notes to Literature*, tr. S. W. Nicholsen, 2 vols. (New York, 1991–2).

——*Quasi una fantasia: Essays on Modern Music*, tr. R. Livingstone (London, 1992).

——*Aesthetic Theory*, tr. R. Hullot-Kentor (Minneapolis, 1997).

ALBRIGHT, D., *Representation and the Imagination: Beckett, Kafka, Nabokov, and Schoenberg* (Chicago, 1981).

ALPERSON, P., 'Schopenhauer and Musical Revelation', *Journal of Aesthetics and Art Criticism*, 40/2 (1981), 155–66.

——*Philosophies of Arts: An Essay in Differences* (Ithaca, NY, 1997).

——(ed.), *What is Music? An Introduction to the Philosophy of Music* (New York, 1987).

——(ed.), *The Philosophy of Music*, Special Issue, *Journal of Aesthetics and Art Criticism*, 52/1 (1994).

ALLISON, D. B., and BABICH B. E. (eds.), *New Nietzsche Studies*, Special Issue: *Nietzsche and Music*, 1/1 (Fall–Winter 1996).

ARATO, A., and GEBHARDT, E. (eds.), *The Essential Frankfurt School Reader* (New York, 1982).

ATTALI, J., *Noise: The Political Economy of Music*, tr. B. Massumi (Minneapolis, 1985).

BABBITT, M., 'On Having Been and Still Being an American Composer', *Perspectives of New Music*, 27/1 (Winter 1989), 106–12.

BALLANTINE, C., *Music and its Social Meanings* (New York, 1984).

BARTHES, R., *Writing Degree Zero*, tr. A. Lavers and C. Smith (New York, 1968).

BARTHES, R., *Image–Music–Text*, tr. S. Heath (London, 1977).

——*The Responsibility of Forms: Critical Essays on Music, Art, and Representation*, tr. R. Howard (Berkeley, Calif., 1991).

BARZON, J., *Berlioz and his Century: An Introduction to the Age of Romanticism* (Chicago, 1982).

BATTCOCK, G., and NICKAS, R. (eds.), *The Art of Performance: A Critical Anthology* (New York, 1984).

BAUDELAIRE, C., *The Painter of Modern Life and Other Essays*, tr. J. Mayne (New York, 1964).

BENJAMIN, W., *Illuminations: Walter Benjamin. Essays and Reflections*, ed. H. Arendt, tr. H. Zohn (New York, 1968).

BERGER, K., '*Diegesis* and *Mimesis*: The Poetic Modes and the Matter of Artistic Presentation', *Journal of Musicology*, 12/4 (1994), 407–33.

BERGERON, K., and BOHLMAN, P. V. (eds.), *Disciplining Music: Musicology and its Canons* (Chicago, 1992).

BERGHAUS, G. (ed.), *Theatre and Film in Exile: German Artists in Great Britain, 1933–45* (Oxford, 1989).

BERLIN, I., *Four Essays on Liberty* (Oxford, 1969; repr. 1990).

BERLIOZ, H., *The Art of Music and Other Essays*, tr. and ed. E. Csicsery-Rónay (Bloomington, Ind., 1994).

BEST, D., *Philosophy and Human Movement* (London, 1978–9).

BETZ, A., *Hanns Eisler, Political Musician*, tr. B. Hopkins (Cambridge, 1982).

BLOCH, E., and ROLLAND, R., *Lettres, 1911–13*, ed. J.-F. Tappy (Lausanne, 1994).

——*Ernest Bloch Society Bulletin*.

BLOCH, E., 'Disrupted Language, Disrupted Culture', *Exiled German Writers, Art, Fiction, Documentary Material*, Special Issue, *Direction* (Dec. 1939), 16–17, 36.

——*Essays on the Philosophy of Music*, tr. and ed. D. Drew (Cambridge, 1985).

BLOCH, S., and HESKES, I. (eds.), *Ernest Bloch: Creative Spirit*, A Program Source Book (New York, 1976).

BÖLL, H., 'Murke's Collected Silences', in *The Stories of Heinrich Böll*, tr. L. Vennewitz (Evanston, Ill., 1986), 495–513.

BONDS, M. EVANS, *Wordless Rhetoric: Musical Form and the Metaphor of Oration* (Cambridge, Mass., 1991).

BORCHMEYER, D., *Richard Wagner: Theory and Theatre*, tr. S. Spencer (Oxford, 1991).

BOULEZ, P., *Orientations: Collected Writings*, ed. J.-J. Nattiez, tr. M. Cooper (Cambridge, Mass., 1986).

BOURDIEU, P., *Distinction: A Social Critique of the Judgment of Taste*, tr. R. Nice (Cambridge, Mass., 1984).

—— *The Rules of Art: Genesis and Structure of the Literary Field*, tr. S. Emanuel (Stanford, Calif., 1995).

BOWIE, A., *Aesthetics and Subjectivity from Kant to Nietzsche* (Manchester, 1990).

—— *From Romanticism to Critical Theory: The Philosophy of German Literary Theory* (London, 1997).

BOYERS, R. (ed.), *The Legacy of the German Refugee Intellectuals* (New York, 1972).

BRECHT, B., *Selected Poems*, tr. H. R. Hays (New York, 1947).

BRENNAN, T., and JAY, M. (eds.), *Vision in Context: Historical and Contemporary Perspectives on Sight* (New York, 1996).

BRINKMANN, R., and WOLFF, C. (eds.), *'Driven into Paradise': The Musical Migration from Nazi Germany to the United States* (Berkeley, Calif., forthcoming).

BRONNER, S. E., *Of Critical Theory and its Theorists* (Oxford, 1994).

—— and Kellner, D. M. (eds.), *Critical Theory and Society: A Reader* (London, 1989).

BROWN, W., *States of Injury: Power and Freedom in Late Modernity* (Princeton, 1995).

BUCK-MORSS, S., *The Origin of Negative Dialectics* (New York, 1977).

BUDD, M., *Music and the Emotions: The Philosophical Theories* (London, 1985).

BUDICK, S., and ISER, W., *Languages of the Unsayable: The Play of Negativity in Literature and Literary Theory* (New York, 1989).

BUJIĆ, B. (ed.), *Music in European Thought, 1851–1912* (Cambridge, 1988).

—— 'Delicate Metaphors', *Musical Times* (June 1997), 16–22.

BURBIDGE, P., and SUTTON, R. (eds.), *The Wagner Companion* (London, 1979).

BURNHAM, S., *Beethoven Hero* (Princeton, 1995).

BUSONI, F., *Entwurf einer neuen Ästhetik der Tonkunst* (Frankfurt, 1974).

CAGE, J., *Silence: Lectures and Writings* (Middletown, Conn., 1939).

CARPENTER, P., 'Musical Form and Musical Idea: Reflections on a Theme of Schoenberg, Hanslick, and Kant', in Strainchamps *et al.* (eds.), *Music and Civilization*, 394–427.

CATHER, W., *Youth and the Bright Medusa* (New York, 1975).

—— *The Song of the Lark* (Lincoln, Nebr., 1978).

CAVELL, S., *Must we Mean what we Say? Modern Philosophical Essays in Morality, Religion, Drama, Music and Criticism* (New York, 1969).

—— *The World Viewed: Reflections on the Ontology of Film* (Cambridge, Mass., 1979).

CERF, S. R., 'False Dawn: How Hans Sachs' Warning at the End of *Die*

Meistersinger Echoes through German History', *Opera News*, 16 Jan. 1993, 10–12, 44.

CERTEAU, M. de, *The Practice of Everyday Life*, tr. S. Rendall (Berkeley, Calif., 1984).

CHANCELLOR, J., *Wagner* (London, 1978).

CHEFDOR, M., QUINONES, R., and WACHTEL, A. (eds.), *Modernism: Challenges and Perspectives* (Urbana, Ill., 1986).

CHYTRY, J. J., *The Aesthetic State: A Quest in Modern German Thought* (Berkeley, Calif., 1989).

CICORA, M. A., '"Eva in Paradies", An Approach to Wagner's *Meistersinger*', *German Studies Review*, 10/2 (1987), 321–33.

CLÉMENT, C., *Opera, or the Undoing of Women*, tr. B. Wing (Minneapolis, 1988).

CLIFFORD, J., 'Diasporas', *Cultural Anthropology*, 9/3 (1994), 302–38.

COHEN, T., and GUYER, P. (eds.), *Essays in Kant's Aesthetics* (Chicago, 1982).

——— and PUTNAM, H. (eds.), *Pursuits of Reason: Essays in Honor of Stanley Cavell* (Lubbock, Tex., 1993).

COOK, N., *Music, Imagination, and Culture* (Oxford, 1990).

COOKE, D., *I Saw the World End: A Study of Wagner's* Ring (Oxford, 1979).

DAHLHAUS, C., *Richard Wagner's Music Dramas*, tr. M. Whittall (Cambridge, 1979).

——— *Between Romanticism and Modernism*, tr. M. Whittall (Berkeley, Calif., 1980).

——— *Esthetics of Music*, tr. W. Austin (Cambridge, 1982).

——— *Foundations of Music History*, tr. J. B. Robinson (Cambridge, 1983).

——— *Realism in Nineteenth-Century Music*, tr. M. Whittall (Cambridge, 1985).

——— *Schönberg and the New Music*, tr. D. Puffett and A. Clayton (Cambridge, 1987).

——— *The Idea of Absolute Music*, tr. R. Lustig (Cambridge, 1989).

——— *Nineteenth-Century Music*, tr. J. Bradford Robinson (Berkeley, Calif., 1989).

DANTO, A., *Beyond the Brillo Box: The Visual Arts in Post-Historical Perspective* (New York, 1992).

——— *After the End of Art: Contemporary Art and the Pale of History* (Princeton, 1997).

DANUSER, H., 'Zur Aktualität musikalischer Interpretationstheorie', *Musiktheorie*, 1 (1996), 39–51.

DAVERIO, J., *Nineteenth-Century Music and the German Romantic Ideology* (New York, 1993).

DAVIES, S., *Musical Meaning and Expression* (Ithaca, NY, 1984).

DEAS, S., *In Defence of Hanslick* (London, 1940).

DEATHRIDGE, J., and DAHLHAUS, C., *Wagner*, The New Grove (London, 1984).

DEBUSSY, C., BUSONI, F., and IVES, C., *Three Classics in the Aesthetic of Music* (New York, 1962).

DENNIS, D. B., *Beethoven in German Politics, 1870–1989* (New Haven, 1996).

DENSELOW, R., *When the Music's Over: The Story of Political Pop* (London, 1990).

DOWNING, T. A., *Music and the Origins of Language: Theories from the French Enlightenment* (Cambridge, 1995).

DUMONT, L., *German Ideology from France to Germany and Back* (Chicago, 1994).

DUNSBY, J., *Performing Music: Shared Concerns* (Oxford, 1995).

DWORKIN, G., *The Theory and Practice of Autonomy* (Cambridge, 1988).

EAGLETON, T., *The Ideology of the Aesthetic* (Cambridge, 1990).

——*Ideology: An Introduction* (London, 1991).

EDWARDS, A., *Flawed Words and Stubborn Sounds: A Conversation with Elliott Carter* (New York, 1971).

EISLER, H., *A Rebel in Music: Selected Writings*, ed. M. Grabs (New York, 1978).

EWEN, D., *American Composers: A Biographical Dictionary* (New York, 1982).

FITZGERALD, W., 'The Questionability of Music', *Representations*, 46 (Spring 1994), 121–47.

FLEMING, D., and BAILYN, B. (eds.), *The Intellectual Migration: Europe and America, 1930–1960* (Cambridge, Mass., 1969).

FOX, M. (ed.), *Schopenhauer: His Philosophical Achievement* (Brighton, 1980).

FRANKLIN, P., *The Idea of Music: Schönberg and Others* (London, 1985).

FRISBY, D., *Fragments of Modernity* (Cambridge, Mass., 1986).

FRISCH, W. (ed.), *Brahms and his World* (Princeton, 1990).

FRITH, S., *Performing Rites: On the Value of Popular Music* (Oxford, 1996).

——(ed.), *Performance Matters*, Special Issue, *New Formations: A Journal of Culture/Theory/Politics*, 27 (Winter 1995–6).

FUBINI, E., *A History of Music Aesthetics*, tr. M. Hatwell (London, 1990).

FULCHER, J., *The Nation's Image: French Grand Opera as Politics and Politicized Art* (Cambridge, 1987).

GADAMER, H.-G., *Truth and Method*, tr. and rev. J. Weinheimer and D. G. Marshall (New York, 1994).

GAY, P., *Freud, Jews, and Other Germans: Masters and Victims in Modernist Culture* (Oxford, 1978).

GELLEY, A. (ed.), *Unruly Examples: On the Rhetoric of Exemplarity* (Stanford, Calif., 1995).

GERMANISCHES NATIONALMUSEUM NÜRNBERG, *Die Meistersinger und Richard Wagner. Die Rezeptionsgeschichte einer Oper von 1868 bis heute* (1981).

GILLIAM, B. (ed.), *Music and Performance during the Weimar Republic* (Cambridge, 1994).

——'The Annexation of Anton Bruckner: Nazi Revisionism and the Politics of Appropriation', *Musical Quarterly*, 78/3 (Fall 1994), 584–609.

GILLIES, M. (ed.), *Bartók Remembered* (New York, 1990).

GOEHR, L., *The Imaginary Museum of Musical Works: An Essay in the Philosophy of Music* (Oxford, 1992).

——'Writing Music History', *History and Theory*, 31/2 (1992), 182–99.

——'Music has no Meaning to Speak Of: On the Politics of Musical Interpretation', in Krausz (ed.), *The Interpretation of Music*, 177–90.

——'Political Music and the Politics of Music', in Alperson (ed.), *The Philosophy of Music*, 99–112.

——'Schopenhauer and the Musicians: An Inquiry into the Sounds of Silence and the Limits of Philosophizing about Music', in Jacquette (ed.), *Schopenhauer, Philosophy, and the Arts*, 200–28.

GOETHE, J. W., *Wilhelm Meister's Apprenticeship*, ed. and tr. E. A. Blackall (New York, 1989).

——*Elective Affinities*, tr. R. J. Hollingdale (Harmondsworth 1971).

GOLDBERG, A., 'The Sounding Board', *Los Angeles Times*, sect iv, 14, 21 and 28 May 1950.

GOLDSTEIN, R. J., *Political Censorship of the Arts and the Press in Nineteenth-Century Europe* (New York, 1989).

GOULD, G., *The Glenn Gould Reader*, ed. Tim Page (New York, 1984).

GOULD, T., 'The Audience of Originality: Kant and Wordsworth on the Reception of Genius', in Cohen and Guyer (eds.), *Essays in Kant's Aesthetics*, 179–93.

GRASSL, W., and SMITH, B., 'A Theory of Austria', in *From Bolzano to Wittgenstein: The Tradition of Austrian Philosophy* (Vienna, 1986), 11–30.

GREY, T. S., *Wagner's Musical Prose: Texts and Contexts* (Cambridge, 1995).

——'Metaphorical Modes in Nineteenth-Century Music Criticism: Image, Narrative, and Idea', in Scher (ed.), *Music and Text*, 93–117.

GRIMM, R., and HERMAND, J. (eds.), *Re-Reading Wagner* (Madison, Wis., 1993).

GROOS, A., 'Constructing Nuremburg: Typological and Proleptic Communities in *Die Meistersinger*', *19th-Century Music*, 16/1 (Summer 1992), 18–34.

GUCK, M. A., 'Rehabilitating the Incorrigible', in Pople (ed.), *Theory, Analysis, and Meaning in Music*, 57–73.

HABERMAS, J., *Theory and Practice*, tr. J. Viertel (Boston, 1973).

HAHN, R., *On Singers and Singing: Lectures and an Essay*, tr. L. Simoneau (Portland, Oreg., 1990).

HAMLYN, D. W., *Schopenhauer: The Arguments of the Philosophers* (London, 1980)

HAMPSHIRE, S., *Innocence and Experience* (Cambridge, Mass., 1989).

HANSLICK, E., *Music Criticisms, 1846–99*, tr. H. Pleasants (Baltimore, 1950).

——*Vienna's Golden Years of Music, 1850–1900*, tr. and ed. H. Pleasants (New York, 1950).

——*On the Musically Beautiful*, tr. G. Payzant (Indianapolis, 1986).

——*Aus Meinem Leben* (Basel, 1987).

——*Sämtliche Schriften*, ed. D. Strauss (Vienna, 1993).

HANSON, A. M., *Musical Life of Biedermeier Vienna* (Cambridge, 1985).

HASSAN, I., *The Literature of Silence: Henry Miller and Samuel Beckett* (New York, 1966).

HEGEL, G. W. F., *Aesthetics: Lectures on Fine Art*, tr. T. M. Knox, 2 vols. (Oxford, 1975).

HEIDEGGER, M., *Poetry, Language, Thought*, tr. A. Hofstadter (New York, 1971).

HEIN, H., 'Performance as an Aesthetic Category', *Journal of Aesthetics and Art Criticism*, 28 (1970), 381–6.

HEINE, H., *The Works of Heinrich Heine*, tr. C. G. Leland, 20 vols. (New York, 1920).

HEISTER, H.-W., ZENCK, C. M., and PETERSEN, P. (eds.), *Musik im Exil: Folgen des Nazismus für die internationale Musikkultur* (Frankfurt, 1983).

HELD, D., *An Introduction to Critical Theory: Horkheimer to Habermas* (Berkeley, Calif., 1980).

HENZE, H. W., *Music and Politics: Collected Writings, 1953–81*, tr. P. Labanyi (London, 1982).

HESSE, H., *The Glass Bead Game (Magister Ludi)*, tr. R. and C. Winston (New York, 1969).

HINDEMITH. P., *A Composer's World: Horizons and Limitations* (Cambridge, Mass., 1969).

HINTON, S. (ed.), *The Threepenny Opera* (Cambridge, 1990).

HOBSBAWM, E., and RANGER, T. (eds.), *The Invention of Tradition* (Cambridge, 1983).

HODGE, J., 'Aesthetic Decomposition: Music, Identity, and Time', in Krausz (ed.), *The Interpretation of Music*, 247–58.

HÖLBLING, W., and WAGNLEITNER, R. (eds.), *The European Emigrant Experience in the USA* (Tübingen, 1992).

HOFFMAN, E., *Lost in Translation: A Life in a New Language* (New York, 1989).

HOFFMANN, E. T. A., *Musikalische Novellen und Aufsätze*, i, ed. E. Istel (Regensburg, 1919).

—— 'Tobias Martin, Master Cooper, and his Men', in *The Best Tales of Hoffmann*, ed. E. F. Bleiler (New York, 1967), 236–84.

—— *E. T. A. Hoffmann's Musical Writings: Kreisleriana, The Poet and the Composer, Music Criticism*, ed. D. Charlton, tr. M. Clarke (Cambridge, 1989).

HOWELL, C., 'Sartre and the Commitment of Pure Art', *British Journal of Aesthetics*, 18/2 (1978), 172–82.

HUME, D., *Essays: Moral, Political, and Literary*, ed. E. F. Miller (Indianapolis, 1987).

HURAY, P. LE, and DAY, J., *Music and Aesthetics in the Eighteenth and Early-Nineteenth Centuries* (Cambridge, 1981).

ISSACHAROFF, M., and JONES, R. F. (eds.), *Performing Texts* (Philadelphia, 1988).

JACKMAN, J. C., and BORDEN, C. M. (eds.), *The Muses Flee Hitler: Cultural Transfer and Adaptation, 1930–1945* (Washington, 1983).

JACOBSON, R., *Reverberations: Interviews with the World's Leading Musicians* (New York, 1974).

JACQUETTE, D. (ed.), *Schopenhauer, Philosophy, and the Arts* (Cambridge, 1996).

JAMES, W., *The Varieties of Religious Experience* (New York, 1982).

JAMESON, F. (ed.), *Aesthetics and Politics* (London, 1980).

JANSEN, S. C., *Censorship: The Knot that Binds Power and Knowledge* (Oxford, 1988).

JAY, M., *Adorno* (Cambridge, Mass., 1984).

—— *Permanent Exiles: Essays on the Intellectual Migration from Germany to America* (New York, 1986).

—— *The Dialectical Imagination: A History of the Frankfurt School and the Institute of Social Research, 1923–1950* (Berkeley, Calif., 1996).

JOHNSON, M., *The Body in the Mind: The Bodily Basis of Meaning, Imagination, and Reason* (Chicago, 1987).

JOSEPHSON, D., 'Documentation of the Upheaval and Immigration in *The New York Times* and the *Grove Dictionaries*', (6 May 1994).

KANE, L., *The Language of Silence: On the Unspoken and the Unspeakable in Modern Drama* (London, 1984).

KANT, I., *Critique of Pure Reason*, tr. N. Kemp Smith (1929; New York, 1965).

—— *Critique of Judgment*, tr. W. S. Pluhar (Indianapolis, 1987).

KAPLAN, A., *French Lessons: A Memoir* (Chicago, 1993).

KATZ, R., *The Powers of Music: Aesthetic Theory and the Invention of Opera* (Princeton, 1994).

KERMAN, J., *Opera as Drama* (Berkeley, Calif., 1988).

——*Write all these Down: Essays on Music* (Berkeley, Calif., 1994).

KIERKEGAARD, S., *Either/Or*, tr. D. F. and L. M. Swenson, 2 vols. (New York, 1959).

——*Søren Kierkegaard's Journal and Papers*, ed. H. V. Hong and E. H. Hong (Bloomington, Ind., 1979), iv.

——*Fear and Trembling: Dialectical Lyric by Johannes de Silentio*, tr. A. Hannay (Harmondsworth, 1985).

KINGSBURY, H., *Music, Talent, and Performance: A Conservatory Cultural System* (Philadelphia, 1988).

KIPPENBERG, H. G., and STROUSMA, G. G. (eds.), *Secrecy and Concealment: Studies in the History of Mediterranean and Near Eastern Religions* (Leiden, 1995).

KIVY, P., *Music Alone: Philosophical Reflections on the Purely Musical Experience* (Ithaca, NY, 1990).

——*Philosophies of Arts: An Essay in Differences* (Ithaca, NY, 1997).

KLEIST, H. VON, 'St Cecelia or the Power of Music', *The Marquise of O and Other Stories*, tr. D. Luke and N. Reeves (Harmondsworth, 1978), 217–30.

KNAPP, B. L., *Exile and the Writer: Exoteric and Esoteric Experiences. A Jungian Approach* (University Park, Penn., 1991).

KODALY, Z., *Fifty-Five Two-Part Exercises*, ed. P. M. Young (London, 1955).

KOESTENBAUM, W., *The Queen's Throat: Opera, Homosexuality, and the Mystery of Desire* (New York, 1993).

KOURY, D. J., 'Orchestral Performance Practices in the Nineteenth Century: Size, Proportions, and Seating', Ph.D. thesis, University of Michigan, 1986.

KOWALKE, K., and EDLER, H. (eds.), *A Stranger here myself: Kurt Weill-Studien* (Hildesheim, 1993).

KRACAUER, S., *The Mass Ornament: Weimar Essays*, tr. and ed. T. Y. Levin (Cambridge, Mass., 1995).

KRAUS, K., *Half-Truths and One-and-a-Half Truths: Selected Aphorisms*, tr. H. Zohn (Chicago, 1990).

KRAUS, R. C., *Pianos and Politics in China: Middle Class Ambitions and the Struggle over Western Music* (Oxford, 1989).

KRAUSZ, M. (ed.), *Relativism: Interpretation and Confrontation* (Notre Dame, Ind., 1989).

——(ed.), *The Interpretation of Music: Philosophical Essays* (Oxford, 1993).

KRENEK, E., *Music Here and Now* (New York, 1939).

KRENEK, E., 'Self-Analysis', *New Mexico Quarterly*, 23 (Spring 1953), 5–57.

——— *Exploring Music*, tr. M. Shenfield and G. Skelton (New York, 1966).

——— 'America's Influence on its Émigré Composers', tr. D. Harran, *Perspectives of New Music*, 'Colloquy and Review' (Spring–Summer, 1970), 112–17.

——— *Die Amerikanischen Tagebücher, 1937–1942. Dokumente aus dem Exil*, ed. C. M. Zenck (Vienna, 1992).

KRISTEVA, J., *Strangers to Ourselves*, tr. L. S. Roudiez (New York, 1991).

KROHN, C.-D., *Intellectuals in Exile: Refugee Scholars and the New School for Social Research*, tr. R. and R. Kimber (Amherst, Mass., 1993).

KROPFINGER, K., *Wagner and Beethoven: Richard Wagner's Reception of Beethoven*, tr. P. Palmer (Cambridge, 1991).

KRUKOWSKI, L., *Aesthetic Legacies* (Philadelphia, 1992).

LACOUE-LABARTHE, P., *Musica Ficta (Figures of Wagner)*, tr. F. McCarren (Stanford, Calif., 1994).

LAMB, C., 'A Chapter on Ears' (Essays of Elia), *The Complete Works and Letters of Charles Lamb* (New York, 1935), 35–8.

LANGER, S. K., *Philosophy in a New Key: A Study in the Symbolism of Reason, Rite, and Art* (New York, 1951).

LAVIN, T. (ed.), *Meaning in the Visual Arts: Views from the Outside. A Centennial Commemoration of Erwin Panofsky (1892–1968)* (Princeton, 1995)

LELAND, C. G., *The Music-Lesson of Confucius and Other Poems* (Boston, 1872).

LEPPERT, R., *The Sight of Sound: Music, Representation, and the History of the Body* (Berkeley, Calif., 1993).

——— and MCCLARY, S. (eds.), *Music and Society: The Politics of Composition, Performance, and Reception* (Cambridge, 1987).

LEVI, A. W., *Humanism and Politics: Studies in the Relationship of Power and Value in the Western Tradition* (Bloomington, Ind., 1969).

LEVIN, D. J. (ed.), *Opera through Other Eyes* (Stanford, Calif., 1994).

——— (ed.), *Richard Wagner*, Special Issue, *New German Critique*, 69 (1996).

LÉVI-STRAUSS, C., *The Raw and the Cooked: Mythologies*, i, tr. J. and D. Weightman (Chicago, 1983).

LIE KUEN TONG, 'The Meaning of Philosophical Silence: Some Reflections on the Use of Language in Chinese Thought', *Journal of Chinese Philosophy*, 3 (1976), 169–83.

LIPMAN, S., 'Wagner as Anti-Semite', *Commentary*, 87/1 (1987), 57–60.

LIPPMAN, E., *A History of Western Musical Aesthetics* (Lincoln, Nebr., 1992).

LISZT, F., *The Letters of Franz Liszt to Olga von Meyendorff, 1881–1886*, tr. W. R. Tyler (Cambridge, Mass., 1979).

LOCKE, R. P., *Music, Musicians, and the Saint-Simonians* (Chicago, 1986).

LORD, A., *The Singer of Tales* (Cambridge, Mass., 1960).

LÖWITH, K., *From Hegel to Nietzsche: The Revolution in Nineteenth-Century Thought*, tr. D. E. Green (New York, 1964).

——*My Life in Germany before and after 1933*, tr. E. King (Urbana, Ill., 1994).

LYON, J. K., *Bertolt Brecht in America* (Princeton, 1980).

McCLARY, S., *Feminine Endings: Music, Gender, and Sexuality* (Minneapolis, 1991).

MAGEE, B., *The Philosophy of Schopenhauer* (Oxford, 1983).

MANEA, N., *On Clowns: The Dictator and the Artist* (New York, 1992).

MANN, A., 'A European at Home Abroad: An Autobiographical Sketch', *Eighteenth-Century Music in Theory and Practice: Essays in Honor of Alfred Mann*, ed. M. A. Parker (New York, 1994), 289–328.

MANN, T., *Doctor Faustus*, tr. H. T. Lowe-Porter (Harmondsworth, 1947).

——*Essays of Three Decades*, tr. H. T. Lowe-Porter (New York, 1947).

——*Reflections of a Nonpolitical Man*, tr. W. D. Morris (New York, 1987).

MARCUSE, H., *Negations: Essays in Critical Theory*, tr. J. J. Shapiro (Boston, 1968).

——*The Aesthetic Dimension: Toward a Critique of Marxist Aesthetics* (Boston, 1978).

MARTIN, N., *Nietzsche and Schiller: Untimely Aesthetics* (Oxford, 1996).

MAYNARD, P. (ed.), *Perspectives on the Arts and Technology*, Special Issue, *Journal of Aesthetics and Art Criticism*, 55/2 (1987).

MENDELSSOHN, BARTHOLDY, F., *Letters of Felix Mendelssohn Bartholdy, 1833–1847*, tr. Lady Wallace, ed. J. Rietz (Boston, 1863).

MERLEAU-PONTY, M., *Sense and Non-Sense*, tr. H. L. and P. A. Dreyfus (Evanston, Ill., 1964).

——*The Visible and the Invisible*, ed. C. Lefort, tr. A. Lingis (Evanston, Ill., 1968).

——*The Prose of the World*, ed. C. Lefort, tr. J. O'Neill (Evanston, Ill., 1973).

MERRICK, P., *Revolution and Religion in the Music of Liszt* (Cambridge, 1987).

MEYER, L. B., *Style and Music: Theory, History, and Ideology* (Philadelphia, 1989).

MIDGETTE, A., '*Die Meistersinger*', *Opera News*, 9 Dec. 1995, 24–6, 72.

MILL, J. S., *Utilitarianism, On Liberty and Considerations on Representative Government*, ed. H. B. Acton (London, 1972).

MILLINGTON, B., *Wagner* (Princeton, 1984).

MINER, M., *Resonant Gaps: Between Baudelaire and Wagner* (Athens, Ga., 1995).

MITCHELL, W. J. T. (ed.), *The Politics of Interpretation* (Chicago, 1983).

MOON, D., *Constructing Community: Moral Pluralism and Tragic Conflicts* (Princeton, 1993).

MORGENSTERN, S. (ed.), *Composers on Music: An Anthology of Composers' Writings from Palestrina to Copland* (New York, 1956).

MÜLLER, U., and WAPNEWSKI, P. (eds.), *Wagner Handbook*, tr. ed. J. Deathridge (Cambridge, Mass., 1992).

NATANSON, M. (ed.), *Essays in Phenomenology* (The Hague, 1966).

NATTIEZ, J.-J., *Music and Discourse: Toward a Semiology of Music*, tr. C. Abbate (Princeton, 1990).

—— *Wagner Androgyne*, tr. S. Spencer (Princeton, 1993).

NEUBAUER, J., *The Emancipation of Music from Language: Departure from Mimesis in Eighteenth-Century Aesthetics* (New Haven, 1986).

NEWMAN, E., *The Wagner Operas* (New York, 1949).

NIETZSCHE, F., *Basic Writings of Nietzsche*, tr. and ed. W. Kaufmann (New York, 1968).

—— *Complete Works*, tr. and ed. W. Kaufman (New York, 1968).

—— *Twilight of the Idols and the Anti-Christ*, tr. R. J. Hollingdale (Harmondsworth, 1968).

—— *Untimely Meditations*, tr. R. J. Hollingdale (Cambridge, 1983).

—— *Human, all too Human: A Book for Free Spirits*, tr. M. Faber and S. Lehmann (Lincoln, Nebr., 1986).

—— and WAGNER, R., *The Nietzsche–Wagner Correspondence*, ed. E. Foerster-Nietzsche (New York, 1921).

NISBET, H. B. (ed.), *German Aesthetic and Literary Criticism: Winckelmann, Lessing, Hamann, Herder, Schiller and Goethe* (Cambridge, 1985).

NORRIS, C. (ed.), *Music and the Politics of Culture* (London, 1989).

NYIRI, J. C., and SMITH, B. (eds.), *Practical Knowledge: Outlines of a Theory of Traditions and Skills* (London, 1988).

OAKESHOTT, M., *Rationalism in Politics and Other Essays* (Indianapolis, 1991).

ORWELL, G., 'The Prevention of Literature', in *The Collected Essays, Journalism and Letters of George Orwell*, iv: *In Front of your Nose, 1945–1950*, ed. S. Orwell and I. Angus (New York, 1968), 59–72.

—— *A Collection of Essays* (San Diego, Calif., 1981).

OSBORNE, C., *The Complete Operas of Richard Wagner* (London, 1990).

OTT, B., *Lisztian Keyboard Energy/Liszt et la pédagogie du piano: An Essay on the Pianism of Franz Liszt*, tr. D. H. Windham (Lewiston, NY, 1992).

PADDISON, M., *Adorno's Aesthetics of Music* (Cambridge, 1993).

PALMER, C., *The Composer in Hollywood* (London, 1990).

PAYZANT, G., *Glenn Gould: Music and Mind* (Toronto, 1992).

—— 'Hanslick, Sams, Gay, and "Tönend Bewegte Formen"', *Journal of Aesthetics and Art Criticism*, 40/1 (1981), 41–8.

PERLOFF, M., *Wittgenstein's Ladder: Poetic Language and the Strangeness of the Ordinary* (Chicago, 1996).

PERRIS, A., *Music as Propaganda: Art to Persuade, Art to Control* (Westport, Conn., 1985).

PLATO, *Five Dialogues: Euthyphro, Apology, Crito, Meno, Phaedo*, tr. G. M. A., Grube (Indianapolis, 1981).

POE, E. A., 'The Purloined Letter', *Selected Tales*, ed. K. Graham (London, 1967), 318–37.

POLANYI, M., *The Tacit Dimension* (New York, 1966).

POPLE, A. (ed.), *Theory, Analysis, and Meaning in Music* (Cambridge, 1994).

RAHN, J. (ed.), *Perspectives on Musical Aesthetics* (New York, 1994).

RAPHAEL, R., *Richard Wagner* (New York, 1969).

RAWLS, J., *Political Liberalism* (Cambridge, Mass., 1993).

RAYNER, R. M., *Wagner and* Die Meistersinger (London 1940).

RAYNOR, H., *Music and Society since 1815* (London, 1976).

REIJEN, W. VAN, SCHIEFELBEIN, P., and LOHMANN, H.-M., *Adorno: An Introduction*, tr. D. Engelbrecht (Philadelphia, 1992).

RICH, A., *On Lies, Secrets, and Silence: Selected Prose, 1966–1978* (New York, 1979).

RICHTER, M., *The History of Political and Social Concepts: A Critical Introduction* (Oxford, 1995).

RINK, J., *The Practice of Performance: Studies in Musical Interpretation* (Cambridge, 1995).

ROBINSON, M. (ed.), *Altogether Elsewhere: Writers on Exile* (Boston, 1994).

ROBINSON, P., 'Sartre on Music', *Journal of Aesthetics and Art Criticism*, 31/4 (1973), 451–7.

——*Opera and Ideas from Mozart to Strauss* (Ithaca, NY, 1985).

ROLLAND, R., *Romain Rolland's Essays on Music*, ed. D. Ewen (New York, 1922).

ROREM, N., 'Random Notes from a Diary', *Music from Inside Out* (New York, 1967).

ROSE, P. L., *German Question/Jewish Question: Revolutionary Anti-semitism from Kant to Wagner* (Princeton, 1990).

——*Wagner: Race and Revolution* (New Haven, 1992).

ROUSSEAU, J.-J., *Œuvres Complètes* (Paris, 1837), iii. *Dictionnaire de Musique*.

——*Rousseau: The Discourses and Other Early Political Writings*, tr. and ed. V. Gourevitch (Cambridge, 1997).

RUBSAMEN, W. H., 'Schoenberg in America', *Musical Quarterly*, 37/4 (Oct. 1951), 469–89.

SACKS, S. (ed.), *On Metaphor* (Chicago, 1979).

SAFRANSKI, R., *Schopenhauer and the Wild Years of Philosophy*, tr. E. Osels (Cambridge, Mass., 1990).

SAID, E. W., *Musical Elaborations* (London, 1991).

—— *Representations of the Intellectual* (New York, 1994).

SALMEN, W. (ed.), *The Social Status of the Professional Musician from the Middle Ages to the 19th Century*, tr. H. Kaufman and B. Reisner (New York, 1983).

SANDOW, G., 'At Spring's Command', *Opera News*, 16 Mar. 1985, 36–7.

SARTRE, J.-P., *Situations*, tr. B. Eisler (Greenwich, Conn., 1965).

—— *'What is Literature?' and Other Essays* (Cambridge Mass., 1988).

SCHECHNER, R., and APPEL, W. (eds.), *By Means of Performance: Intercultural Studies of Theatre and Ritual* (Cambridge, 1990).

SCHEFFLER, I., *Reason and Teaching* (Indianapolis, 1989).

SCHER, S. P. (ed.), *Music and Text: Critical Inquiries* (Cambridge, 1992).

SCHILLER, F., *An Anthology for our Time*, tr. F. Ungar (New York, 1959).

—— *On the Aesthetic Education of Man*, tr. R. Snell (New York, 1965).

—— and KÖRNER, C. G., *Correspondence of Schiller with Körner*, tr. L. Simpson, 3 vols. (London, 1849).

SCHLEGEL, F., *Philosophical Fragments*, tr. P. Firchow (Minneapolis, 1991).

SCHOENBERG, A., *Arnold Schoenberg Letters*, ed. E. Stein, tr. E. Wilkins and E. Kaiser (London, 1964).

—— *Style and Idea: Selected Writings of Arnold Schoenberg*, ed. L. Stein, tr. L. Black (Berkeley, Calif., 1975).

SCHOENBERG, B. ZEISL, 'The Reception of Austrian Composers in Los Angeles: 1934–1950', *Modern Austrian Literature*, 20/3–4 (1987), 135–44.

SCHONBERG, H. C., *The Great Conductors* (New York, 1967).

SCHOPENHAUER, A., *The World as Will and Representation*, tr. E. F. J. Payne, 2 vols. (New York, 1969).

—— *Essays and Aphorisms*, tr. R. J. Hollingdale (Harmondsworth, 1970).

SCHUMANN, R., *Schumann on Music: A Selection from his Writings*, tr. and ed. H. Pleasants (New York, 1965).

SCHUTZ, A., 'The Stranger: An Essay in Social Psychology', *American Journal of Sociology*, 49/6 (1944), 499–507.

—— and GURWITSCH, A., *Philosophers in Exile: The Correspondence of Alfred Schutz and Aron Gurwitsch, 1939–1959*, ed. R. Grathoff, tr. J. Claude Evans (Bloomington, Ind., 1989).

SHARPE, B., and BROWNE, B., 'The Problem of Wagner', *Cogito* (Spring 1994), 45–52.

SHAW, G. B., *Shaw on Music: A Selection of the Music Criticism of Bernard Shaw*, ed. E. Bentley (New York, 1955).

SHEPHERD, J., *Music as Social Text* (Cambridge, 1991).

SIEGEL, L., *Music in German Romantic Literature: A Collection of Essays, Reviews, and Stories* (Novato, Calif., 1983).

SIMMEL, G., *Schopenhauer and Nietzsche*, tr. H. Loiskandl, D. Weinstein, and M. Weinstein (Amherst, Mass., 1986).

SKELTON, G., *Wagner in Thought and Practice* (Portland, Oreg., 1991).

SLUGA, H., *Heidegger's Crisis: Philosophy and Politics in Nazi Germany* (Cambridge, Mass., 1993).

SOLIE, R. A. (ed.), *Musicology and Difference: Gender and Sexuality in Music Scholarship* (Berkeley, Calif., 1993).

SONNECK, O. G. (ed.), *Beethoven: Impressions by his Contemporaries* (New York, 1954).

SPITZER, L., *Classical and Christian Ideas of World Harmony: Prolegomena to an Interpretation of the Word 'Stimmung'*, ed. A. G. Hatcher (Baltimore, 1963).

SPOTTS, F., *Bayreuth: A History of the Wagner Festival* (New Haven, 1984).

STEIN, E., *Form and Performance* (New York, 1962).

STEINBERG, M. P., 'The Musical Absolute', *New German Critique*, 56 (1992), 17–42.

—— 'Music, Language, and Culture', *Musical Quarterly*, 77 (1993), 397–400.

STEINER, G., *Language and Silence* (New York, 1967).

STENDAHL, *The Life of Rossini*, tr. R. N. Coe (London, 1985).

STEVENS, W., *The Collected Poems of Wallace Stevens* (New York, 1955).

STEWART, J. L., *Ernst Krenek: The Man and his Music* (Berkeley, Calif., 1991).

STRAINCHAMPS, E., and MANIATES, M. R. (eds.), *Music and Civilization: Essays in Honor of Paul Henry Lang* (New York, 1984).

STRAUS, E. W., and GRIFFITHS, R. M. (eds.), *Phenomenology of Will and Action* (Pittsburgh, 1967).

STRAUSS, L., *Persecution and the Art of Writing* (Chicago, 1952, 1980).

STRAVINSKY, I., *An Autobiography* (New York, 1936).

—— *The Poetics of Music in the Form of Six Lessons* (Cambridge, Mass., 1942).

—— and CRAFT, R., *Dialogues and a Diary* (London, 1968).

STRAVINSKY, V., *Stravinsky in Pictures and Documents* (New York, 1978).

STRUNK, O. (ed.), *Source Readings in Music History: From Classical Antiquity through the Romantic Era* (New York, 1950).

SUBOTNIK, R. R., *Developing Variations: Style and Ideology in Western Music* (Minneapolis, 1991).

TAMBLING, J., *Opera and the Culture of Fascism* (Oxford, 1996).

TANNER, M., *Wagner* (Princeton, 1996).

TARUSKIN, R., *Text and Act: Essays on Music and Performance* (Oxford, 1995).

TAYLOR, R., *Kurt Weill: Composer in a Divided World* (Boston, 1991).

THOM, P., *For an Audience: A Philosophy of the Performing Arts* (Philadelphia, 1993).

THOMPSON, H., *Wagner and Wagenseil: A Source of Wagner's Opera* Die Meistersinger (London, 1927).

THOMSON, V., *Virgil Thomson* (London, 1967).

TILLICH, P., 'Mind and Migration', *Social Research*, 4 (1937), 295–305.

TODD, R. Larry. (ed.), *Mendelssohn and his World* (Princeton, 1991).

TOKER, L., *Eloquent Reticence: Withholding Information in Fictional Narrative* (Lexington, Ky., 1993).

TREITLER, L., *Music and the Historical Imagination* (Cambridge, Mass., 1989).

—— 'What Obstacles Must be Overcome, Just in Case we Wish to Speak of Meaning in the Musical Arts', in Lavin (ed.), *Meaning in the Visual Arts*, 285–303.

TROTSKY, L., *Art and Revolution: Writings on Literature, Politics, and Culture* (New York, 1970).

VALÉRY, P., *Selected Writings of Paul Valéry*, tr. M. Cowley (New York, 1950).

VAUGHAN WILLIAMS, U., *Silence and Music* (Fair Lawn, NJ, 1959).

WACKENRODER, W. H., and TIECK, L., *Outpourings of an Art-Loving Friar*, tr. E. Mornin (New York, 1975).

WAGNER, C., *Cosima Wagner's Diaries*, An Abridgement, ed. G. Skelton (New Haven, 1994).

WAGNER, R., *Gesammelte Schriften und Dichtungen*, ed. W. Golther (Leipzig, 1913).

—— *Briefe an Hans von Bülow* (Jena, 1916).

—— *The Letters of Richard Wagner*, ed. and tr. W. Altmann, 2 vols. (London, 1927).

—— *Wagner Writes from Paris . . . Stories, Essays and Articles by the Young Composer*, ed. and tr. R. L. Jacobs and G. Skelton (London, 1973).

—— *My Life*, tr. A. Gray, ed. M. Whittall (Cambridge, 1983).

—— *Richard Wagner Dichtungen und Schriften*, ed. D. Borchmeyer (Frankfurt, 1985).

—— *Selected Letters of Richard Wagner*, tr. and ed. S. Spencer and B. Millington (New York, 1987).

—— *Stories and Essays*, ed. C. Osborne (La Salle, Ill., 1991).

——*Die Meistersinger*, tr. S. Webb, Metropolitan Opera Libretto Series, ed. P. Gruber (New York, 1992).

——*Richard Wagner's Prose Works*, tr. W. A. Ellis, 8 vols. (Lincoln, Nebr., 1995).

WALKER, A., *Franz Liszt: The Virtuoso Years* (Ithaca, NY, 1983).

WALLACE, R., *Beethoven's Critics: Aesthetic Dilemmas and Resolutions during the Composer's Lifetime* (Cambridge, 1986).

WALZER, M., *The Company of Critics: Social Criticism and Political Commitment in the Twentieth Century* (New York, 1988).

WARRACK, J., 'Stravinsky', *Tempo*, 81 (1967), 7–9.

——(ed.), *Die Meistersinger von Nürnberg*, Cambridge Opera Handbooks (Cambridge, 1994).

WARTOFSKY, M. W., *Feuerbach* (Cambridge, 1977).

WEBER, C. M. VON, *Carl Maria von Weber: Writings on Music*, ed. J. Warrack, tr. M. Cooper (Cambridge, 1981).

WEBER, M., *Selections in Translation*, ed. W. G. Runciman, tr. E. Matthews (New York, 1978).

WEBER, W., and LARGE, D. C. (eds.), *Wagnerism in European Culture and Politics* (Ithaca, NY, 1984).

WEEKS, A., *German Mysticism from Hildegard of Bingen to Ludwig Wittgenstein: A Literary and Intellectual History* (New York, 1993).

WEGENER, C., *The Discipline of Taste and Feeling* (Chicago, 1992).

WEIL, J., *Mendelssohn is on the Roof*, tr. M. Winn (New York, 1991).

WEINER, M., *Richard Wagner and the Anti-Semitic Imagination* (Lincoln, Nebr., 1995).

WEISS, P., and TARUSKIN, R. (eds.), *Music in the Western World: A History in Documents* (New York, 1984).

WESTERNHAGEN, C. VON., *Wagner: A Biography*, tr. M. Whittall (Cambridge, 1978).

WILDE, O., *The Works of Oscar Wilde* (Leicester, 1993).

WILLIAMS, B. A. O., *Ethics and the Limits of Philosophy* (London, 1985).

WILSON, C., *On Music* (London, 1967).

WINCKELMANN, J. J., *Reflections on the Imitation of Greek Works in Painting and Sculpture*, tr. E. Heyer and R. C. Norton (La Salle, Ill., 1987).

WIORA, W., *Das Musikalische Kunstwerk* (Tützing, 1983).

WITTGENSTEIN, L., *Philosophical Investigations*, tr. G. E. M. Anscombe (Oxford, 1958).

——*Tractatus Logico-Philosophicus*, tr. D. F. Pears and B. F. McGuinness (London, 1961).

——*Culture and Value*, tr. P. Winch, ed. G. H. von Wright (Oxford, 1980).

WOLFF, J., *Resident Alien: Feminist Cultural Criticism* (New Haven, 1995).

WOOD, D., *Philosophy at the Limit: Problems of Modern European Thought* (London, 1990).

YERUSHALMI, Y. H., 'The Moses of Freud and the Moses of Schoenberg: On Words, Idolatry, and Psychoanalysis', in *The Psychoanalytic Study of the Child*, xlvii (New Haven, 1992), 1–20.

Index

Index